THE CROWN AND THE TOWER:
THE LEGEND OF RICHARD III

THE CROWN
AND THE
TOWER
The Legend of Richard III

A condensation of Caroline Amelia Halsted's
important biography of 1844, *Richard III as
Duke of Gloucester and King of England*, with
the views of other authors and additional
commentary.

Researched and edited
by
William H. Snyder

RICHARD III SOCIETY, INC.
1981

Let Truth and Falsehood grapple; who ever knew Truth put to the worse, in a free and open encounter.

John Milton, *Areopagitica*, a Speech for the Liberty of Unlicensed Printing, to the Parliament of England, November, 1644.

There is a principle which is a bar against all information, which is proof against all argument, and which cannot fail to keep a man in everlasting ignorance. That principle is condemnation before investigation.

Herbert Spencer

Published by Richard III Society, Inc.,
P.O. Box 217, Sea Cliff, New York 11579.

LIBRARY OF CONGRESS
CATALOG CARD NO.: 79-92797

Printed in Great Britain by
Redwood Burn Limited, Trowbridge, Wiltshire, for
Alan Sutton Publishing Limited,
17a Brunswick Road, Gloucester GL1 1HG

*Cover design and genealogical charts
by William Hogarth*

CONTENTS

FOREWORD

Was Richard III the deformed villain pictured by Shakespeare and tradition? Or is his story, as it has come down to us, a hoax?

Interest in Richard III continues and is even more intense almost 500 years after Bosworth Field because his story poses a question relevant in all ages and especially now: How do we recognize truth in a welter of fable, fiction, and propaganda? What picture of Richard emerges when we review the facts?

I do not claim to present newly discovered evidence. But I hope that, by including the views of a number of writers and scholars in one concise review, I may give the reader a broader perspective from which to evaluate one of the great mysteries of history.

My aims are:
    to state the facts we do know about Richard's actions;
    to record the opinions of those who knew him best, especially
       his brother, Edward IV;
    to show how the legend of the evil King started; and
    to present the views of some leading authorities.

Since Caroline A. Halsted's 1,027 page, two volume 'Richard III', London, 1844, incorporates a significant body of research, I have prepared a brief condensation as a framework for this review, using her own words as far as possible. And as Richard's story becomes more complex, I have summarized the views of other writers in my own words, except for selected quotations.

Because of the controversy about Richard III's true character, it is especially important that the reader be able to test for himself the adequacy of the evidence. To facilitate his review, I have departed from custom and placed the citations in the text, as is common in legal briefs and court decisions.

Readers who prefer to start with a summary should read Chapter XXI first.

William H. Snyder
Silver Spring, Maryland, 1980

1

ENGLAND IN THE MIDDLE AGES

Once upon a time, there was a wicked, deformed Duke of Gloucester who usurped the throne of England as Richard III by murdering the two young sons of his dead brother, Edward IV.

Such is the legend firmly fixed in the public mind by Shakespeare's brilliant *Richard III*. Yet we should not confuse the dramatic Richard III with the historical Richard III. Modern scholars admire Shakespeare's dramatic genius but discredit his historical accuracy, since the only sources available to him were works by prejudiced chroniclers writing for Richard III's successor, Henry VII. And Shakespeare was interested in dramatizing a study of evil rather than in writing an accurate history. He has Richard engaged in battles when, in fact, Richard was an infant. Henry VII's chroniclers depicted Richard III as a hunchbacked monster to make Richard appear capable of having murdered his two small nephews, thus bolstering Henry's own very weak claim to the throne.

Two men, Henry VII and the Duke of Buckingham, had strong motives to kill the two young Princes. Richard III had none. He was lawfully King of England by reason of *Titulus Regius*. *Titulus Regius*? That was the act of Parliament settling the crown upon Richard and his issue. The first thing Henry did upon becoming King was to order all copies of *Titulus Regius* destroyed on pain of severe punishment. One copy, however, escaped destruction. It was found in the Tower of London and was one of the first sources of the true history of Richard III.

There is more — much more. In 1768, Horace Walpole said: 'Shakespeare's immortal scenes will exist, when such poor arguments as mine are forgotten. Richard at least will be tried and executed on the stage, when his defense remains on some obscure shelf of a library'. But thanks to modern scholars who have exposed the prejudice and corruption in the early chroniclers about Richard III, his defense has not remained 'on some obscure shelf of a library'.

There are enough undisputed facts about Richard's actions and his reputation during his lifetime to give us a reasonable basis for evaluating his character. This book is an attempt to review these facts, to evaluate his reputation among the people who knew him best, especially his brother, King Edward IV, and to summarize the views of some prominent authors.

Was Richard III England's worst king, a deformed murderer who killed his dead brother's children to reach the throne? Or has Richard's memory been blackened forever by an usurper who, by treachery and cunning, seized the throne?

Before dealing with these questions, which represent probably the biggest mystery in English history, let us take a very brief look at the England into which Richard Plantagenet, later Duke of Gloucester and King of England, was born, October 2, 1452.

Turbulence Since 1066

From the time that William, the bastard Duke of Normandy, invaded England, defeated King Harold Godwineson at Hastings in 1066, and became known as William the Conqueror, there were only a few consecutive years when peace prevailed in England. The longest conflict, the Hundred Years War between England and France, started in 1337. By 1429, the English and their Burgundian allies held almost all of France north of the Loire, including Paris and Rheims.

But in that year, Joan of Arc, inspired by the voices of Saint Margaret, Saint Catherine, and Saint Michael, stemmed the tide, raised the siege of Orleans, and attended Charles VII when he was crowned King of France at Rheims Cathedral. Fifteen months later, the Burgundians captured Joan and sold her to the English. Charles VII made not one move to save her, and she was burned at the stake in 1431.

Still inspired by Joan's leadership, however, the French continued to beat back the English. When the Hundred Years War ended in 1453, England's holdings in France had been reduced to only Calais and the Channel Islands and her dream of continental power was finished. Conflict would again erupt soon, however — the Wars of the Roses between the Lancastrians (the red rose) and the Yorkists (the white rose). The England that was fought over by the Lancastrians and Yorkists, however, was very different from the England we know today.

The Developing Nation

Population

England in the 1400's was a quite different place from the England of today. She had a population of about 2½ million people, ninety percent of whom lived on the land. Among her few towns, London had about 50,000 and York about 12,000. Small as London was by today's standards, she was regarded as the richest city in Europe.

Towns and Guilds

For defense, the towns were surrounded by walls, limiting the space within the walls. Houses and shops were crowded together in the narrow streets which were closed in by the overhanging upper storeys of the larger buildings. There were no sidewalks, and mud and filth lay in the gutters. Most houses were small, especially outside the cities, and were poorly lighted. Windows were mostly shuttered; few had glass. Smoke rose through the house and escaped through a hole in the roof. So, people spent most of their time in the streets, which were a riot of activity and noise.

Guilds — associations of persons in the same craft or business — had local control over the craft or business, fixing prices, setting standards, training apprentices, and providing social status. They were quite powerful and often were the real rulers of the town.

The Black Death

The crowded, noisy and dirty conditions of the cities, and the ignorance of even elementary principles of sanitation, inevitably led to the spread of the bubonic plague or Black Death, which was caused by a bacterium transmitted to man by infected rats. In the fourteenth century, returning Crusaders had spread the plague which killed probably three fourths of the population of Europe and Asia. England was not spared. The Black Death struck there in 1348, and within one year had killed at least one third of the population. It would strike again in the great plague of 1665.

Roads

The Roman roads, built of stone 1,200 years before, were still good. But smaller thoroughfares might be only tracks, poorly marked and maintained, so that local guides might be necessary.

Language

The English of today can be traced back to the language of the fifth century Germanic invaders of England — the Angles, Saxons, and Jutes — but an Englishman in Richard III's time would not have understood the language of 500 or the English of today. Following the Norman Conquest, 1066, French supplanted English as the language of the court and officialdom. By the end of the fourteenth century, English became again the language of the upper classes, although there was a wide diversity in spelling. The new standard was a London dialect from which Modern Standard English grew.

In 1362, Parliament decreed that all pleading and judgements should be in English. Henry IV probably used French, but spoke in English when he claimed the throne in 1399, whilst Henry V wrote in English, but quite different from the English we know. In Bruges, William Caxton and Colard Mansion printed *The Recuyell of the Historyes of Troy* in 1475, the first book printed in English. In 1477, at Westminster, Caxton printed *Dictes or Sayengis of the Philosophres*, the first dated book in English printed in England.

Education of The Nobility and Upper Classes

Only about 30 percent of the population could read; fewer could write. However, the ability of the nobility and upper classes to read and write English was steadily increasing.

It was a common practice to send a young son to another household to serve as a page and apprentice in knighthood. Here, he would first learn reading, writing, Christian doctrine, and some French and Latin, and later the manly arts, including knightly conduct and the use of weapons. Thus, Richard III, as a boy, entered the household of the Earl of Warwick, and Sir Thomas More was raised in the household of John Morton, Bishop of Ely.

An upper class girl would also be placed in the household of a noble or other person of quality to learn the arts needed to attract a husband — singing, dancing, dress, manners, and posture.

Feudalism and Livery and Maintenance

The King was at the top of the feudal structure, followed by a hierarchy of nobles. Their castles were armed fortresses as well as houses. The lord of the castle received his land from the King or a higher lord. In return, he pledged loyalty and military support. Then, in turn, he might make grants of his land to lesser nobles who would swear fealty and military support to him. At the bottom of the scale were the peasants, villeins, and serfs who provided food for all. The lord of the manor granted them only the use of the land and his protection in return for their services.

The feudal system of the Middle Ages was based on the principle of patronage and protection. The system arose because of the unsettled conditions of the times, stemming from the lack of a standing army and a police force. Local government was feeble. Juries could be bribed or intimidated, and a lord might, and often did, take the law into his own hands. An alliance of several powerful lords could pose a serious threat to the King. Thus, in 1399, Henry Bolingbroke, with the aid of other nobles, forced Richard II to abdicate and usurped the throne as Henry IV.

Gradually, the feudal system gave way to livery and maintenance or 'bastard feudalism'. Instead of grants of land, lords received services by pay. The retainer wore the livery or cognizance of his employer, for example, the rising sun of York, but he could seek a new master. Because of the instability introduced by 'bastard feudalism', nobles often had to struggle by peaceful or violent means to maintain or increase their wealth and numbers of retainers in order to preserve their authority and well being.

Parliament

In 1407, the Commons had secured from Henry IV formal recognition of its exclusive right to initiate financial grants. Using its power to consider petitions for the redress of grievances and to submit these petitions to the King, Parliament developed the practice of withholding financial grants until the King had acted on the petition. This tight hold on finances greatly increased Parliament's power and added to the problems facing the troubled Kings.

The Troubled Kings :
The House of Lancaster vs. The House of York

Richard II, 1367-1400; King of England, 1377-1399

Richard II, the son of Edward, the Black Prince, distinguished himself at an early age when, only 14, he personally confronted the leaders of Wat Tyler's peasant rebellion and won their allegiance. He successfully pursued a peace policy, achieved a sound level of crown finances, and tried to deal with the Irish problem.

In 1398, he banished Henry of Bolingbroke, Duke of Hereford, for quarrelling with the Duke of Norfolk. When, in 1399, Richard II left for the Irish wars, Bolingbroke returned to England and assembled his forces. Richard, upon learning of Bolingbroke's return, hastened back to England, only to find his own forces dissolving. Henry induced Richard, by lying promises, to surrender to him, and then usurped the throne as Henry IV, founding the Lancastrian dynasty. Within several months, Richard II was dead by starvation or murder. The House of Lancaster continued to rule England through Henry's son and grandson, Henry V and Henry VI, but the seeds had already been sown for the conflict in the next century since known as the Wars of the Roses, between the Lancastrians (the red rose) and the Yorkists (the white rose).

Henry IV, 1367-1413; King of England, 1399-1413

Henry IV's reign was marked by unrest and rebellion caused in part by the example of his own usurpation of the throne and in part by his failure to keep his promises of better government. His undutiful son and heir, Prince Henry, twice tried to pressure his father into abdicating, but these disputes ended in reconciliation before Henry IV's death.

Henry V, 1387-1422; King of England, 1413-1422

Henry V spent most of his reign, and much of England's resources, trying to enforce what he sincerely regarded as a just cause — the English claim to the French crown. With his warm personality and personal bravery, he was a popular King, but he was harsh, crafty, and cruel toward his enemies.

Shakespeare's famous play, *Henry V*, glorified Henry as a national hero when his small forces decimated a vastly superior French army at Agincourt, 1415. In 1420, Charles VI, Henry V, and Philip the Good of Burgundy signed the Treaty of Troyes recognizing Henry as heir of France, and Henry married Charles' daughter, Katherine. The dauphin would repudiate the Treaty when, in 1429, he was crowned as Charles VII, following Joan of Arc's military triumphs.

But history regards Henry V's achievements as barren and futile and his reign as a disaster for England. When he died, he left a heavy legacy of military problems, disorder, and debt. To complicate the problems confronting Henry's heir, the nobles who had helped Henry Bolingbroke usurp the throne had consolidated their power to such an extent that they could pose a threat to the crown.

To cope with these overwhelming problems, Henry V left an infant son, eight months old, who inherited the madness of his grandfather, Charles VI of France.

Henry VI, 1421-1471; King of England, 1422-1461 and 1470-1471

Henry VI was pious but weak-willed and subject to periods of insanity, and he had no capacity for, or interest in, governing. So, throughout his lifetime, he was the pawn of warring factions. At first his infancy, and later his occasional insanity and total incapacity to rule the nation, led to the development of two contending forces.

The Lancastrian faction was led by his agressive Queen, Margaret of Anjou, whose relationship with her favorites raised considerable doubt as to the legitimacy of Henry's son, Edward of Lancaster. The Yorkist faction was led by the most powerful noble in the kingdom, Richard, Duke of York (father of Richard III) whose claim to the throne was indisputably better than that of Henry VI, who claimed through the usurper, Henry IV. Although the Duke of York was twice appointed Protector during Henry VI's two long sieges of insanity, he refrained from trying to seize the throne or revenging himself on his enemies. His attempts to be recognized as successor to Henry VI, over Henry's son, Edward, would result in the first battle of the Wars of the Roses, at St. Albans, May 22, 1455, and the conflict would not end until August 22, 1485, on Bosworth Field.

Thus we find an England, on October 2, 1452, ripe for civil war, with these problems:

> a King representing a usurping Lancastrian dynasty, who was at times mad, who totally lacked ability to govern, and who had lost English claims to France;

> the rule of the nation in the hands of Margaret of Anjou, a foreigner, and her favorites, first William de la Pole, Earl of Suffolk, and then Edmund Beaufort, Duke of Somerset;

> an unruly nobility who could command more power than the King; and

> two factions at court contending for supreme power.

On this day, October 2, 1452, was born the son of the Duke of York, Richard Plantagenet, afterward Duke of Gloucester and, as Richard III, King of England.

HALSTED'S RICHARD III (CONDENSED) AND SUMMARIES OF OTHER VIEWS

NOTE: The summaries of the views of Professors A.R. Myers (University of Liverpool), H.G. Hanbury and E.F. Jacob (University of Oxford), and other scholars, are identified in bold captions, thus: **Myers, Jacob**, etc. These summaries are by the Editor, and appear throughout the text.

PREFACE

The era of King Richard III is the darkest, the most complex and the worst-authenticated portion of English history. The 'authorities' were swayed by the violent prejudices and strong antipathies natural where civil discord had long existed. Shrinking from corrupt and uncertain authority, history becomes silent. The defeat of the historian is the triumph of the poet. The former — reduced to chronicling doubts and suspicions — his tale is tame and uninviting and takes no hold on the public mind. The latter pours into the 'too credulous ear' his thrilling and attractive tale. Such must always be the case when history leaves her work to be done by the poet.

Despite opinions so long held and so deeply rooted, no prejudice can withstand the truth when fairly and simply displayed. Because errors and misstatements have been promulgated in less enlightened times and received in succeeding ages as historical facts, should they continue to be perpetuated in spite of all the evidence which modern research has made available?

Chapter 1

MYTH, LEGEND, AND HISTORY

Introduction

Few men have been more bitterly reviled than Richard III. From our childhood his name is pronounced with terror. Supernatural appearances both at his birth and death have been alleged to increase the odium of one who, from his cradle, was marked as a monster. By the aid of the drama, the representations of adversaries have been impressed on the minds of succeeding generations through the innocent genius of Shakespeare.

It is time for justice to be done to Richard III as a monarch, however opinions may vary as regards his guilt as a man. This can be done only by banishing traditional legends and trying to form an impartial decision from well-attested facts, derived not from the statements of over-zealous friends on the one hand or virulent enemies on the other, but from contemporary authority and un-biased witnesses.

Why was Richard III vilified?

Why, of all the sovereigns of England, was Richard III so peculiarly the prey of rancour and malevolence? Richard was a defeated monarch. He was the last Plantagenet King and the object of hatred and jealousy by the Woodvilles and his rival, Henry Tudor. It was crucial to the usurper, Henry VII, who had no legitimate claim to the throne, to blacken the name of the monarch he had deposed. The art of printing was as yet scarcely known, so that all accounts were written in manuscript with great cost and labour. Many of these were wholly destroyed or mutilated in later times from warfare and also from the destruction of the religious houses during the reign of Henry VIII.

No historian or biographer flourished during the reign of King Richard to narrate the circumstance which led to his aspiring to the crown and to describe his acts and regulations. These are recorded in the national archives and corroborated by rare manuscripts.

On the other hand, biographers of ability in the pay of Henry VII sought favour and advancement by eulogising the reigning monarch and vilifying the fallen king. Those friends who could best have testified to Richard's good deeds, or have defended his memory from unjust aspersions, were slain with him at Bosworth Field.

Caxton, the first English printer, dedicated one of his rarest works (The Booke of the Order of Chivalry or Knighthoode: Caxton, 1484) to Richard III and, in the preface, bore eloquent testimony to his chivalrous feelings and princely demeanor.

Richard III was destined to terminate with his brief reign that unceasing period of feudal oppression and civil war, the 'middle ages', which began with the Norman Conquest, 1066, and ended with his defeat at Bosworth, 1485.

As the image of the deceased king faded from remembrance, deformity of body, without proof, was gradually associated with alleged deformity of mind.

Contemporary Sources

The Chronicler of Croyland: Valuable authority, but his narrative is brief. The author was 'a doctor of canon law, and one of King Edward the Fourth's councillors' (*Cont. Croy.* in Gale, vol. 1, p. 557)

Rous: Dedicated his work *Historia Regum Anglicae* to Richard's rival, Henry VII, and therefore cannot be considered an impartial authority. He discredited himself by praising Richard III in an account written during Richard's lifetime and then writing a contradictory account for King Henry VII.

Harleian Manuscript No. 433: Contains registers of grants, letters, and other state papers during the reign of King Richard III, consisting of no less than 2,378 articles. Also No. 18 contains manuscripts and collections from the Parl. Rolls of Richard III, and No. 22 a short abstract from the Parl. Rolls of the private acts during the reign of Richard III — See Preface to the *Catalogue of the Harl. MSS.*, p. 16.

Later Sources

Provincial Histories, Municipal Records, Correspondence,

Diaries: Drake's *History of York* (Eboracum), Surtee's *History of Durham*, Whittaker's *History of Richmondshire*, Publications of the Camden Society, The Paston Correspondence.

Bernard Andre: Andre was Henry VII's official biographer, his poet laureate, and tutor to Prince Arthur, his eldest son. His work was never published, but the manuscript is in the Cott. MSS. Dom. A. xviii, written in 1500.

Polydore Vergil: Vergil was Dean of Wells and historiographer to Henry VII. He completed his history, which was begun 1505, under the immediate patronage of that monarch's second son and successor, King Henry VIII.

Fabyan: Fabyan, the city chronicler, was a zealous Lancastrian, and compiled his work during the reign of Henry VII.

Sir Francis Bacon: Bacon's *Life of Henry VII*, though not written until after the accession of James I, was a transcript from the Tudor historians, from whose works he obtained his information — see *Archaeologia*, vol. xxvii, p. 153.

Chapter II

THE STORY OF LANCASTRIAN USURPATION

Usurpation by the House of Lancaster

The contesting forces in Richard's lifetime were shaped by events which occurred many years before. Let's look at some of these events. Edward III reigned 50 years — 1327 to 1377. His eldest son, Edward the Black Prince, died shortly before his father, so that the crown devolved on the Black Prince's only son, Richard II.

Richard was deposed in 1399 by his cousin Henry of Bolingbroke (Henry IV), heir to John of Gaunt, Duke of Lancaster, the *fourth* son of Edward III. Parliament, however, had previously nominated as successor to Richard II (who had married Ann of Bohemia but without issue) Roger Mortimer, Earl of March, the grandson of Lionel, Duke of Clarence (the *third* son of Edward III and *elder* brother to John of Gaunt). Mortimer was the legitimate heir to the throne, Prince William, Edward's second son having died young.

The House of *Lancaster* retained possession of the usurped sceptre and transferred it to their lineal successors for three consecutive reigns — Henry IV, who forcibly seized it, his son Henry V, and Henry VI, his grandson — representing the Lancastrian dynasty.

But their sway, though uninterrupted for over 50 years, was neither peaceful nor uncontested. Despite the alleged abdication of Richard II, and the fact that Parliament ratified the usurpation of Henry IV, the claims of the descendants of Lionel, Duke of Clarence, third son of Edward III, were considered at Richard II's death indisputable by the laws of inheritance.

Execution of Earl of Cambridge

The Earl of Cambridge (grandfather of Richard III), son of Edmund of Langley, Duke of *York* and *fifth* son of Edward III, had married Anne Mortimer, great-granddaughter of Lionel, Duke of Clarence, the *third* son of Edward III. He was not of a temperament quietly to abandon his child's just claims. Consequently, on the eve of the departure of Henry V on an expedition into France, he joined in a conspiracy with some leading nobles to depose the King and restore the lawful heir to the throne in the person of Edmund Mortimer, brother of Anne Mortimer. He was betrayed, however, and was beheaded with the other conspirators in 1415.

Thus, upon the deaths of the Earl of Cambridge and Edmund Mortimer, Richard Plantagenet — the only son of the Earl of Cambridge and Anne Mortimer — united in his own person the representation of King Edward's third and fifth sons. By virtue of direct heirship from the *third* son, he became the lineal inheritor of the crown of England which had been usurped by Henry Bolingbroke of the House of Lancaster.

Richard Plantagenet's Claim

Richard Plantagenet, Duke of *York* (father of Richard III) was characterized by writers of that period as courageous, intrepid, humane, and beneficent. He was appointed by Henry VI and served wisely and well as —

> Constable of England at 16 (1434) when Henry VI went to France to be crowned;
>
> Regent of France at 17 (1435);
>
> Lieutenant General and Governor General of France at 22 (1440).

The Duke of York gave no encouragement for many years to cabals or conspiracies in his behalf. He ruled justly and wisely as viceregent of Henry VII. But a combination of events in later years forced him eventually to take a decisive part in the domestic struggles that agitated England, and finally, in self-defence, to enforce his claim to the crown which he clearly inherited from Edward III, through his mother, Anne Mortimer.

England — A scene of disorder and contention

From the time that Henry VI ascended the throne in 1422 as an infant but eight months old, England was little less than one continual scene of disorder and contention. From his earliest childhood, he became the victim of ambitious guardians and continued through life to be the tool of designing and selfish ministers. The measure of his misfortunes was completed by his marriage with Margaret of Anjou, who, by her violent temper and inordinate ambition, fed the discontent that arose from the misgovernment of those evil counsellors who influenced the simple-minded King in his unpopular measures.

Parliament elects Duke of York 'Protector'

The illness of Henry VI, in the thirtieth year of his reign, ending in imbecility, openly rekindled the long-smothered contention between the rival branches of the House of Plantagenet. The Duke of York, by the death of members of the reigning family without issue, became first prince of the blood and, consequently, next in order of succession to the throne, apart from his dormant maternal claims. He was unanimously elected by Parliament 'protector and defender of the realm', and in April 1454, invested with all the state and importance attached to heir presumptive of the crown.

The birth of an heir apparent, Edward, Prince of Wales (October 13, 1453), at this critical juncture, and under circumstances of suspicion regarding his legitimacy, increased rather than diminished the strength of the opposing party. The prospect of the similar evils of a long minority occurring in the person of this infant son aroused a feeling of discontent in the supporters of the rights of primogeniture, which was daily fostered by the imperious conduct of the Queen, Margaret of Anjou, and the obnoxious measures of her ministers.

House of Lords places Duke in line of succession

An open rupture resulted, and for ten years the animosity, hatred, and spirit of vengeance which characterized the Houses of York and Lancaster can be estimated by the principal battles which disgraced this age. At the end of that period, October, 1460, the Duke of York, being irritated to extremity by the political and personal opposition of the Queen, and goaded by his incensed party to revenge the insults which had been repeatedly offered to them, at length publicly appealed to Parliament. He requested recognition of his title to the throne as the descendant of Lionel, Duke of Clarence, *third* son of Edward III (as compared with Henry VI, who claimed through John of Gaunt, Duke of Lancaster, *fourth* son of Edward III).

The House of Lords recognized the Duke of York's claims to the throne by enacting (*Rot. Parl.* p. 317) that Henry VI should retain the sceptre for the remainder of his life, but that succession to the throne should devolve, on his decease, to the Duke of York and his heirs.

Spurning with indignation an enactment which deprived her son of his inheritance and limited her own and her husband's regal position to the mere sufferance of Parliament, Queen Margaret fled to Scotland. Here she assembled, with the aid of her northern partisans, the Earl of Northumberland and the Lord Clifford, a powerful force in such an incredibly short time that it enabled her to defy Parliament's decision and the commands of her pusillanimous husband, Henry VI.

Death of Duke of York

The Duke of York, unprepared for such prompt measures, hastened to crush this opposition to his recently admitted claims to the crown. Accompanied by his second son, Edmund, Earl of Rutland, he reached his Castle of Sendal with about 6,000 men on December 21, 1460. He was to have been speedily joined by his eldest son, Edward, the Earl of March, whom he had hastily dispatched to Wales to summon his vassals.

The intrepid Queen reached the gates of York before the Duke was in any position to encounter her fomidable force. Heedless of the advice of his friends, and regarding only the taunts of his enemies, the Duke sallied forth from the Castle, and was induced under peculiarly disadvantageous circumstances to encounter his foes. The Battle of Wakefield, December 30, 1460, was brief. The Duke was overpowered by superior numbers and was captured.

He was dragged in mockery to an ant-hill, crowned by a diadem of knotted grass, and insultingly placed there as on a throne. His enemies deridingly made their submission, exclaiming, 'Hail! king without a kingdom. Hail! prince without a people'. He was at length beheaded. His head, fixed on a lance, was presented in triumph to the Queen and, by her command, placed over the gates of York, surmounted with a paper crown. The Earl of Rutland, the Duke's son, was also captured and killed. Such was the tragedy of the career of Richard, Duke of York who, like his illustrious parent, Richard, Earl of Cambridge, was suddenly cut off by a violent and untimely death.

Crowning of Edward IV

The Yorkists speedily rallied their full force round the eldest surviving son of the Duke of York, Edward, the Earl of March, who was not quite 19. Victory followed upon victory. Henry VI, Queen Margaret, and their son, Edward, Prince of Wales, fled into Scotland. Edward of March, now Duke of York, proceeded to London where he was proclaimed King Edward IV and crowned at Westminster, March 4, 1461, within three months of his father's death.

Thus, we have briefly portrayed the state of public affairs, from the usurpation of the line of Lancaster (from Richard II) in the person of Henry IV, to the period up to the accession of the House of York in that of King Edward IV. It is now the fitting time to chronicle the history of the Prince who is the subject of this history. His feelings and impressions, from the earliest dawn of reason, could not fail to be influenced by the violent deaths of his grandfather, the Earl of Cambridge, and his father, the Duke of York, and by the passions and struggle for power which marked the period in which was born Richard of Gloucester.

Chapter III

RICHARD'S BIRTH — LEGENDS

Richard born at Fotheringhay

Richard Plantagenet, usually designated Richard of Gloucester, was born at Fotheringhay Castle on October 2, 1452. Fotheringhay Castle was erected by Edmund of Langley, first Duke of York, the fifth son of Edward III, and the great grandsire of Richard of Gloucester. Richard was the youngest son and the eleventh of twelve children of the Duke of York, whose busy and illustrious life closed so tragically at the Battle of Wakefield, December 30, 1460.

Cecily, Duchess of York

The mother of Richard III, Cecily, Duchess of York, was one of the most eminent women of her age and occupied a very prominent position in the eventful life of her youngest son. Of high birth and superior attainments, her rare and exquisite beauty obtained for her in childhood the name of the 'Rose of Raby'. She showed greatness of mind during periods of unexampled trial, and displayed zeal and rectitude of purpose in the active performance of conjugal and maternal duties. She is more an object of respect and admiration than of sympathy for the poignant sorrows which marked her sad and eventful career.

This distinguished lady was the youngest of twenty-two children of Ralph Neville, Earl of Westmoreland. Though by birth a Lancastrian — her mother being half-sister to the usurper, Henry of Bolingbroke (Henry IV) — yet from very early childhood, the Lady Cecily was the companion of the attainted heir of the House of York, who was brought up and educated in her father's house. The wardship of the young Plantagenet, her future husband, had been bestowed by Henry V upon the Earl of Westmoreland shortly after the execution of Richard's father, the Earl of Cambridge. Of the place or the precise period at which the marriage of Richard, Duke of York, with the Lady Cecily was solemnized, no record has been found. The Lady Cecily was about two years younger than her noble consort, having been born on the 3rd of May, 1415. The loyalty of the young couple, their entire submission to King Henry VI (who was first cousin, once removed, to Neville's daughter), and the interest and attachment felt by that monarch for them is shown by the fact that he stood godfather to their eldest son, who was named Henry in deference to his royal sponsor and kinsman.

The illustrious couple were blessed with twelve children — eight sons and four daughters. On the demise of the Duke of York, three sons and three daughters alone survived him:

Edward of York, the second son, Earl of March, his heir and successor, born at Rouen, April 28, 1442, during his father's regency in France, who succeeded (as Edward IV) to the dignities of his house and obtained that crown for which the life of his sire and his grandsire had been prematurely sacrificed.

George of York, the sixth son, afterwards Duke of Clarence, born October 21, 1449, at Dublin, during his parents' abode in Ireland.

Richard of York, the eighth son, afterwards Richard III, born October 2, 1452, at the Castle of Fotheringhay, the patrimonial seat of his ancestors.

Ann of York, Duchess of Exeter, the eldest child, born at Fotheringhay, August 10, 1439; married first to Henry Holland, Duke of Exeter, secondly to Sir Thomas St. Leger, Knight.

Elizabeth of York, born at Rouen, April 22, 1444; married to John De La Pole, Duke of Suffolk.

Margaret of York, born at Fotheringhay, May 2, 1446; married to Charles, Duke of Burgundy.

Inattention to the vast difference of age — almost 10½ years — between Edward, Earl of March, the third child, and Richard of Gloucester, the eleventh child, has been one leading cause of confusion as to dates. It has resulted in many conflicting statements on important events in which Richard is considered to have acted a prominent part but which, it will be hereafter seen, was improbable if not actually impossible by reason of his extreme youth.

To the Lady Cecily, in great measure, may be attributed the superior acquirements of her family, who were most carefully educated by her. We have substantial proof of the uniform manner in which the household of the Duchess of York was probably conducted and of the religious and moral sentiments there inculcated in a valuable and highly interesting document which has been preserved to the present day ('In a collection of papers now at the Board of Green Cloth, St. James's' — 1844), narrating the order, rules, and regulations observed in her establishment and evincing the sound principles and strict discipline enforced by its noble mistress:

> 'She useth to arise at seven of the clock, and hath readye her chapleyne to saye with her mattins of the daye, and mattins of our lady, and when she is fully readye she hathe a lowe mass in her chambre; and after mass she taketh something to recreate nature and soe goeth to the chapelle, hearinge the devine service and tuo lowe masses. From thence to dynner, durringe the tyme whereof she hath a lecture of holy matter, either a "Hilton of Contemplative and Active Life" or other spiritual and instructive works. After dinner she giveth audyence to all such as hath any matter to shewe unto her by the space of one hower, and then sleepeth one quarter of an hower, and after she hath slepte she contynueth in prayer unto the first peale of evensonge. In the tyme of supper she recyteth the lecture that was had at dinner to those that be in her presence. After supper she disposeth herself to be famyliare with her gentlewomen, to the seasoning of honest myrthe; and one houre before her going to bed she taketh a cuppe of wyne, and after that, goeth to her pryvie closette and taketh her leave of God for all nighte, makinge end of her prayers for that daye, and by eighte of the clocke is in bedde'.

Although the record whence the foregoing was extracted was drawn up at a much later period of her life, yet the same spirit that influenced her conduct in after years also animated this eminent lady in the regulation of her domestic circle with a well-devised system which reflects such honour on her memory. Similar ordinances were framed for the regulation of the household of her son George, Duke of Clarence, long after he was emancipated from maternal influence, and by her eldest son, King Edward IV, for the observance of his own offspring, in which many of the regulations closely correspond with those pursued by his mother.

Affection of young Plantagenets for parents

Original letters vividly portray the true and natural character of individuals, by depicting their inmost thoughts and feelings. This letter, dated June 3, 1454, was written when the Earl of March was twelve and the Earl of Rutland was eleven years of age. The obsolete spelling has been modernized:

> 'Right high and mighty Prince, our most worshipful and greatly redoubtable lord and father, — In as lowly wise as any sons can, or may, we recommend us unto your good lordship; and please it your

highness to wit, that we may have received your worshipful letters yesterday by your servant William Cleton, bearing date at York the 29th of May (apparently acquainting them he had triumphed over the Duke of Suffolk and been appointed "protector and defender of England", to which office he was appointed in April 1454).

'By the which William, and by the relation of John Milewater, we conceive your worshipful and victorious speed against your enemies; to their great shame, and to us the most comfortable things that we desired to hear. Whereof we thank Almighty God of his gifts; beseeching him heartily to give you that good and cotidian fortune, hereafter to know your enemies, and to have the victory of them. And if it please your highness to know of our welfare at the making of this letter, we were in good health of body, thanked be God; beseeching your good and gracious fatherhood of your daily blessing. And where ye command us by your said letters to attend specially to our learning in our young age, that should cause us to grow to honour and worship in our old age, please it your highness to wit, that we have attended our learning since we came hither, and shall hereafter, by the which we trust to God your gracious lordship and good fatherhood shall be pleased. Also we beseech your good lordship, that it may please you to send us Harry Lovedeyne, groom of your kitchen, whose service is to us right agreeable, and we will send you John Boynes to wait on your good lordship.

'Right high and mighty Prince, our most worshipful and greatly redoubted lord and father, we beseech Almighty God give you as good life and long, as your own princely heart can best desire.

Written at your castle of Ludlow the 3rd of June.

'your humble sons,
'E. Marche.
'E. Rutland.

'To the right high and mighty Prince, our most worshipful and greatly redoubted lord and father, the Duke of York, protector and defender of England'.

(Previous to the reign of Henry V, specimens of English correspondence are rare. Letters before that time were usually written in French or Latin, chiefly by the great and learned. The earliest royal signature is the signature of Richard II.)

Legends about Richard's birth

Not the slightest foundation exists for reports so outrageous to common sense as those propagated regarding the birth of Richard of Gloucester. No trace of them can be found in contemporary records with the single exception of John Rous, 'the monk of Warwick', whose narrative (*Hist. Reg. Ang.*, p. 214) has been pronounced by Lord Orford (Horace Walpole), after careful and critical examination, 'too despicable and lying even amongst monkish authors' to merit quotation.

Whatever Rous chose to say of Richard III after his death, for the ears of Henry VII, he gave a very different account of him in his roll which he left as a monument of the earls and town of Warwick. Here is the inscription as it is written by Rous's own hand: 'The most mighty Prince Richard, by the grace of God, King of England and of France, and Lord of Ireland: . . . by heir male lineally descending from King Harry the Second, all avarice set aside, ruled his subjects in his realm full commendably, punishing offendors of his laws, especially extortioners and oppressors of his commons, and cherishing those that were virtuous, by the which discreet guiding he got great thank of God and love of all his subjects, rich and poor, and great laud of the people of other lands about him'. (From the original MS roll, now in the College of Arms, published in Lord Orford's Works, vol. ii, p. 215.)

All other annalists of credit belonging to that period, including the Chronicler of Croyland, William of Wyrcester, and the Abbot of St. Alban's, make no mention or allusion to such reports. Even Sir Thomas More, whose history has been the main source whence modern writers have derived their prejudices against Richard of Gloucester, prefaces his marvellous report by the modifying sentence, 'it is for truth reported' or 'as the fame runneth'. By adding 'whether men of hatred reporte above the truth' he shows that his statement was founded on no authority but on report alone and implies his own suspicion of the rancorous feeling whence the tradition emanated.

No authentic record, indeed, is extant respecting the birth of Richard Plantagenet beyond the date of time and place where it occurred. Mr Hutton asserts that 'the idle tales of Richard's birth are beneathe the notice of history, and that his infancy was spent in his father's house, where he cuckt his ball and shoot (sic) his taw with the same delight as other lords' (Hutton's Bosworth, p. xvii). Laing, in his valuable 'Dissertation on the crimes imputed to Richard III, after quoting the statement by Rous regarding the alleged birth of Richard with teeth and hair reaching to his shoulders', adds: 'The historian who deduces Richard's crimes from a calculation of his nativity, may attest the popular belief and rumour; but his private information must rest where he has placed it

— on the authority of the stars'.(Appendix at the close of Henry's *History of England*, vol. xii, p.424).

Treachery at Ludlow

Richard was only about seven when he was called upon to experience the severe vicissitudes and personally share in the disastrous consequences of nearness to the throne. For three generations that proximity had perilled the lives and nearly ruined the fortunes of his illustrious House of York. It was in October 1459 that the armies of the Houses of Lancaster and York — the Red and White Roses — having been roused to the highest degree of fury, assembled in order of battle near the town and Castle of Ludlow. But Sir Andrew Trollope, with the chief soldiers of Calais, suddenly departed secretly in the night and joined the royal banner. This desertion, the dismay it created, and the uncertainty how many would imitate the treachery, unnerved the courage of the rest, and they dispersed before dawn.

The Duke of York, taking with him his second son, Edmund, Earl of Rutland, aged sixteen, departed secretly at midnight from his stronghold at Ludlow and sought refuge in the wilds and fastnesses of Ireland. Here he was received with enthusiasm and served with fidelity because of the popularity he had acquired during his former just but mild government of that country. Edward, Earl of March, his eldest son, aged seventeen, escaped into France with his kinsmen, the Lords of Salisbury and Warwick, leaving to the mercy of their foes the Duchess of York and her infant sons, George and Richard Plantagenet, aged ten and seven. By command of King Henry VI, the Lady Cecily and her young offspring were immediately made prisoners of state and consigned to the custody of her elder sister, the Duchess of Buckingham, who was espoused to one of the firmest supporters of the line of Lancaster, Humphrey, Duke of Buckingham.

The Lady Cecily, with her younger children, found herself a prisoner with them and bereft of home and all her goods. She was overwhelmed by the conviction of the utter and irretrievable ruin of the House of York, because of the severe measures adopted towards the House. Its leaders were all exiles or outlawed as traitors. Every branch of her own family was attainted for the share which they had taken in the rebellion or, like herself, deprived of their rich possessions, and utterly in the power and at the mercy of their foes. But

26

her husband's cause was not so desperate as it first appeared. It was too popular and had been espoused too warmly to be ruined by a single dispersion of his followers.

The Yorkists regain the ascendancy

The pretensions of the Duke of York to the throne being upheld by the powerful influence of his wife's kindred, and aided by their vast wealth, fortune once more began to smile on the exiled chief and his family. The young Edward of March was encouraged in the ensuing year to return to England and face his opponents. With the leaders of the Yorkist faction, he unfurled the standard of rebellion and gave battle to the Lancastrians at Northampton, July 10, 1460.

So signal a victory did they achieve over the royal army that Henry VI was taken prisoner and the chief of his adherents scattered or slain. Queen Margaret of Anjou and her young son, Edward, Prince of Wales, were compelled to seek safety in flight. The Duke of York was summoned from his exile in Dublin by his triumphant party to assume a still higher position than that which had led to his attainder in the previous year.

The Lady Cecily had privately sought an asylum for herself and young children at the law-chambers of Sir John Paston, a faithful friend and ally of the family, in the Temple. The following excerpts from a contemporary letter convey one of the few well-authenticated memorials of the childhood of Richard III:

> 'To the Right Worshipful Sir and Master John Paston at Norwich, be this letter delivered in haste.
> 'Right worshipful Sir and Master, . . . there come hither to my master's place . . . the harbinger of my Lord of March, desiring that my Lady of York might be here until the coming of my Lord of York and her two sons, my Lord George and my Lord Richard, and my Lady Margaret her daughter, which I granted . . . my lord (the Duke of York) sent for her, that she should come to him to Hereford; and thither she is gone, and she hath left here both the sons and the daughter, and the Lord of March cometh every day to see them.
> 'Written by a confidential servant of John Paston, one Christopher Hausson, October 12, 1460'.

Here we see exemplified in a very striking manner the strong affection which was evidently a spontaneous and inherent feeling in the children of the House of York. Edward, its heir, though only 18, and commanding his father's garrison with the firmness and vigour of an experienced leader, yet affectionately attended to the comfort of his younger brothers and sister. Despite his political difficulties and the importance of his military claims, the Earl of March found time to visit them each day.

Duke of York's claims conceded by Parliament

On October 10, 1460, the Duke and Duchess of York reached London and at Baynard's Castle the long-separated branches of the illustrious family of York were once more happily reunited. The political events consequent on this sudden emancipation of the Duke of York have been already narrated in Chapter II. It will be remembered that up to this period he had not actually claimed the crown but merely urged his right of succession. When, however, this latter point was conceded to him and his heirs, not only by act of Parliament but by the assent of Henry VI, there needed little else to render his triumph complete. This result speedily followed for Parliament further enacted that henceforth, 'to encompass the Duke of York's death should be considered high treason', and the justness of his rights were acknowledged by his being created 'Prince of Wales, Duke of Cornwall and Earl of Chester' in addition to the lofty title of 'protector of the realm'.

Thus, after years of storm and tempest, the sun of prosperity seemed at last to shine with renewed lustre upon the House of York, as if to compensate for the many reverses of fortune that had, in the end, terminated so happily for them.

Lancastrians regain ascendancy

But it was a prosperity too brilliant to be lasting. A few weeks of reunion and domestic happiness were destined to usher in a future fraught with degradation and death to the father, sorrow and calamity to his widow, and ultimate misery to his descendants and their offspring. The Duke of York was hastily summoned to oppose Queen Margaret in the North. Once more, he took young Edmund of Rutland as his companion, dispatched the Earl of March into Wales to assemble their feudal adherents in the marches (boundaries between England and Wales), and left Lady Cecily to watch over the lives of the junior branches of their family. The Duke proceeded with a small but trusty band to his fortress at Sendal, near Wakefield.

There, on December 30, 1460 (as narrated in Chapter II), he received a paper crown in lieu of that much-coveted diadem for which he had so long fought and bled. Then, he and young Rutland met a speedy and tragic death.

The Chronicler of Croyland, in narrating the effect of the battle of Wakefield on the minds of King Henry's supporters, states that 'elated with their victory, they rushed like a whirlwind over England, and plundered without respect of persons or place. They attacked the churches, took away their vessels, books, and clothes; even the sacramental pyxes, shaking out the eucharist, and slew the priests who resisted. So they acted for a breadth of thirty miles, all the way from York nearly up to London'. (*Chron. Croy.*, p. 531)

Chapter IV

RICHARD'S ALLEGED DEFORMITY

Duchess of York secretly conveys sons to Utrecht

The widowed Duchess of York was overwhelmed at the disastrous intelligence of her husband's defeat and death and the murder of her son, the Earl of Rutland, at Wakefield, December 30, 1460. She promptly took measures for secretly conveying out of the kingdom her two young sons, George and Richard Plantagenet, aged 11 and 8, respectively. Philip, Duke of Burgundy, gave them a friendly reception and speedily established them, with suitable governors, in the City of Utrecht. They continued to abide there until the House of York regained ascendancy and their brother, King Edward IV, was established permanently on the throne.

Accession and coronation of Edward IV

It was in the famed metropolitan abode of the late good Duke Richard, Baynard's Castle, that the youthful representative of the House of York, Edward, assumed the title and dignity of king as Edward IV, March 4, 1461. After witnessing the triumphant return of her son, and beholding in due time his accession and coronation, June 28, 1461, Cecily retired to the privacy of Berkhampstead. By this act, the Lady Cecily evinced that true nobleness of character for which she was so remarkable. She might, as the surviving parent of the victorious sovereign, have continued to occupy that high position which the spirit of the times rendered so enviable. But in her husband's grave the widow of the noble York appears to have buried all her aspiring views.

Tranquility at length being somewhat restored to the desolated kingdom, Edward IV dispatched trusty messengers to Burgundy to bring home his young brothers. He invested Prince George, his eldest surviving brother, with the Duchy of Clarence and created Prince Richard, the youngest, Duke of Gloucester in November 1461. In February 1462, he further constituted Clarence lieutenant of Ireland.

Richard of Gloucester, whom the King had made admiral of the sea, was speedily nominated to even greater honours. The preamble of the patent conveying these honours, viz., 'The king, in consideration of the sincere fraternal affection which he entertained towards his right well-beloved brother Richard, Duke of Gloucester, and admiral of the sea', strongly marks, even at this early period, the peculiar interest and attachment entertained for Richard by his royal brother.

It is apparent that Richard was fondly cherished by his kindred, early endowed with immense wealth, distinguished by marks of singular favour and openly expressed strong affection from his sovereign and elder brother. Could he have been the monster of depravity which posterity has been taught to believe him — 'malicious, wrathful, envious from his birth' — or have given indication during infancy and boyhood of that fiend-like temperament which hitherto has been generally considered the characteristic of the Duke of Gloucester?

Alleged deformity of Richard, Duke of Gloucester

No contemporary account except that of Rous affords even a shadow of foundation for the distorted figure and repulsive lineaments so universally ascribed to Richard in after ages. The testimony of eye-witnesses or contemporary authorities can alone be deemed conclusive on such points. It is thus a very startling circumstance that, except for the prejudiced Rous, all the writers to whom the Duke of Gloucester could have been personally known, and from whose remarks the only genuine accounts of him can at the present day be obtained, are silent on the subject, thus tacitly proving that there was no such deformity to note.

The Chronicler of Croyland, the Abbot of St. Alban's, the author of Fleetwood's Chronicle, the correspondents of the Paston family, and many other writers, lived at the same period with Richard, Duke of Gloucester. William of Wyrcester, for example, when detailing the enthusiasm of the populace at the election of Edward IV in St. John's Field, says, 'I was there, I heard them, and I returned with them into the city'. The author of the fragment relating to Edward IV published by Hearne proves his intimate acquaintance with the House of York by stating 'My purpose is, and shall be, as touching the life of Edward IV, to write and show such things as I have heard of his own mouth; and also impart of such things in the which I have been personally present, as well within the royaulme as without, during a certain space, more especial from 1468 to 1482'.

This period embraces a most important part of Richard of Gloucester's life — a period when he was on all public occasions associated with his royal brother. Yet this writer nowhere mentions any deformity in Richard. Neither is it noticed or in any way alluded to by any of the other writers mentioned above, though each must have known the fact had it existed. In these writers we have extant a series of connecting links extending from Gloucester's infancy to his death. Yet nowhere in any one of them is there to be found a foundation even for the report of a deformity. Were it true, it is opposed to all reason to believe it could have escaped comment or mention by writers who narrated so minutely the passing events of their day.

Honest Philip de Comines (as he has been termed), a Flemish historian of undoubted veracity and uninfluenced by party views, neither asserts nor insinuates anything remarkable in the external appearance of Richard of Gloucester. This historian twice mentions 'that Edward IV was the most beautiful prince that he had ever seen, or of his time'. He was well known to the three brothers — Edward, George and Richard — and frequently saw them all. Certainly de Comines, who had mentioned the extraordinary beauty of form and feature of Edward IV and the Duke of Clarence, would also have alluded, by way of comparison, to a deformity in their young brother had there been the slightest foundation for that revolting aspect with which later writers have invested him.

The only account which supports the fables so long imposed on posterity is that of John Rous, the recluse of Warwick, whose history in Latin of the Kings of England was dedicated to Henry VII. But, though an avowed Lancastrian and a bitter enemy of the line of York, this historian simply alleges that Gloucester 'was small of stature, having a short face and uneven shoulders, the left being lower than the right'.

Polydore Vergil, author of the *Anglica Historia*, which strongly favours the House of Lancaster, describes King Richard as 'slight in figure, in face short and compact, like his father'. Sir George Buck, the first historian who had sufficient hardihood to attempt Richard's defence, appears to have had access to documents no longer extant, though quoted by him as then in Sir Robert Cotton's manuscript library. He not only warmly defends Richard against the current accusation of moral guilt, but confesses himself unable to find any evidence whatever warranting the imputation of personal deformity.

32

Horace Walpole, Lord Orford, who bestowed the most un-wearied pains in searching for the source of the extraordinary reports of Gloucester's alleged misshapen appearance, could find no corroboration of rumours so long believed. On the contrary, in his *Historic Doubts*, this able writer produces contemporary state-ments to prove the beauty of Richard's features and the fact of his generally prepossessing appearance. He says the old Countess of Desmond, who had danced with Richard, declared he 'was the handsomest man in the room except for his brother Edward, and was very well made'. Sharon Turner, in his *Middle Ages*, says 'His face was handsome'.

After the most attentive examination of contemporary sources, the evidence regarding the personal appearance of Richard, Duke of Gloucester, will be found to amount to this:

> 'In figure slight'. 'Like his father's, short and compact'. — Polydore Vergil, p. 544.
> 'Small of stature'. 'Mild in countenance'. — Rous, p. 215.
> 'Of low stature'. — John Stow, p. xiii.
> 'Thy face worthy of the highest empire and command'. — Oration of the Scottish Ambassador, Buck, lib. v, p. 140.
> 'His face always thin'. — Cont. Croy., p. 574.
> 'Lowlye of countenance'. — More.

(Note: The reader will find the London National Gallery's portrait of Richard utterly devoid of those features attributed to him by his enemies.)

Origin of rumours — More's *Historie* — Bishop Morton

'There never was in any man a greater uniformity of body and mind than was in him, both of them equally deformed. Of body he was but low, crook'd-backed, hook-shouldered, splay-footed and goggle-eyed; his face little and round, his complexion swarthy, his left arm from his birth dry and withered; born a monster in nature, with all his teeth, with hair on his head and nails on his fingers and toes. And just such were the qualities of his mind'. Baker's *Chronicle*, p. 234.

'The tyrant King Richard was born', says Rous, 'with teeth, and hair reaching to his shoulders . . .'.

Whence, then, arose an idea so firmly believed that it has stood the test of ages and been transferred for almost five centuries from the grave pages of history to the simplest elementary tales connected with our national biography? It was unsupported by the testimony of writers immediately succeeding the period in which those that have been quoted flourished. This is apparent not merely from Polydore Vergil and the authorities above named but also from John Stow, whose writings have always been esteemed for their honest, clear and correct details.

Stow, in his valuable work, *The Survey of London*, declared that 'he could find no such note of deformity in King Richard III as historians commonly relate'. He had spoken with some ancient men who, from their own sight and knowledge affirmed that Richard was of bodily shape comely enough, only of low stature. Now, as 'honest John Stow' was born in 1525, only 40 years after Richard's decease, he must have had many facilities for speaking with those who had both known and seen the King. Stow was also remarkable for his circumstantial detail of the persons of princes, and 'very inquisitive', too, in the description of their persons and features. (Life of Stow, prefixed to his *Survey of London*, p. xviii, ed. 1720)

This note of deformity and other rumours equally unfair to King Richard were at first only suggested but afterwards speedily asserted as fact by succeeding chroniclers to flatter the reigning sovereign of the new dynasty, Henry VII. There can be little doubt that they emanated exclusively from the writings of Thomas More, specifically *The Historie of King Rycharde the Thirde, written by Master Thomas More, then one of the Under Sheriffes of London; about the year of our Lord 1513.*

More was then not Saint Thomas More, nor Sir Thomas More, nor Lord Chancellor of England. He was an undersheriff of London, aged 35 — born February 7, 1478. Thus, he was only 7 when Richard III was killed at Bosworth Field and must have gotten the material for his Historie from hearsay. He was raised in the house of Bishop Morton, Richard's bitterest enemy. Moreover, Morton was a personal friend, a companion in exile, and a chief agent in establishing Henry VII on the throne.

Yet even More, violent as he was against Richard of Gloucester, by no means vouches for the truth of the startling assertions which he was the means of promulgating. 'Richard was deformed', he says, 'as the fame ranne of those that hated him'. What contradiction more efficient than his own few words, 'as menne of hatred reporte'? It at once shows that the rumours of Richard's deformity, which received no corroboration from contemporary sources, evidently proceeded from the hatred, prejudice, and malignity of his enemies.

Nevertheless, More's *Historie* is the acknowledged origin of the preposterous tales alluded to by Stow and speedily refuted by that historian. These tales were, however, afterwards revived and exaggerated by the Tudor chroniclers and, through them, indelibly perpetuated by the master hand of their copyist, the immortal Shakespeare. In many of the great dramatist's most striking passages connected with this period he has merely versified the language of those early historians who based their authority on More.

One very remarkable fact should be considered — *no writer, except the prejudiced Rous, describes the person of Richard during his lifetime.*

It is quite clear from the testimony of More's biographer (Singer's reprint of More, pp. viii, ix) that 'the mistakes, discrepancies and falsifications' of the Historie, together with the 'hideous portrait of Richard' contained in it, were derived from details and conversation in boyhood from Morton. He was Richard's avowed enemy and bitter persecutor, who sought that monarch's destruction on every occasion, and by whose death Morton was eventually elevated by Henry VII to be Lord Chancellor of England. Henry VII eventually obtained for Morton the dignity of a cardinal. (Modern historians agree that Morton either wrote the Historie or supplied most of the information to More.)

Lord Bacon says, when summing up the character of Cardinal Morton: 'Hee was a wise man and an eloquent, but in his nature harsh and haughtie; much accepted by the king, but enveyed by the nobility and hated by the people. Hee wonne the king with secrecie and diligence, but chiefly because he was his old servant in his lesse fortunes; and also for that (in his affections) he was not without an inveterate malice against the House of York, under whom he had been in trouble'. (Bacon's *Henry VII*, p. 198)

Richard's boyhood and training

Resuming the narrative with the nomination of Richard to the Dukedom of Gloucester, it is apparent that the young Prince could have taken no part in the turbulent opening years of the reign of his brother, Edward IV. Richard had just attained the age of nine, his creation as Duke of Gloucester occurring November 4, 1461, in the first Parliament held by King Edward IV after his coronation.

Richard evidently remained in his mother's care up to the usual age of seven but, from this period, his name is no longer mentioned in connection with the Lady Cecily. It appears most probable that on his return from Flanders, Gloucester was forthwith submitted to the prescribed probation of the succeeding seven years in the abode of some powerful baron. This was the usual course for those that were to perform the duties of a warrior knight.

This surmise appears to be correct because, in the fifth year of his brother's reign, an entry on the issue roll of the Exchequer (Anno 5 Edw. IV, p. 490, 8vo. 1837) records that money was 'paid to Richard, Earl of Warwick, for costs and expenses incurred by him on behalf of the Duke of Gloucester, the king's brother'. No other public document relating to Richard is on record, except for letters from King Edward conferring honours and possessions upon his young brother. Richard was 13 at the time of this entry (1465). This corresponds precisely with the intermediate probationary term exacted by the laws of chivalry for the knightly instruction of noble youths of that period. This fact, and the omissions of all mention of the Prince's name in political affairs during the intervening years and the particular wording of this document, seems to warrant the conclusion that the renowned Earl of Warwick, the 'king maker' and the King dethroner, was the warrior lord selected by King Edward IV for initiating his young brother into the practice of arms.

The young Richard of Gloucester probably passed his boyish days at Middleham Castle. There, too, perhaps Richard first bestowed his affections on his gentle cousin Anne, Warwick's younger and more lovely daughter.

Edward's great affection for Richard

One thing at least remains undisputed regarding Richard, namely, King Edward's strong and unabated affection for him and his anxious desire to promote his young brother's advancement to the highest and most honourable posts. If the written memorials of Richard's history are few, yet on this one point they are authentic and valuable. No more convincing proof could be desired than Richard's election, at fourteen, to the high honour of a knight of the most noble Order of the Garter, an institution which made England the centre of chivalry. It was one of the most ancient lay orders in the world, and at that time was limited to twenty-six companions. The rarity of the distinction is evinced by its not having been bestowed by the founder, Edward III, even upon his own son, Thomas, Duke of Gloucester.

If then but little of actual importance remains on record concerning the early youth of Richard III, it is an indication of his peaceable and tranquil career that no verified tales of horror or accusations against him can be fairly charged. King Edward might have nominated his young brother to important offices and appointments as a means of preventing the power thus nominally bestowed from being turned against himself by treachery or rebellion. But unless this monarch had considered Richard as worthy to bear and fitting to adorn one of the most distinguished positions in the sovereign's power to advance him — one exclusively of honour — he would scarcely have been induced to invest the young Richard, at the early age of fourteen, with so high a distinction as the order of the Garter.

Chapter V

WARWICK AND CLARENCE REVOLT; EDWARD ABDICATES

Re-interment of Duke of York and Earl of Rutland at Fotheringhay

Richard of Gloucester was but a stripling of 14 when he was created a Knight of the Garter in 1466, and his entrance into a most active public career may be dated from this period. Almost the first act of Edward IV, after his accession to the crown in 1461 was to remove the head of his illustrious parent, the Duke of York, from its ignominious spot over the gates of York and honourably inter his remains beside those of the young Earl of Rutland at Pontefract. When firmly established on the throne, and after a few years of tranquility had somewhat replenished the impoverished coffers of the kingdom (1466), the young monarch further evinced his strong affection for the memory of his deceased father and brother. He decided to remove their remains to the burial place of their family, in the chancel of the collegiate church founded at Fotheringhay by their ancestor, Edward Plantagenet, second Duke of York.

Edward IV selected Richard of Gloucester, on this important occasion, to transport the remains of their father, and to accompany them in state the whole way, following next after the corpse, supported by the chief of the nobility and officers. The funeral was one of the most splendid and sumptuous on record. The King stood at the entrance of the churchyard, arrayed in the deepest mourning, to receive the relics from Gloucester, and to precede the revered remains of his relatives to the altar of Fotheringhay Church. No mention is made of Clarence, though many noble personages are enumerated by Sandford as aiding the monarch in the solemn ceremony which he minutely describes. It is quite evident, therefore, that Clarence was not present. This cannot but suggest a strong conviction that George of Clarence must early have forfeited the esteem and confidence of his royal brother. His rebellious spirit was discerned and resented by the King, while the firmness and decision which characterized the young Richard of Gloucester, equally apparent to his elder brother, formed the groundwork of that unity of feeling which throughout their lives existed between Edward IV and Richard.

The characters of the three brothers

Personal bravery was characteristic of the House of York, and King Edward IV was unexampled in English history for the frequency and completeness of his victories and the number and high character of his appointments. But though an able general, and of invincible courage, he was averse to business, devoted to pleasure, vain of his person, and self-willed in his actions. Thus, although he was by nature endowed with an understanding of no ordinary power, he was generally looked upon by his nobles as a weak though fascinating King. However, he won the hearts of his people: *'There never was any prince of this land attaining the crown by battle,'* observed Sir Thomas More (*Rychard III*, p. 2), *'so heartily beloved with the substance of the people . . . '.*

George, Duke of Clarence, was 'a goodly and noble prince' (More, p. 7), scarcely inferior to the King in beauty of person and dignity of demeanour. The Chronicler of Croyland, speaking of him and his young brother of Gloucester, says that 'the said princes possessed so much talent that all men, even those learned in the law, wondered' at them (p. 557). But Clarence, though possessed of warm and kindly feelings, was a fickle and unstable Prince and easily became the prey of designing men who were far beneath him in goodness of heart and intellectual endowments.

Richard of Gloucester, ten years younger than the King, and three years junior to Clarence, was gifted with such vigorous powers of intellect that, in spite of the disparity of years, he is found on all occasions associated with his brothers. Even his bitterest enemy, Cardinal Morton, speaks of his 'good qualities being fixed on his memory' (Grafton, p. 147). The evidence of his brother, Edward IV, in a public document still extant, affords proof of the probity, virtue, and integrity which he felt to be deserving of public notice and of substantial reward:

'The king especially, considering the gratuitous (sic), laudable, and honourable services in manywise rendered to him by his most dear brother, Richard, Duke of Gloucester, his innate probity and other deserts of manners and virtues, and willing, therefore, to provide him a competent reward,' etc., bestows on him, by letters patent, a fitting remuneration for his fidelity and honourable conduct (Cott. MSS. Julius, book xii, fol. iii).

These virtues of his young age were matured in after years, and continued to influence his actions. A Parliamentary Roll (Rot. Parl., vol. vi, p. 240) notes 'the great wit, prudence, justice, princely courage, memorable and laudable acts, in divers battles, which we by experience know ye heretofore have done for the salvation and defence of this same realme'. It attests the opinion entertained of his character and conduct, not merely by his lordly compeers but by the great mass of the people who flourished in his time.

Such was Richard, Duke of Gloucester — such the much execrated monster long believed and long represented as deficient in every quality, except such as were revolting to humanity.

Marriage of Edward IV
— mortification of Warwick

Never did monarch assume a crown under brighter prospects, never did the tide of royal fortune flow more propitiously than during the opening years of the reign of Edward IV. Let us recall that he was accepted as King, March 4, 1461. Prosperity, however, was less suited to exalt the character of this monarch than were the harder lessons of adversity. He soon became careless, indifferent, and short-sighted, except in the pursuit of pleasure. King Edward, in an un-guarded moment, was subdued by the beauty and virtues of a Lancastrian widow pleading in all lowliness of heart forgiveness and favour for herself and her offspring. He secretly married the Lady Elizabeth Grey, May 1, 1464, and made her Queen of England. Elizabeth, the consort of King Edward IV, was the daughter of Sir Richard Wydeville, knight, and the widow of Sir John Grey, of Groby, slain fighting against Edward at the battle of St. Alban (Sandford, book v, p. 385). Thus, Edward placed the regal circlet on the brow of one not only a subject, but the relict of an attainted rebel and the associate and ally of the Lancastrian faction still hated by his own devoted partisans. Edward IV was the first monarch of this realm who selected a subject to share the regal honours.

It has generally been asserted that the Earl of Warwick was at the precise time of this marriage in France, having been sent there by King Edward IV expressly to treat for the hand of Princess Bona of Savoy, sister to the Queen of France, and then resident with her at the

French court. This, however, appears to be one of the many errors of later historians. It is disproved not only by the silence of the French chroniclers as regards any such embassy, but also by the positive contradiction of contemporary writers (see Hearne's Fragment, p. 292, and Cont. Croyland, p. 551).

In common with the nobles of the Yorkist party, Warwick felt indignant at so unseemly an alliance. In his case, that feeling was heightened by having two daughters co-heiresses to his enormous wealth. If a subject were to be selected, he may have thought one of his daughters better entitled by birth and consanguinity and in reward of his own services to be raised to the distinquished position of King Edward's Queen, rather than the widow of Edward's enemy and opponent.

Jealous of the authority and weary of the thralldom in which he was kept by the despotic Earl of Warwick and other powerful lords who had helped to seat him on the throne of his ancestors, Edward IV sought to neutralize the power of the ancient aristocracy of the realm by a counteracting and newly created nobility. Hence, he raised to the highest dignities the relatives of the Queen and conferred on her connections those places of profit and emolument which were greatly coveted by the impoverished gentry of his own party and which, indeed, were justly due to them for their faithful service, thus inducing universal discontent.

Marriage of Clarence

Though many disappointments and mortifications were experienced by the Earl of Warwick, his fidelity towards his acknowledged sovereign and his peaceable demeanour towards the Queen and her relatives continued unbroken. But, by their influence with the King, Edward IV was induced to disregard the advice and remonstrance of his powerful kinsman and accept a treaty of marriage from Philip, Duke of Burgundy, for uniting Philip's heir, Prince Charles, with the Lady Margaret Plantagenet, the sovereign's youngest sister. 'This', says the Chronicler of Croyland, in his most valuable history (p. 551), 'I consider to be the true cause of the dispute between the king and the earl', as the latter was at personal enmity with Prince Charles and wished, moreover, to promote an alliance between the House of York and the court of France, with whom of late he had been amicably connected and was, in fact, secretly allied. The union was postponed for a brief period on account of the sudden demise of

Philip, the reigning duke, but Margaret was united to the Prince of Burgundy July 3, 1468.

Having been foiled in his hopes of seeing one of his co-heiresses raised to that throne on which he had helped to place her cousin, Edward IV, the Earl of Warwick henceforth bent all his thoughts on Clarence, then the first Prince of the blood royal. He sought to appease his mortification by striving to promote the union of his daughter, the Lady Isabelle, with the next male heir to the crown. The decided opposition of the King to this union and the efforts he made to crush all connections between Warwick and Clarence served to complete the exasperation of that proud and haughty baron. Clarence, too, was easily led by Warwick to consider the King's opposition to his marriage as a personal grievance. It was a common cause of offence, then, which really united in firm alliance the Earl of Warwick and the Duke of Clarence.

Enticing the young Prince to Calais, of which dependency Warwick was then governor, he there bestowed on him (July 12, 1468) his elder daughter, Isabelle, in marriage, with a settlement upon them of one-half of the Countess of Warwick's rich inheritance. He obtained a dispensation from Pope Paul III, since the two cousins were related within the forbidden degrees of consanguinity. From this point, the reigning family of England must be viewed in a divided and twofold light, the Duke of Clarence siding with his father-in-law and kinsman, the Earl of Warwick, and the Duke of Gloucester supporting with all zeal and favour the royal prerogative and defending with energy and warmth his brother, Edward IV.

It is apparent that the King was attached to Gloucester in no common degree. The parliamentary documents and state records of that monarch's reign show that scarcely a year passed, from his accession to his death, without some public testimony of it. From henceforth, the elder and younger brother will be found acting in concert on every important affair, actuated apparently by mutual confidence and united by the warmest attachment.

Open rebellion

Margaret of Anjou, the exiled Queen of Henry VI, ever watchful to restore her husband to liberty and reinstate the Prince of Wales in his hereditary honours, hailed with joyful feelings the divisions amongst the Yorkist leaders. Her partisans in England, animated by her unsubdued spirit, rallied their forces again, so that open rebellion was proclaimed in the north of England. Under the command of a popular leader, Robin of Redesdale (Sir John Conyers), the insurgents numbering 60,000 men commenced their march towards London in June 1469. The royal troops were everywhere defeated, and King Edward himself fell into the hands of Warwick and Clarence. Although not as yet openly leagued with the Lancastrian party, they hoped to intimidate the monarch by temporary captivity and mould him again to their views by this display of strength and power. He was first sent to Warwick Castle and thence to Middleham in August. However, his treacherous kinsman, the Earl of Warwick, had no actual authority for detaining his sovereign a prisoner. Having reason to fear a rescue from the more moderate of the Yorkist party, Warwick soon voluntarily released the King. But Edward never forgot the indignity and injury he had suffered, which were, in truth, an unexampled and bitter insult.

Unnatural warfare speedily ensued between Edward IV and the Duke of Clarence, after the former had regained his liberty. This fact, and the defiance by her nephews, the Nevilles, of the acknowledged sovereignty of their King, once more induced the Lady Cecily to publicly exercise maternal rebuke. She procured a meeting at Baynard's Castle between the two brothers and her impetuous kindred, but the reconciliation was transient and insincere. A series of vindictive conflicts followed the recommencement of civil war in which, for a brief period, King Edward gained the ascendancy. In April 1470, Clarence and Warwick were compelled to fly to France.

The twelve months following April 1470 saw a bewildering series of reversals of fortune hardly paralleled in all history. The Earl of Warwick and Clarence were most courteously received because of the friendship long secretly fostered between Louis XI and Warwick. In France they found Margaret of Anjou with Prince Edward of Lancaster, her son. All hope of pardon from King Edward appeared futile by reason of their avowed rebellion, and all connection with the Yorkist faction seemed irrevocably broken by their abandonment of their royal chief, notwithstanding his conciliatory proclamation. Thus, they were induced by the French monarch openly to espouse the cause of the exiled Queen and Henry VI and publicly to avow their intention of reinstating that sovereign on the throne of England. To bind this extraordinary alliance, a marriage was contracted on July 25, 1470, between Margaret of Anjou's only son, the Prince of Wales (16) and the Lady Anne Neville (15), younger daughter of the Earl of Warwick, whose sister, Isabelle, had been united to the Duke of Clarence about a year previously. The fulfilment of the contract

43

was made to depend on the dethronement of Edward IV and restoration of Henry VI to the throne.

Edward IV abdicates throne
— Richard shares his exile

Receiving prompt and considerable aid from Louis XI, both in men and shipping, Warwick was soon able, accompanied by the Duke of Clarence, to effect a landing in England (September 1470). He issued proclamations denouncing Edward of York as a usurper and declaring the imprisoned Henry of Lancaster to be the lawful sovereign. Upon this, the young Duke of Gloucester was immediately appointed warden of the northern marches. He was hastening there with the King and his adherents to quell the insurrection in those revolted districts, when disturbing information was privately conveyed to them. Warwick and Clarence had landed on the southern coast, and King Edward was once more about to be treacherously betrayed by others of his perfidious relatives in the north.

Thus openly defied and basely entrapped, the recently idolized monarch found himself, in a brief period, a King in name only. Perceiving his liberty to be again endangered and his situation growing desperate, his own brother being arrayed against him, Edward of York was compelled to abdicate his throne. With Richard of Gloucester and a small band of faithful followers, he fled the kingdom. He embarked from Lynn, in Norfolk, September 1470, and sailed to Flanders where he besought asylum from his sister Margaret, at the court of Burgundy. So extreme was his poverty, because of his precipitate flight, that it was said his kingly robe, lined with martin skins, was all he had to pay the brave men who conveyed him across the seas.

Restoration of Henry VI — attainder
of Edward IV and Richard

The insurgents hastened with all speed to London and released from captivity the unfortunate Henry VI. On October 13, 1470, just nine years after his dethronement, the hapless monarch resumed the crown and again ostensibly exercised the royal prerogative. Finding

44

him wholly incapacitated for government, Warwick and Clarence were compelled to summon in all haste Parliament so their acts might receive legitimate sanction without waiting for the arrival of the Queen, as had been stipulated by her. In this assembly, Henry of Lancaster was again acknowledged King, Edward IV was declared a usurper, and both he and his brother, Richard, Duke of Gloucester, were attainted and outlawed. The long-exiled supporters of the House of Lancaster were restored to their honours and estates. The Earl of Warwick and the Duke of Clarence were empowered to act as regents during the minority of the Prince of Wales, and in default of issue to him, George, Duke of Clarence, was declared successor to the throne. An impartial review of the whole tenour of the conduct of the Earl of Warwick, from the period of Edward's marriage with Elizabeth Wydeville to his expulsion from the throne by Warwick's means, brings home the conviction that he destined his own offspring to share the throne, by allying them with whosoever swayed the sceptre.

The Duke of Gloucester, young as he was, was of no temperament to be ensnared by the dangerous policy which had duped the un-reflecting George of Clarence. Faithful to the interests of his family, and true to his sovereign who was its head, he preferred, when affairs had reached so desperate a crisis, exile and poverty with his royal brother to dishonourable elevation at the hands of his enemies. The sacrifice induced by such a decision can scarcely be understood at the present day, though its extent is made sufficiently apparent by the chroniclers of those disastrous times. 'I saw', says Philip de Comines (vol. i, p. 239), 'the Duke of Exeter barefoot and ragged, begging his meate from door to door, in the Low Countries', although that nobleman and the Prince of the country had married two sisters, the sisters of Edward IV and Richard of Gloucester. Yet Gloucester voluntarily shared Edward's privations in Burgundy, and served him in his adversity with as much cheerfulness and fidelity as when he had accepted with grateful feelings in days of prosperity the high honours and wealthy endowments which the monarch so early bestowed upon him.

A comparison cannot fail to be here drawn between the unworthy feelings that influenced Clarence to accelerate the downfall of his brother, Edward IV and the behavior of the much defamed Richard, Duke of Gloucester. Richard, traditionally reputed to be devoid of every kind and generous sentiment was, nevertheless, the willing companion and friend in adversity of that brother who had so tenderly fostered him in childhood. Though elevated at this crisis to a degree of authority and importance far beyond that usual to a youth of seventeen, Richard sacrificed all wealth, honours, and independence to become a houseless wanderer and an outcast from his home, and participated in the attainder that deprived King Edward and himself of every possession whether hereditary or acquired.

Chapter VI

BATTLES OF BARNET AND TEWKESBURY; DEATH OF HENRY VI

Edward and Gloucester return to England

The return to England of Queen Margaret of Anjou and her son Edward, Prince of Wales, with additional troops and subsidies from France, seemed alone needed to complete the extraordinary revolution discussed in the previous chapter. Margaret and her son were supported by the entire power of Louis XI. Yet the advanced season of the year, added to perpetual storms and an accumulation of the most untoward casualties, retarded them month after month from landing.

The deposed King Edward IV and his young brother of Gloucester were not of dispositions tamely to submit to a reverse of fortune as sudden as it was severe. They rallied their forces enough to return to England, with the private help of Charles of Burgundy and before Margaret could fulfill any portion of her contract with the Earl of Warwick.

Having only a small body of troops, King Edward was more than once deterred from landing on the coasts which Warwick's vigilance so well guarded. At length, Edward landed at Ravenspur, in Yorkshire, March 14, 1471. Here, he burned his ship, resolving to regain his throne or die. (See Turner's [pp. 278-293] and Markham's [p. 45] stirring accounts of Edward and his 500 followers meeting Richard and his tiny band of 300, after their landing.)

Edward approached the gates of York, not ostensibly as a sovereign, but merely a claimant for his hereditary right of the Duchy of York, bestowed on the Duke of Clarence after King Edward's attainder and expulsion from the throne. 'And he said to the mayor and alderman (sic), that he never would claim no title, nor take upon hande to be King of England, nor would have done afore that time, but by the exciting of the Earl of Warwick; and thereto before all people he cried, "A King Henry! A King and Prince Edward!" and

47

weared an ostrich feather, Prince Edward's livery; and after this, he was suffered to pass the city, and so held his way southward; and no man let him nor hurt him'. (Warkworth's Chronicle, p. 14).

The leading cause, however, of that success which enabled King Edward to throw off the mask which he had assumed was the indication given by the Duke of Clarence of defection from the rebellious standard of Warwick. The rival of his House of York, the monarch of Lancaster, was to be substituted for his exiled brother. In grasping at a vain shadow, he had, in reality, removed himself one degree farther from the possible possession of a crown which he had so laboured and so degraded himself for the purpose of attaining. The now-repentant Duke lamented his defection and saw the folly and weakness of his conduct. The shallow policy which he had pursued in becoming the dupe of Warwick, when fancying himself protesting solely against the undue influence of Edward's Queen, was now apparent.

Cecily, the Duchess of York, with her daughters, the Duchesses of Exeter, Suffolk, and Burgundy, laboured unceasingly to win back the misguided Clarence to his family and his faction. Clarence, inconsistent and restless, ever hasty in action but weak in purpose, again changed sides. He secretly promised that, if his royal brother could land and effect a junction with him, he would aid him with his support towards re-establishment on that throne from which he had been so active an agent in expelling him a few months previously.

Gloucester chiefly instrumental in reconciling his brothers

By Edward's consummate generalship, and movements well devised and ably executed, Warwick was paralysed at the boldness of an undertaking which baffled even his foresight and penetration. Thus, King Edward reached within three miles of the Duke of Clarence's encampment without a single conflict or the slightest opposition being offered to his progress. The fate of the brothers, indeed, of the kingdom at large, now hung on the final decision of the wavering Clarence.

Gloucester, the much-defamed but consistent Gloucester, firm in his allegiance to the one, yet feelingly alive to the degradation of the other, was the chief agent in finally effecting a reconciliation. He achieved a reunion of interests which in a few hours overthrew the deep policy of France, the long-laboured schemes of Warwick, and the sanguine hopes of the Lancastrian Queen, Margaret of Anjou, founded on the apparent annihilation of the Yorkist dynasty.

This anxious desire to restore one brother to the crown and to reclaim the other from dishonour must at least serve to qualify the opposing statements of a subsequent age and throw discredit on the tradition that makes Richard destitute of every kindly sentiment. It satisfactorily explains the nature of 'the gratuitous, laudable, and honourable services', 'the innate probity and other virtues', which King Edward publicly recorded in the letters patent which perpetuated the merits and the rewards which be bestowed on the Duke of Gloucester. (Cottonian MSS, Julius B xii, fol. III.)

The meeting between the brothers — so important to the future destinies of England — is thus simply, but feelingly, narrated by an eye-witness, in a manuscript preserved in the Harleian collection, little known until within the last few years:

> 'The king, upon an afternoon issued out of Warwick with all his fellowship, by the space of three miles, into a fair field, towards Banbury, where he saw the duke, his brother, in fair array, come towards him with a great fellowship; and when they were together within less than half a mile, the king set his people in array, the banners displayed, and left them standing still, taking with him his brother of Gloucester, the Lord Rivers, Lord Hastings, and a few others, and went towards his brother of Clarence, and in likewise the duke, for his part, taking with him a few noblemen and leaving his host in good order, departed from them towards the king: and so they met betwixt both hosts, where was right kind and loving language betwixt them too'. . . . 'And then in likewise spake together the two Dukes of Clarence and Gloucester, and after the other noblemen being there with them, whereof all the people there that loved them were right glad and joyous, and thanked God highly of that joyous meeting, unity and accord, hoping that thereby should grow unto them prosperous fortune in all that they should after that have to do'. . . . 'And so with great gladness both hosts, with their princes, together went to Warwick (city), and there lodged, and in the country near adjoining'.

(collected from a MS in the Harleian Library entitled *Historie of the Arrivall of Edward IV in England, and final Recoverye of his Kingdom*, sometimes entitled *Fleetwood's Chronicle*, and edited and published by J. Bruce, Esq., for the Camden Society, p. 11.)

King Edward recovers the throne

Strong efforts were made to induce the rebellious Neville, Earl of

Warwick, to return to his allegiance, but in vain. King Edward, therefore, by the advice of his brothers, Clarence and Gloucester, and accompanied by them, continued his march to London with all possible dispatch, where he was joyfully received by the citizens. Taking possession of the Tower and of the person of the unhappy Henry VI, he found himself once more established on the English throne. Edward achieved this dramatic change exactly six months after his abdication and expulsion and within only one month of his landing at Ravenspur, under the most unfavourable and unpropitious circumstances that could be conceived.

Edward IV reached London on April 9, 1471, On the 11th, having entire possession of the city, he proceeded first to St. Paul's, to render thanks to Heaven for his triumph, and thence to the Sanctuary at Westminster, to 'comforte' his Queen, who 'presentyd hym at his comyne' with a 'fayre son a prince (afterwards Edward V), to his hert's singular comforte and gladness'. Releasing the royal Elizabeth from her gloomy asylum, the King returned the same evening to London and, carrying her to Baynard's Castle, 'they lodged at the lodgynge of my ladye his mother, where they heard divine service that night and upon the morn, Good Friday'. (*Fleet. Chron.*, p. 17.)

Battle of Barnet — Earl of Warwick slain

The Earl of Warwick was at first paralysed at Edward's rapid movements, and subsequently dismayed at the desertion of Clarence. However, he was too firmly pledged to Queen Margaret, and his honour was too deeply involved, to desert a cause which he had so warmly and strenuously undertaken. Tidings were communicated to Edward IV, in the midst of his domestic rejoicing, of his opponent's approach to the capital. The partisans of the House of York, who had emerged from their sanctuaries, were speedily assembled. After resting in London for the remainder of Good Friday, to refresh his wearied troops, Edward placed himself the following morning at the head of his army. Quitting London, he met the Lancastrian leaders on a plain near Barnet, about ten miles north of the capital where, on Easter eve, the hostile forces encamped preparatory to the approaching conflict which took place on Easter Sunday, April 14, 1471.

King Edward showed, in the arrangement of his forces, the different opinions he entertained of the good faith and fidelity of his two brothers. The 'vaward was commanded by the Duke of

Gloucester; the rear, by the Lord Hastings; the main battle, by himself; but George, Duke of Clarence, commanded not in any way in chief that day'. (Habington's Edw. IV, p. 81.) Prior to the battle, Clarence is said to have most earnestly desired a reconciliation, but Warwick's response was sharp. 'Go, tell your master', he said in reply to Clarence's emissaries, 'that Warwick, true to his word, is a better man than the false and perjured Clarence'. (Lingard, vol. V, p. 208.)

From four in the morning until ten in the forenoon, both armies fought with unexampled fury. Prodigies of valour were performed, but by none more than the young Duke of Gloucester who was immediately opposed to the Earl of Warwick himself. If any proof could invalidate the fabled traditions of Richard's misshapen form and nerveless arm, his conduct in this battle may well be considered an adequate test. It was the first in which he had been engaged. Though only eighteen, he bore down all before him and 'entred so farre and boldly into the ennemies' army, that two of his esquires, Thomas Parr and John Milewater, being nearest to him, were slain; yet by his owne valour he quit himselfe, and put most part of the enemies to flight'. (Buck's *Life of Rich.* III, lib. i, p. 9.)

The Earl of Warwick, after a time, dismounted and fought on foot. Surrounded by his enemies, he fell victim to his misplaced zeal, ungovernable pride, and fatal ambition. His death decided the day. King Edward's foes fled in all directions. Many, who had remained neutral until then, joined his victorious banner, willing to share in the triumph which attended their sovereign's return to the metropolis and to participate in the acclamation which greeted his final re-assumption of the throne. He offered up at St. Paul's, at evensong the same day, his own standard and that of the Earl of Warwick, trophies alike of his signal victory and the utter discomfiture of his enemies.

Battle of Tewkesbury

The ex-Queen, Margaret of Anjou, and her son, Edward of Lancaster, the young Prince of Wales — about a year younger than Gloucester — landed at Weymouth on the very day that Warwick's fate was sealed on Barnet field. Sad indeed was the disastrous intelligence conveyed to the royal fugitives. Yet their spirits were not altogether broken. King Henry still lived, although again a captive, and Edward of York filled a throne which they felt to be theirs by right and by the inheritance of three generations.

Each party prepared for another trial of strength. Only twenty days elapsed before the antagonists of Barnet once again confronted each other near the town of Tewkesbury, Saturday, May 4, 1471. All the chivalry were there arrayed, either under the banner of the Red Rose, again unfurled by the intrepid Queen and her son, or under the banner of the White Rose of Edward IV. Edward of Lancaster took the command of his father's army. King Edward again entrusted the post of honour and peril to his young brother, the Duke of Gloucester. The trust reposed in Richard was not misplaced, and Edward's judicious arrangement was demonstrated by the result. It is generally acknowledged that the success of the battle of Tewkesbury may in great measure be ascribed to the cool determination and able generalship of Gloucester.

Death of Edward, Prince of Wales

The Queen's army was entirely routed, and the Yorkist monarch gained a complete victory. No conquest could be more decisive. Queen Margaret herself was captured within a few days, and Edward, Prince of Wales, forfeited his life in the first battle in which he had unsheathed his sword in defence of his royal parents, his inheritance, and his crown. He was 'taken fleeinge to the town-wards, and slain in the field'. (Fleetwood's *Chron.*, p. 30.)

The mode of young Edward's death involves one of the most serious accusations which tradition has imputed to Richard, Duke of Gloucester. Nearly all of the popular and standard histories of England agree, from the earliest printed chronicles of the sixteenth century to the abler productions that closed the eighteenth century. They represent the Lancastrian Prince as brought before Edward IV after the battle and as incurring the resentment of that King by his dauntless and bold assumption to his face of right to the throne. After stating this, and that he was struck by the irritated monarch with his gauntlet, as a signal of defiance, it is further represented that he was finally dispatched by the sword of Richard of Gloucester.

Whence, however, is this information obtained? Not, certainly, from eye-witnesses of the event nor from contemporary chroniclers. These reports emanate from the annalists of the Tudor times. They afford but one of innumerable instances of the prejudiced and corrupt source whence accusations against the character and repu-tation of Richard III were derived and have been perpetuated. Shakespeare follows Holinshed, as did Hume; Holinshed copied

Hall; and Hall (with his own additions) Polydore Vergil, who was not only a staunch Lancastrian, but asked by Henry VII to compile the history and the reports of his period.

Sir George Buck was the first who ventured, by reference to early and contemporary writers, to dispute the legendary tales of a subsequent period. Though adopting the view of the Prince as being slain in cold blood, he expressly asserts, on the testimony of a 'faithful MS Chronicle of those times' (Chron. in quarto, MS, apud Dom. Regis, Rob. Cotton) that the Duke of Gloucester 'only, of all the great persons present, stood still and drew not his sword'. (Buck, lib. iii, p. 81.)

Recent researches have at length proved how well founded were the doubts of the defenders of Richard III, arising from the corrupt source whence the charges were originally derived and afterwards propagated. These researches have led to the publication of interesting manuscripts and diaries written by men who lived in those troubled time and, in some cases, witnessed the things they detailed. Of this description are two very remarkable narratives penned about the same period and by contemporary writers. A broad distinction separates their views, however. One author was on the side of the House of York — a servant who personally attended upon Edward IV: *History of the Arrivall of Edward IV in England* printed by the Camden Society from the Harl. MSS., No. 543. The other author was a staunch and violent Lancastrian who, in his party zeal, minutely enumerates every evil trait that could in any degree sully the fame of the enemies of his own faction: *A Chronicle of the thirteen Years of Edward IV*, by John Warkworth, D.D., master of St. Peter's College, Cambridge, published by the Camden Society from the MS. now in the library of that College.

These two coeval diaries invalidate, if not absolutely refute, the charge of Gloucester's participation in the murder of the young Prince of Wales. They add force to the neutral position of later writers who, uninfluenced by party feeling, were silent upon accusations for which there appear no solid or sufficient foundation. They rose long after the death of those who were present or who narrated at the time the events of that fearful day. (See Rapin's Hist. of England, p. 615; also, Carte, Sharon Turner, and others, all of whom doubted or impugned the veracity of the Lancastrian tales.)

The Yorkist narrative mentioned above, commonly termed 'Fleetwood's Chronicle', simply states that 'Edward, called Prince, was taken fleeing to the townwards, and slain in the field'. Warkworth, the Lancastrian authority, says, 'and there was slain in the field Prince Edward, which cried for succour to his brother-in-law, the Duke of Clarence'. This latter testimony adds great weight to the assertion of the Yorkist chronicler. Not only do both use precisely the same expression, 'slain in the field', but both couple the name of the Lancastrian Prince with that of the Earl of Devon who is well known to have been, in its most literal sense, 'slain in the field'.

But there is another circumstance which speaks most forcibly for the truth of the above statements from men who were violently opposed to each other. Their account is substantially supported by the Chronicler of Croyland — a man of education, high in the church, learned in the law, and the most impartial and able authority of the time. He says, 'At last King Edward gained a signal victory, there being slain on the part of the queen, as well in the field as afterwards, by the revengeful hands of certain persons, the Prince Edward, the only son of King Henry, the defeated Duke of Somerset, the Earl of Devon, and other lords universally well remembered'. (Chron. Croy., p. 555.) Here, he corroborates as much as could be expected from authors who did not mutually compare their writings the statements in the above-quoted diaries, viz., that Prince Edward and the Earl of Devon were slain in the field.

Perhaps the next most valuable evidence in defence of Gloucester is the striking fact that Sir Thomas More and Lord Bacon, both violently opposed to Richard III, make no mention whatever of the death of Edward, Prince of Wales, or even hint at any report having implicated the Duke of Gloucester. (See More's *Rycharde III*, p. 9 and Bacon's *Hen. VII*, p. 2.)

But, even if it were true that Edward of Lancaster was brought to the King's tent and therefore, if killed, may still be said by a flower of speech to have been 'slain in the field', there yet remains not a shadow of proof for fixing the act on the young Richard of Gloucester. Fabyan, the earliest authority for the young Prince being assassinated, makes no mention of the perpetrator of the crime being Richard of Gloucester. His version of the tale is that the King 'there strake him with his gauntlet upon the face, after which stroke by him received, he was by the king's servants incontinently slain'. (Fabyan, p. 662.) Neither of the royal dukes is named by him even as present at the time.

Thus, reference to Gloucester's own times, and to the precise period when the calumnies arose, is the best and most substantial proof of the prejudices that prevailed against him after death. They inclined the chroniclers of the succeeding age to associate Gloucester's name indiscriminately with every unworthy act committed during his lifetime rather than having solid authority or testimony from a valid source.

'There is little in reason', observes the late Mr. Courtney who, in his *Commentaries on Shakespeare's Historical Plays*, has bestowed infinite labour and research in seeking the earliest original authorities, 'for believing any part of the story . . . ' . . . 'It is quite clear that there is nothing like evidence either of Prince Edward's smart reply to the king or of his assassination by anybody; and there is not even the report of one who lived near to the time of the participation of either of the king's brothers in the assassination, if it occurred'. Truly, if this commentator on our great dramatic bard could afford to make this admission of the poet's corrupt source, the historian — professing to discard romance and to be guided alone by plain, simple, and well authenticated facts — may well be content to divest his mind of long-received impressions, if they rest on no firmer basis than these legendary tales.

(For a convincing example of how the Tudor historians distorted history see Chapter XXI, 'The growth of a legend: the death of Edward Prince of Wales at Tewkesbury, 1471'. This graphic portrayal starts with a brief account from the Tewkesbury Abbey Chronicle, 1471, listing among the lords slain in the battle Prince Edward slain *in the field*. Starting with this simple three-line account in 1471, the growth of the legend can be clearly traced. Succeeding historians writing for Henry VII and Henry VIII added to the story, apparently from their own imaginations. Finally, we come to Edward Hall, writing in 1542, 71 years after the battle and the simple account in the Tewkesbury Abbey Chronicle. Hall expands the story to 18 lines and repeats the tale from the Great Chronicle that the Prince was brought to Edward IV's tent after the battle, struck by King Edward with his gauntlet, and killed by Richard.)

Insurrection of Falconbridge

Leaving as competent judges the Lords of Gloucester and Norfolk to decide the fate of his victims of Tewkesbury, Edward IV proceeded with speed to Coventry to quell the further progress north of the insurgents. There, Margaret of Anjou was delivered into his hands as a prisoner, having been captured in a church adjoining Tewkesbury, with the ladies of her suite, shortly after the battle, Here, such intelligence reached the King as compelled him in all haste to proceed to London, with the bereaved Queen as part of his train.

During the brief restoration of Henry VI, and upon the attainder of Richard, Duke of Gloucester, the Earl of Warwick had nominated as vice-admiral of the English Channel, his near kinsman, Thomas Neville, the illegitimate son of his uncle, known in history as 'the bastard of Falconbridge'. Feeling that his distinguished command was forfeited by the decisive battle of Barnet and the restoration of the Yorkist line, Falconbridge boldly attempted to surprise London and release Henry VI from captivity. The battle of Tewkesbury took place on May 4, 1471. On May 11, Sir William Stanley delivered the ex-Queen as a prisoner to the King at Coventry. On May 12, Falconbridge attacked London. On May 16, the King quit Coventry and summoned to his aid Richard of Gloucester. On May 21, the two brothers entered London in triumph, carrying with them Queen Margaret. So rapid were the movements, so momentous the events that were crowded into the brief space of seventeen days!

Finding he had no chance of success in his desperate project, Falconbridge made overtures to surrender if pardon were extended towards him. The Duke of Gloucester saw the policy of converting into an ally so formidable a foe — one who had at his command 47 ships and 17,000 men. 'Wherefore', says the chronicler (Fleetwood, p. 32) 'the king sent thither his brother Richard, Duke of Gloucester, to receive them in his name and all the ships; as he so did the 26the day of the same month'. 'Falconbridge, after he had submitted, was not only pardoned, but knighted and again appointed vice-admiral. This happened in May, 1471, but was of short continuance; for between the 13th and 29th of September following, he was beheaded, though whether for a fresh crime or not, is uncertain'. (Paston Letters, vol. ii, p. 75.)

Duke of Gloucester unjustly accused of murder of Henry VI

During the interval which elapsed between the battle of Tewkesbury and the quelling of Falconbridge's insurrection, an event occurred which, with one exception, has contributed more than all others to sully the reputation of the Duke of Gloucester. This event is the mysterious death of the unhappy and care-worn Henry VI.

On May 22, 1471, the morning after King Edward the Fourth's triumphant entry into London, Henry VI was found lifeless in the Tower. Towards the close of the same day, the corpse of Henry of

Lancaster, 'upon a bier, and about the bier more glaives and staves than torches', (Cott. MSS., Vitell. A. xvi, vol. 133) was brought from the Tower to St. Paul's, and there publicly exposed to view preparatory to being conveyed to Chertsey for interment.

Every ireful feeling was doubtless rekindled in Edward's heart by Falconbridge's attempt to release the Lancastrian monarch and also by his setting fire to the metropolis. Warwick, the kingmaker, was slain; Margaret of Anjou was a prisoner and childless; the young Prince of Wales was numbered with the dead; and the ex-King was not only in close confinement, but incapable of active measures, whether in mind or body. Yet Falconbridge had proved, within eight days of the battle of Barnet, that King Henry's name alone was sufficient to render Edward's throne unstable. Thus, there is a strong ground for believing that the death of his unhappy rival was a matter previously determined upon by the Yorkist monarch even if, as was alleged, nature, worn out and exhausted, had really anticipated the decree by a tranquil and natural dissolution.

But the fate of the hapless Henry, whatever it may have been, and Edward's character and policy, are not subjects for discussion here. The subject is the part which is said to have been acted by Richard, Duke of Gloucester. Gloucester has been unsparingly vilified as the actual murderer of Henry VI. But there is not one single document extant to warrant the imputation, or even to afford reasonable ground of belief for so hateful, and indeed unnecessary, a crime. In this case, as in the reputed killing by Gloucester of Edward, Prince of Wales, the implication can be gradually and clearly traced, commencing with the ambiguous terms 'it is said' or 'as the fame ranne', and ending at last in decided and positive assertion of the alleged fact. Much as these inaccuracies in our national annals are to be deplored, yet it is an evil well known and acknowledged. So imperfect and contradictory are the statements relating to this period of history by such as are termed the 'Tudor historians' that on many matters of vast import scarcely two agree. This arises from the practice of adding, without competent authority, to the original manuscripts from which they professed to copy.

It is from annalists who were living in the period when the event occurred that the truth can alone be elicited. These revolve themselves into three: the two small fragments already quoted, under the titles of Fleetwood's and Warkworth's Narrative, and the able ecclesiastical historian, the Chronicler of Croyland. These three writers penned the events they record before Henry was regarded as a martyr and before Richard III was maligned to gratify the reigning

Henry VII and to extenuate his seizure of the crown. The statements of these three coeval writers are as follows.

The Yorkist narrative, after detailing the imprisonment of Queen Margaret, the death of the young prince, and the total discomfiture of the Lancastrians, thus describes the death of the unhappy monarch: 'The certainty of all which came to the knowledge of the said Henry, late called king, being in the Tower of London: not having afore that knowledge of the said matters, he took it to so great despite, ire and indignation, that of pure melancholy he died, the 23rd day of the month of May'. (Fleet. *Chron.*, p. 38.)

Plausible as is this account, it is inconsistent with these circumstances: (1) Henry VI was discovered dead on the only day that King Edward was in London; (2) the King had recently placed Henry in a position of such peril at Barnet — he was placed in front of the battle as a mark 'to be shot at' (Fleet. Chron., p. 18) — that his preservation seemed little less than miraculous; and (3) King Edward had written to the Duke of Clarence 'To keep King Henry out of sanctuary' (Leland, *Collectanea*, Vol. ii, p. 108). These circumstances support a strong assumption that the Lancastrian account approaches nearest to the truth: 'And the same night that King Edward came to London, King Henry, being inward in prison in the Tower of London, was put to death, the 21st day of May, on a Tuesday night, betwixt 11 and 12 of the clock'. (Warkworth, p. 21.)

The evidence of the third contemporary, the prior of Croyland, not only supports the assumption of Henry's death having been accelerated by violence but his guarded expression indicated that he considered it was the act of King Edward: 'During this interval of time, the body of King Henry was found lifeless in the Tower: may God pardon and give time for repentance to that man, whoever he was, that dared to lay his sacrilegious hands upon the Lord's anointed! The doer may obtain the name of a tyrant; the sufferer of a glorious martyr'. (Chron. Croyl., p. 557.)

A passage in Warkworth will probably explain the origin of this crime having been laid to the charge of the Duke of Gloucester. After describing the murder in the words quoted above, he adds, 'Being then at the Tower, the Duke of Gloucester, brother to King Edward, and many other'. (Wark. Chron., p. 21.) But why was Richard there and who were the 'many other' then at the Tower? No less illustrious personages than the whole of the royal family, the court, and the council who are said to have decreed King Henry's murder! The Duke of Gloucester appears at this period to have had no distinct residence in London, but lived with King Edward and his court.

Consequently, there was nothing remarkable in the young Prince being at the Tower with the rest of the royal family. The Tower of London was not, at this period, merely a state prison. It was the metropolitan palace and the ordinary residence of our monarchs at periods of insurrection and danger.

There are three other important facts: (1) Richard of Gloucester had no command within the Tower and no power over its inmates. So far from it, the governorship was held by the Lord Rivers at the time. Owing to the jealousy between the Queen's connections and the King's family, the Duke of Gloucester had perhaps even less access to the royal prisoner than the 'many other' named by Warkworth as 'being then in the Tower'. (2) King Edward indeed was deeply interested in the death of Henry VI, for the Lancastrian monarch alone stood between him and undisputed possession of the sceptre of England. Not so his young brother of Gloucester. The one had almost regained the object of his ambition; the other had only just entered upon his public career. (3) Richard was altogether removed from succession to the crown since a direct male heir to the house of which he was the youngest member had been born to King Edward during his brief exile in Burgundy.

In short, the accusations against Richard III do not rest upon any imputation of the deed by contemporary writers or upon any substantial basis on which to fix the accusation beyond the simple fact that he, in common with 'many other' was then at the Tower. But this fact, as justly observed by Mr. Courtenay, 'affords no proof of the murder'. (Courtenay's *Commentaries*, Vol. ii, p. 54.)

Rous, the earliest historian who propagates the rumour of the crime being attributed to the Duke of Gloucester, writes evidently in entire ignorance of the circumstances. Rous wrote his work for a Lancastrian monarch, Henry VII, the very one who vanquished Richard III and who sought to canonise Henry VI. 'He killed by others or, as many believe, with his own hand, that most sacred King Henry VI'. Fabyan, the 'city chronicler', whose chronicle was not published until upwards of thirty years after these events, says 'that of the death of the Prince (Henry VI) divers tales were told, but the most common fame went that he was stikked with a dagger by the hands of Richard of Gloucester'. (Fabyan, p. 662.) 'Common fame' is no evidence of guilt. Yet a bad name, once acquired, is an apology for every imputation. The charge by Fabyan and later writers derives more from the impression they had received of him after his death than from any authenticated deed that could tarnish the honour of the youthful career of Richard, Duke of Gloucester.

Polydore Vergil, who is the next historian in chronological order to Fabyan, only certifies, when repeating the tale, that 'the common report' implicated the Duke of Gloucester. Philip de Comines adds but little to confirm this in prefacing the same report by the words 'if what was told me by true'. The MS. London Chronicle, preserved in the Cotton. MSS., expressly adds 'how he was dead, nobody knew'. (Cotton. MSS., Vitell. A, xvi, fol. 133.)

Holinshed (who copied Hall, the follower of Polydore Vergil, and who was the authority selected by Shakespeare for his historical plays) observes that 'Poor King Henry VI, a little before deprived (as we have heard) of his realm and imperial crown, was now in the Tower, despoiled of his life by Richard, Duke of Gloucester (as the constant fame ran) who to the intent that his brother Edward might reign in more surety, murdered the King Henry with a dagger'. (Holin. *Chron.*, p. 324.)

In all these quotations, no one single allegation is brought home to the young Prince beyond that of mere suspicion based on his known fidelity to his brother and attachment to his cause rather than from any alleged malignity of purpose. The probable truth seems to have been given by Habington who sums up his narrative by saying that 'the death of King Henry was acted in the dark, so that it cannot be affirmed, who was the executioner; only it is probable it was a resolution of the state; the care of the king's safety and the public quiet in some sort making it, however cruel, yet necessary'. (Habington, *Life of Edward IV*, p. 104.) This view is further confirmed by two very early MSS. (Sloan MSS., 3479, fol. 6; Arundel MSS., 325, fol. 28) quoted by the editor of *Warkworth's Chronicle* (see Introduction, note to p. xvii). It is also adopted, at least to a certain degree, by all historians whose works are based, not on hearsay or traditional evidence, but upon a full and impartial examination of original documents. It is from reasonings such as these that the truth can alone be elicited.

In reading Horace Walpole's *Historic Doubts*, it is indispensable to take into consideration the prejudice and preconceived opinions with which he had to combat. The conviction of this, as he himself says in the supplement to his work, was the cause of his bestowing the appellation *Historic Doubts* on his first essay. He hoped that some able writer would take up the subject, so as to prevent the reign of Richard III from disgracing our annals by childish improbabilities that place that reign on a level with the story of 'Jack the Giant Killer'.

Buck was the first historian who wrote in defence of Richard. He was hence called a lover of paradoxes, and certainly he injured his cause by seeking to palliate the monarch's imputed crimes by parallel instances. But Sir George Buck agrees with Philip de Comines and with the rolls of Parliament. The research which has of late years been made into our ancient records, state papers, and parliamentary history places Buck's history in a far more credible light than could have been allowed to it some years since, and fixes both him and Lord Orford (Walpole) as higher authority than those historians who wrote professedly to please the Tudor dynasty. (See Walpole's *Supplement* to his *Historic Doubts*, pp. 185, 194; also, his Reply to Hume, to Dr. Masters, and to the learned Dean Mills, published in Lord Orford's works, vol. ii, p. 215.)

Let every contemporary writer be investigated and the source examined whence later historians have drawn their conclusions. It must then be apparent that no valid proof can be adduced to fix the murder of Henry VI or his young heir, Edward of Lancaster, on the Duke of Gloucester.

Gloucester receives thanks of Parliament — rewarded by King

The co-existent diaries all prove that George of Clarence was treacherous to his kindred, false to his colleagues, and faithless in principle and action. The crimes under discussion have never been imputed to him, however. Why? Because his evil deeds were visited by an early and violent death, and by such death he obtained pity and compassion. Richard of Gloucester, on the contrary, faithful in conduct, firm in allegiance, consistent, upright, honourable, is selected as the victim to bear every crime that resulted from the dissensions, ambition, or jealousy of his elder brothers. Were it not that some few recently discovered documents act as beacons to illuminate history, the last monarch of the Plantagenet race might have remained a monument of moral turpitude and unnatural personal deformity.

Fortunately, however, for this much maligned Prince, the honour of our national representatives is concerned in the refutation of both charges. It can scarcely be supposed that the aristocracy of England, her proud barons and lordly peers, could have conveyed the thanks of the Houses of Parliament to a perjured Prince, a convicted regicide, an avowed murderer. For it appears that after Edward IV was finally re-established on the throne, only a few weeks after his landing as an attainted fugitive. Richard, Duke of Gloucester, in the presence of 'his most royal majesty, having before him his lords spiritual and temporal', received the thanks of the House of Commons, through their speaker, William Allington, for his 'knightly demeaning' and for his 'constant faith', with divers other nobles and yeomen being with the king beyond the sea. (Journal of the Lord of Grantham. See Archaeologia for 1836).

The opinion entertained by Edward IV of his brother's faithful conduct is shown in the words of the letters patent yet extant that publicly recorded his sentiments; 'The king, especially considering the gratuitous, laudable, and honourable services in many wise rendered to him by his most dear brother, Richard, Duke of Gloucester, his propinquity in blood, his inmate probity and other deserts of manners and virtues, and willing, therefore, to provide him a competent reward and remuneration . . . ' granted to him certain forfeited estates. (Cottonian MSS., Julius B, xii, fol. iii.) In further reward, he was invested (by patent, in July, 11 Edw. IV, 1471) with the manors of Middleham, Sheriff-Hutton, Penrith, and various lordships belonging to the House of Neville or other nobles who were slain, or had been attainted after the battle of Barnet or in the final contest at Tewkesbury. These important victories were achieved in large measure by the military skill, cool judgment, and determined bravery of the King's brother, Richard, Duke of Gloucester.

Chapter VII

RICHARD MARRIES
ANNE NEVILLE

Distinguished position of Richard,
Duke of Gloucester

Richard of Gloucester, although scarcely 19, had distinguished
himself by his military prowess to a degree almost unprecedented.
He had within the brief space of three weeks, as already detailed,
commanded the foremost ranks of King Edward's army in two of the
most important and fiercely contested battles of that or perhaps any
other age. The triumphant result was fully as much owing to his able
generalship and deep policy as to his determined bravery and
undaunted courage. 'There are but few instances upon record of a
military character rising to fame with the rapidity of Richard of
Gloucester' (Hutton's *Bosworth Field*, p. xliv). He was equally fitted
to aid his brother in civil life as to espouse his cause with the sword.
He voluntarily mediated between King Edward and Clarence and
was selected by Edward to treat with the rebel Falconbridge. Richard
brought both affairs to a happy conclusion, marking the crisis of
Edward's fate.

Richard, young as he was, had nobly exercised those qualities
peculiarly estimated by the really great — undeviating fidelity,
fraternal affection, and unshaken gratitude. And he gained his
reward, as evidenced from the brief records that have been transmitted to posterity (Cott. MSS. Julius B. xii fol. iii). He was henceforth considered fitting to be invested with military authority of the
greatest importance and had civil powers delegated to him that attest
the high regard of his King and the nation.

Richard takes oath of allegiance
to infant Prince of Wales

High as was Richard's position at King Edward's court, and
dangerous as was that position to one so young, there is no one

record extant, either private or public, no historical document, no contemporary statement, to detract from his well-earned fame, before he had entered his twentieth year. By a singular coincidence, the earliest legal instrument extant that bears his signature is the following vow. On 3rd July, 1471, 11 Edward IV, the Duke of Gloucester and other peers, spiritual and temporal, took and subscribed the following oath of recognition of Prince Edward, as heir of King Edward IV:

> 'I acknowledge, take, and repute you, Edward, Prince of Wales, Duke of Cornwayll, and Erle of Chestre, furste begoten son of oure sovereigne lord, as to the corones and reames of England and of France and lordship of Ireland; (the kings of England were simply styled "lords of Ireland" until the reign of King Henry VIII, when that monarch was declared "king of Ireland" by the states of that realm assembled in Parliament. — Camden's *Brit.*, vol. ii, p. 1300) and promette and swere, that incas hereafter it happen, you by Goddis disposition to outleve our seid sovereigne lord, I shall then take and accept you for true, veray, and righteous Kyng of Englond, &c. And feith and trouth to you shall bere. And yn all thyngs truely and feithfully behave me towardes you and youre heyres, as a true and feithfall subject oweth to behave hym to his sovereign lord, and rightiiys Kyng of Englond, &c. So help me God, and Holidome, and this holy Evaungelist'. (*Rot. Parl.*, vol. vi, p. 232.)

Early attachment between Gloucester and Anne

The Lady Anne Neville and her cousin of Gloucester were intimately associated in childhood. One striking instance is cited — the appearance in public of the youthful co-heiresses of the Earl of Warwick with their royal kinsman, the young Duke of Gloucester, at the costly feast which celebrated the installation as Archbishop of York of their uncle, George Neville, Lord Chancellor of England. A very minute and curious detail of this magnificent entertainment may be found in Leland's Collectanea, copied 'out of an old paper roll', and entitled 'The Great Feast at the Enthronization of the Rev. Father in God, George Neville, Archbishop of York and Chancellor of England'.

The narrative first recites 'the goodly provisions made for the same', and then gives the names of the great officers officiating, specifying the Earl of Warwick as steward. It proceeds to describe the 'estates' or order of precedence observed at the feast: 'Estates sitting at the high table in the hall; estates sitting in the chief chamber, where under a canopy, as prince of the blood royal, and upon the dais — a raised platform separating those entitled to such distinction from the rest of the guests — was seated the Duke of Gloucester, the king's brother; on his right hand, the Duchess of Suffolk, on his left hand the Countess of Westmorland, and the Countess of Northumberland, and two of the Lord of Warwick's daughters'. (Leland's *Collect.*, vol. ii, p. 503; vol. vi, p. 2.)

John Leland, the learned historian, was chaplain and librarian to King Henry VIII, who appointed him his antiquary, with a commission to examine all the libraries of the cathedrals, abbeys, colleges, and priories throughout the realm. He spent six years in travelling through the kingdom, and rescued an infinity of valuable records from oblivion and destruction. His Collectanea and Itinerary, published by Hearne, the MSS. of which are preserved in the Bodleian Library, have afforded copious materials of antiquity, biography, and history to succeeding writers. (See Huddelsford's *Life of Leland and Granger's Biog. Hist. of England*, vol. i, p. 98.)

This public association of Richard with Warwick's co-heiresses at York occurred in the summer of 1465, when Richard was in his fourteenth year and Lady Anne was in her twelfth year. The brief notices of Richard's early years are indeed so scattered and have been so distorted that every link that helps to connect his boyish days with the acts of his manhood is invaluable to the historian. The records of past ages become rare in proportion to the distance of time at which they occurred. Domestic feuds, by suppressing some facts and perverting others, add confusion to the scanty details which have happened to escape destruction.

Here, however, is proof that the Lady Anne and Richard of Gloucester were intimately associated in childhood. Their ultimate marriage, in spite of their separation and the innumerable obstacles from all quarters, warrants the assumption that Richard was early attached to his future bride and likewise justifies the inference that the attachment was mutual. The feeling of attachment entertained by Warwick's daughters towards the House of York is distinctly stated by Habington in his Life of Edward IV. In speaking of the sentiments that influenced Isabel, Duchess of Clarence, during that monarch's expulsion from the throne, he says 'she having in her childhood, and those impressions are ever deepest, been instructed to affect the House of York, and approve its title'. (Habington's Edw. IV, p. 60.)

Betrothal of Anne to Edward of Lancaster

In the succeeding spring, February 1466, when Richard was created a knight of the Garter, he was firmly established at court and high in favour with his royal brother. In June 1466, as already narrated, he attended his father's state funeral as chief mourner, by express command of King Edward IV, until the sovereign himself assumed that leading position at the entrance of the church where the royal remains were deposited. From that time, Gloucester was constantly associated with his royal brother, both in his state progresses and on other public and political occasions, until Edward was driven from the throne by Clarence and Warwick in October 1470. This embraces a period of just four years, during which time the Lady Isabel was united to the Duke of Clarence, and her younger sister, Anne, was betrothed to Edward, the heir of King Henry VI.

Anne Neville is represented by all the Tudor chroniclers as having been actually married to Edward of Lancaster, but the far more valuable testimony of contemporary writers completely invalidates this long held and popular tradition. The error most probably arose from the degree of importance attached to betrothments in those days, when they may almost be said to have constituted a portion of the marriage ceremony. A betrothment entered into by both parties with their full and free consent was as binding and valid as a marriage solemnized before the church. Marriage, according to the doctrine of the ancient canon law, held good, however informally administered, provided the consent of the parties concerned was previously obtained.

Warwick's solemn pledge 'on the Gospels' to restore the Lancastrian line made Margaret of Anjou reluctantly consent to ally her only child with the daughter of the bitterest enemy of her house. She well knew, however, that a papal dispensation could absolve her from fulfilling the marriage contract that was to cement by a domestic alliance her political league with the Earl. Deadly hatred had existed between the Queen and the aspiring Warwick. Margaret so mistrusted her former prosecutor that she severely restricted his power until such time as she and Prince Edward should arrive in England. Thus, there can be but little doubt that the implacable consort of Henry VI would sanction no closer union between her youthful heir and Warwick's co-heiress — Anne aged but sixteen, Edward only entering his seventeenth year — than the betrothment usual at this period.

Mere surmise is uncalled for as the fact itself is substantiated by conclusive evidence. A contemporary writer has given a clear account 'of the manner and guiding of the Earl of Warwick at Aungers, from the 15th day of July to the 4th day of August 1470, which day he departed from Aungers, to the French town where the contract was made. Touching the time when the marriage shall be put in ure (shall happen), Item, that from thenceforth the said daughter of the Earl of Warwick shall be put and remain in the hands and keeping of Queen Margaret, and also that the said marriage shall not be perfyted till the Earl of Warwick had been with an army over the sea into England, and that he had recovered the realm of England in the most partie thereof for the King Henry'. (Harl. MSS. 543, fol. 168.)

Most valuable, as corroboration, is the attestation of the Croyland historian who was not only contemporaneous with the chronicler of Aungers but, as a doctor of the canon law, could be accurate upon this point. His words are expressive and decisive: 'To make this promise more binding', says this valuable historian of Warwick's league with the House of Lancaster, 'a marriage *was contracted* between the said prince and Anne, the youngest daughter of the Earl of Warwick; the Duke of Clarence having previously *married* Isabella, her eldest sister'. (*Chron. Croy.*, p. 553.) No reasonable doubt can remain in the unprejudiced mind that it was a mere treaty, dependent for its ratification on the political scheme that was to ensure its ultimate fulfilment. And this implied not the mere release of the royal captive, Henry VI, from prison, but, as explicitly stated by the writer, recovering 'the realm of England in the most partie thereof for the King Henry'. Thus, Anne of Warwick would carry a throne as her marriage portion in exchange for the crown which her father's prowess was to win for her affianced consort.

This great political scheme was never destined to be fulfilled, however. The Earl of Warwick fell at the battle of Barnet; the Lancastrian prince was slain a fortnight afterwards at Tewkesbury; and Lady Anne, with the ill-fated Margaret of Anjou, was taken prisoner within a few days afterwards.

Gloucester seeks Anne's hand

It is on record that, within a few weeks of the fatal battle of Tewkesbury, the Lady Anne was under the entire control of the Duke of Clarence. Richard's early attachment to the Lady Anne was probably well known to the Duke of Clarence. Clearly in anticipation of his brother's probable conduct towards the Duke's sister-in-law, he adopted the most strenuous and extraordinary means of frustrating all communication between them — that of concealing her under the disguise of a kitchen maid.

'Let us now insert that dispute', says the Croyland Chronicler (p. 557), 'with difficulty to be appeased which happened during this Michaelmas term (1471) between the king's two brothers; for after, as is aforesaid, the son of King Henry, to whom the Lady Anne, younger daughter of the Earl of Warwick, was *betrothed*, fell in the battle of Tewkesbury, Richard, Duke of Gloucester, besought that the said Anne should be given to him *to wife*, which request was repugnant to the views of his brother, the Duke of Clarence, who had previously married the Earl's elder daughter. He therefore caused the damsel to be concealed, lest it should become known to his brother where she was; fearing the division of the inheritance which he wished to enjoy alone in right of his wife rather than undergo portion with anyone. But the cunning of the said Duke of Gloucester so far prevailed, that, having discovered the maiden in the attire of a kitchen girl, in London, he caused her to be placed in the sanctuary of St. Martin's; which, having been done, great discord arose between the brothers'.

Richard must have sought his persecuted kinswoman immediately after he was released from his military duties, because it appears he 'had discovered her retreat' before the Michaelmas term following the battle of Tewkesbury; that is to say, between May 4, 1471 and the beginning of the following October. No merely selfish motives could have induced his request that Anne should 'be given to him to wife'. The Lady Anne and her mother, the Countess of Warwick, were under the bill of attainder, and the riches to which she would have been entitled by birth as their co-heiress were now altogether in the gift of the King. The Duke of Gloucester was in so high a position at King Edward's court that, so far from any advantage accruing to him from a union with his impoverished and persecuted cousin, alliances must have been open to him at foreign courts and with the most wealthy subjects in his brother's kingdom. Richard was already endowed with princely possessions and invested with almost regal authority. Why did Clarence 'cause the damsel to be concealed' unless he suspected that the affection which Gloucester had early formed for Anne would lead him immediately to renew his vows of attachment and incline her to listen to them? As the Croyland Chronicler says, 'he feared the division of the inheritance he wished to enjoy alone'. (p. 557.)

What, however, was the part pursued by Richard of Gloucester — that Prince who for 500 years has been held up to scorn and contempt for every base, unmanly, treacherous, and vindictive feeling? Let his conduct be once more contrasted with that of Clarence, who had betrayed and perfidiously deceived every near relative and connection. Clarence was indebted to the very brother whom he was now injuring for his reconciliation with the King and for his restoration to his own forfeited honours and possessions. Instead of outraging her already wounded feelings and taking advantage of her powerless situation, Richard removed her immediately from the degrading garb under which Clarence had concealed her. With the respect due to his mother's niece, he 'caused her to be placed in the sanctuary of St. Martin's', while he openly and honourably sought the King's assent to their marriage.

Thus, before the Lady Anne had passed the age of minority, she had drunk to the very dregs of the cup of adversity. From being the affianced bride of the heir apparent to the throne, and receiving homage at the French court as Princess of Wales, she was degraded to assume the disguise of a kitchen girl in London, reduced to utter poverty by the attainder of herself and parents — a desolate orphan, discarded by the relatives who should have protected her and debased and persecuted by those to whom the law had consigned the custody of her life and person.

Such was the condition of the ill-fated co-heiress of the Nevilles, the Beauchamps, the Despencers, in whose veins flowed the blood of the highest and noblest in the land, when she was affectionately and unceasingly sought for by Richard, Duke of Gloucester, at a time when the sun of prosperity shone upon him so resplendently. Had he been influenced by that mean ambition which has been imputed to him in after years, he would have coveted the daughter of some illustrious prince or the heiress to a crown rather than rescue his dejected kinswoman from her humiliating situation and restore her as his bride to the proud position which she had lost. He placed her in the only asylum where she could feel secure from compulsion and safe alike from his own importunities or his brother's persecution.

Probable date of Gloucester's marriage

It is worthy of remark that throughout the entire narrative of the Croyland historian he speaks most explicitly of the 'betrothment' as such and designates the Lady Anne as 'the damsel', 'the maiden'.

These terms confirm his previous account of the qualified treaty made respecting her destined marriage with Edward of Lancaster. They exonerate Richard from the unfounded charge of seeking the affection of 'Young Edward's bride' before the tears of 'widowhood' had ceased to flow, and equally so of his outraging a custom strictly observed in the fifteenth century which rendered it an offence against the church and society at large for 'a widow' to espouse a second time before the first year of mourning had expired. (Testamenta Vetusta, p. xxxiv.)

As to the precise time or under what circumstances the cousins were at length united there exists no document or satisfactory proof. In consequence of Richard having placed the Lady Anne in sanctuary, 'great discord arose', says the Chronicler. 'At length, by the mediation of the king, it was finally agreed that on Gloucester's marriage he should have such lands as should be decided upon by arbitrators, and that Clarence should have the remainder'. The narrative of the Croyland Chronicler is dated 1471, and by the expression just quoted it is most probable that Gloucester's marriage was solemnized within a few months. The clause evidently implies that the arbitrators could not commence the proceedings on which they were to adjudicate until the young couple were indissoluably united in marriage. From these and other circumstances it is apparent that the cousins must have been united in the spring of 1472.

The young couple are said to have been married at Westminster (*Hearne's Fragment*, p. 283). The ceremony was most probably performed by the Archbishop of York, since it appears that after Gloucester had publicly sought the King's sanction to the alliance, the Lady Anne was removed from her sanctuary at St. Martin's le Grand and placed under the care of her only surviving uncle, George Neville, the prelate of that see.

Gloucester fixed abode at Pomfret Castle

On February 29, in the same year, 1472, the Duke of Gloucester was a second time appointed to the important office of High Constable of England. From this period he seems to have retired from the court and to have altogether fixed his abode in the north of England. On May 20, 1472, he resigned the office of Great Chamberlain (Rymer, Add. MSS. fo. 4614, art. 70). He is shown by contemporary papers in the Plumpton Correspondence (Camden Society, 1839) to have been resident in great state at Pomfret about the same time, by virtue of his office as chief seneschal of the duchy of Lancaster in the northern parts.

Thus, after severe trials and almost unparalleled reverses, did Richard and his youthful bride find that repose which had so long and so painfully been denied to them. He was scarcely nineteen, while his cousin had but just entered her seventeenth year, for only four years had elapsed since their youthful companionship at York. Yet during that interval their lives had been forfeited by attainder. Liberty was only preserved to Richard by flight to a distant land and to Anne by the privilege of sanctuary in her own country. Both had been exiles, both had been outlawed — the one for fidelity to his brother and sovereign, the other as the passive instrument of a rebellious and ambitious parent. Both, within the short space of two years, had been reduced to utter penury by confiscation of lands and possessions. And both, from being homeless wanderers, had experienced also the highest degree of prosperity which could be contrasted with adversity equally poignant.

But fortune upheld them throughout their trials and smiled favourably on their attachment. To a district endeared to them both by the unfading recollections of childhood did Richard convey his young bride. And amidst the bold and wild scenery of the home of their ancestors did the Lady Anne and her princely consort pass the early years of their married life and enjoy those halcyon days of peace that once more dawned upon England. Built on a rock whose rugged surface seemed fully in keeping with the impregnable stronghold that crowned its summit, the Castle of Pontefract (or Pomfret as it is usually called) soared high above the surrounding lands, a fitting abode for the princely seneschals and hereditary high stewards of England. In this celebrated fortress (Sandford, book iii, p. 148; Walsingham, p. 363), Gloucester and his gentle consort, the Lady Anne, enjoyed a peaceful end to their recent persecutions.

Here, in the springtime of their lives and in the fullness of their happiness, they sought, and for a brief interval, enjoyed that rest and tranquillity which Richard had earned by his fidelity and zeal, and which Warwick's daughter must have been well contented to find after her sad reverses.

Chapter VIII

SHAKESPEARE'S RICHARD III — DRAMA NOT HISTORY

Richard's character and Shakespeare's Richard III

The marriage of Richard, Duke of Gloucester, with Anne Neville is an appropriate time to compare the character of the Duke, as it is ordinarily viewed through the works of the immortal Shakespeare, with the evidence of historical records. With great justice has it been observed by the learned author of the History of Durham (Surtee's Hist. of Durham, p. lx) that the 'magic powers of Shakespeare have struck more terror to the soul of Richard than fifty Mores or Barons armed in proof'.

A few years since, it would have been thought little less than sacrilege to impugn the statements of England's mighty dramatist, although truth itself had presided at the inquiry. The hardihood of the undertaking, however, has been considerably lessened by recent researches. It should also be borne in mind that the beauty and power of Shakespeare's dramas are wholly independent of the perverted sources he used in their composition. The important historical discoveries of late years have made apparent inaccuracies and errors so striking that they can no longer escape observation.

If Shakespeare has been the chief means of promulgating the erroneous traditions of the Tudor Chroniclers, he has also been the leading instrument of making these errors known by creating such a lively interest for the periods which he so glowingly describes. But the time has passed when the dramatist is sought as historic authority also. The fabled traditions transmitted by the early chroniclers are now well understood as such. The charm of legendary lore must be discarded to make room for simple but well-authenticated truths. In the tragedy about to be considered the facts will best speak for themselves, disrobed of their attractive dramatic garb but not divested of their touching scenes and such romantic incidents as can be well substantiated.

Shakespeare begins his tragedy of Richard III with the Lady Anne

Neville accompanying, as chief mourner, the corpse of King Henry VI to Chertsey Abbey for interment, and accidentally meeting the Duke of Gloucester on the road. After much angry recrimination, Richard wins the Lady Anne for his bride. It is apparent from facts now fully substantiated (Pell. Records, p. 495) that this Prince and Warwick's daughter could not have met at King Henry's funeral. 'In a barge solemnly prepared with torches', says the Chronicler of Croyland (p. 556), 'the body of King Henry was conveyed, by water, to Chertsey, there to be . . . buryed in our Ladye Chapelle at the Abbey'. (The funeral expenses of King Henry VI have been preserved in the *Issue Rolls of the Exchequer* and completely refute the erroneous statements of Hall, Grafton, and Holinshed that no decent respect was paid to the mortal remains of this unhappy monarch.)

The cousins could not have met until very long after Henry's funeral. Richard was in Kent with his royal brother, King Edward IV, at the time of the interment. The Lady Anne was taken prisoner with Queen Margaret a few days after the battle of Tewkesbury, May 4, 1471. She remained either in state custody or in the charge of Clarence, because of her attainder, until she was discovered in the disguise of a kitchen maid in London during the Michaelmas term following.

It is quite true that Richard sought Warwick's daughter in marriage after the House of Lancaster became extinct. But the alliance was effected by open appeal to his sovereign and not secured, as dramatically represented, either by violence or strategem. The extreme loveliness of the Lady Anne, which Shakespeare commemorates, appears to be founded on fact. At length, by the death of Edward of Lancaster, Richard was enabled to make known to the Lady Anne his long-cherished attachment. But how widely different is the poet's account from the actual fact, as given in the clear and simple narrative of the Croyland Chronicler (page 557 — see Chapter VII). Richard, in the height of his prosperity, sought out in her misery his persecuted cousin. Before applying to King Edward IV for sanction to their union, he placed her in an asylum, the sanctuary of St. Martin's, too hallowed to be violated even by the fiend-like character of the play.

The hideous and deformed appearance ascribed to Gloucester (with which the tragedy commences) has been shown to have resulted from subsequent political malice.

> 'Deform'd, unfinish'd, sent before my time
> Into this breathing world, scarce half made up,

73

And that so lamely and unfashionable
That dogs bark at me as I bolt by them;
Why I, in this weak piping time of peace,
Have no delight to pass away the time,
Unless to spy my shadow in the sun,
And descant on mine own deformity;
And therefore since I cannot prove a lover,
To entertain these fair, well spoken days,
I am determined to prove a villain,
And hate the idle pleasures of these days'.

(*Richard III, Act I, Scene I*)

The historian, discarding all tradition connected with supernatural appearances, finds no foundation for so hateful a picture. On
the contrary, he invalidates the fables which have been so long
published by producing the records of Richard's integrity, of various
rewards bestowed upon him for his fidelity, and of the undeniable
proofs of his firm attachment to his brother, Edward IV. Richard's
allegiance to his sovereign and his peaceful demeanour to the Queen
consort and her family are well attested. There is not a single
document, diary, or contemporary narrative to warrant the
accusations which have been poetically fixed on Richard, Duke of
Gloucester, of hypocrisy to his youthful bride, execration of his
venerable parent, and fiend-like hatred and detestation of his
brothers and his kindred.

Cruel treatment of Elizabeth Wydville

Shakespeare charges Richard III with cruel and inhuman treatment of
King Edward's Queen. Although the Duke of Clarence absented
himself from court immediately after Edward's marriage and openly
gave vent to the most violent and rebellious feelings, it is recorded of
Richard that he was most peaceable and well-conducted towards the
Queen and her kindred. He and the Queen's studious brother, Lord
Rivers, cooperated in re-establishing King Edward on the throne and
in releasing the Queen and her infant from sanctuary. (*Fleetwood's
Chron.*, pp. 2, 3, 11.)

Imprisonment of Duke of Clarence

Shakespeare makes Clarence's imprisonment *precede* Richard's
union with Lady Anne in 1472. However, that imprisonment

occurred some years *afterwards*, in 1478. Furthermore, it would not have been contemplated at the time for Richard had, only a few months earlier, reconciled the rebellious and ungrateful Clarence to his offended sovereign. Furthermore, in the same year in which Richard married the Lady Anne, Clarence was invested, as the husband of the eldest sister, with the title and dignities of his deceased father-in-law, the Earl of Warwick. Edward IV also nominated Clarence to the high appointment of Lord Chamberlain of England for life, which Richard had voluntarily relinquished on fixing his abode in the north. [More (p. 10), Mancini (p. 77), and Kendall (p.454) agree that Richard bitterly opposed Clarence's execution.]

Margaret of Anjou

Shakespeare has the desolate, broken-hearted Margaret of Anjou wander unrestrained through palaces tenanted by her rival, Elizabeth Wydville. However, Margaret was imprisoned from the day preceding her husband's death until she was removed in custody, first to Windsor and then to Wallingford. After five years, she was ransomed by her father, King Rene, and by the French King (Paston Letters, vol. i, p. 89), into whose dominions she was conveyed with little respect and no regal state. Here, bereft of all domestic ties and with a heart seared by trials and withered by afflictions, the heroic Margaret of Lancaster ended her most calamitous career.

Richard's career as dramatically presented vs. historical records

Few persons, on reading the opening scenes of Shakespeare's Richard III, would imagine that the two characters there introduced were young persons in the springtime of life. Gloucester's description is of a misshapen monster, if not hoary in age at least advanced in years and hardened in vice. In fact, Richard was then a youth of nineteen, distinguished by his gallantry, his prowess, and his noble achievements. He had shown unswerving loyalty to his brother, Edward IV, under the most adverse circumstances. Likewise, the sentiments and conduct of the Lady Anne, as depicted in the play, are little in accordance with her youthful age of seventeen. They leave the impression of one well accustomed to the arts of flattery and easily entrapped by the prospect of worldly advancement in however unseemly a form it may appear.

This total disregard of the ages of Richard and Anne appears to be one leading cause of the erroneous views which have been so long entertained about Richard of Gloucester. It explains the discrepancies in dates which occur in Shakespeare when he introduces this Prince in other of his historical plays (Second and Third Parts of Henry VI). It reconciles also many seeming inconsistencies in acts laid to the charge of Richard in these other historical plays as well as in Richard III.

Thus, when a mere infant in arms, nay even before he was born, he is made by Shakespeare to take part in the feuds of the times and to display a callous and hardened nature. Such, for example, is the memorable scene that follows the execution of Jack Cade, in which Richard beards the veteran Clifford in that well-known passage —

> 'Oft have I seen a hot o'erweening cur
> Run back and bite, because he was withheld'
>> (*Second Part of King Henry VI, Act V, Scene I*)

and is rebuked by the warrior —

> 'Hence, heap of wrath, foul indigested lump,
> As crooked in thy manners as thy shape'.
>> (*Ibid.*)

The fact is that Iden, the sheriff of Kent, beheaded the rebel, Jack Cade, in July 1450, two years *before* Richard was born (W. Wyr, p. 470).

At the first battle of St. Albans, Richard is not only named as slaying the Duke of Somerset but is again displayed in an odious light:

> 'Sword, hold thy temper; heart be wrathful still:
> Priests pray for enemies, but princes kill'.
>> (*Ibid., Act V, Scene II*)

And at this very battle the Duke of Gloucester is also represented as thrice saving the life of the valiant Earl of Salisbury:

> 'Three times to-day I holp him to his horse,
> Three times bestrid him, thrice I led him off,
> Persuaded him from any further act'.
>> (*Ibid., Scene II*)

In fact, however, Richard was little more than *two years* old at the time of this battle.

At the battle of Wakefield, in the year 1460, Richard is said to have been present in Sendal Castle and there to have precociously displayed that depravity and ambition which form the basis of Shakespeare's play:

'An oath is of no moment'.

(Third Part of Henry VI, Act I, Scene II)

Again —

'And father, do but think
How sweet a thing it is to wear a crown'

(Ibid.)

Actually, Richard was then but *eight* years of age and, as already mentioned, had been left under the care of his mother, Cecily, Duchess of York, in London.

At the battles of Mortimer's Cross and Towton, Richard is again represented as taking a leading part in the events of the day and inducing the execrations which so abound against the 'foul-mouthed crook-back'. These accustom the mind to invest him with such revolting characteristics and personal deformities as fully to justify the yet more odious picture he is eventually to exhibit in the character of King Richard III. Now, what are the facts? The battle of Mortimer's Cross was fought on February 2, 1461, and the battle of Towton on March 29, 1461. Actually, therefore, Richard was then but a child of *eight*, and both battles occurred *after* he had been sent by his mother, Lady Cecily, to Utrecht for safety.

Shakespeare associates Richard with Edward IV upon every occasion after Edward's accession to the crown. Richard is made to take part with Edward in every battle, as his equal in age, experience, valour, and judgment, though King Edward was but *eighteen* when he ascended the throne and Richard an infant of *eight* years. No document exists to prove Richard acted in any military capacity until ten years following that period, when the King was driven into exile and Gloucester fought to secure his brother's restoration.

Shakespeare misled by corrupt authorities

These striking anomalies may be satisfactorily explained in two ways. *First*, they derive partly from the license permitted to the dramatist relating to time, action, and embellishment of character. The historical events recorded in Shakespeare's tragedy of Richard III occupy a space of about fourteen years, but are frequently confused for the purposes of dramatic representation. The second scene of the first act commences with the funeral of King Henry VI, who is said to have been murdered on May 21, 1471. The imprisonment of Clarence, which is represented previously in the first scene, did not take place, however, until 1477-78.

Second, the anomalies are chiefly to be attributed to the incorrect source whence Shakespeare derived his authority for his deformed portraiture both of Richard's mind and person and for most of the historical scenes. Shakespeare selected as his chief authority Holinshed, the latest and most prejudiced of the Tudor historians. In the painting of Shakespeare preserved in the Town Hall of Stratford-upon-Avon, Holinshed's Chronicles occupy a prominent position in the ground before him. Thus, Shakespeare selected as his guide the chronicler who had most fully incorporated every tradition, every surmise, and every malicious report connected with the last of the Plantagenet monarchs, believing it to be the most standard and true authority.

Here lies the explanation of those long-perpetuated fables which the historian cannot but deeply lament and which have usurped the place of facts. But history was not pursued in Shakespeare's time with the research and attention to chronological exactness which now characterise the study. It was difficult to secure original documents or to ascertain if such records had been preserved, so the annalists of that early period copied the works of preceding chroniclers. Thus, they perpetuated erroneous statements or even increased the mischief of original inaccuracy by engrafting on hearsay reports the embellishments of a wonder-loving age.

The dearth of proper materials for compiling historical works led to the foundation of those valuable libraries which, under the names of the Cottonian, Harleian, Bodleian, and similar collections, have so deservedly commemorated their great founders. (See *Preface to Catalogue of the Harleian Manuscripts*: printed by command of his Majesty, George III, p. 2.)

Early chroniclers' fables furnished Shakespeare with his descriptions

The earliest printed chronicles relating to the period under consideration were not published until after the accession of the Tudor dynasty. It was then the interest of the writers to secure popularity with Henry Tudor, now Henry VII. They did this by aspersing the character of Richard III and perpetuating every report that could strengthen the cause of the reigning sovereign and justify the deposal and death of his rival. 'It is to Polydore Vergil', observes an able writer of the present day, 'that we must look as the source whence the stream of succeeding historians chiefly borrowed their materials'. (See Sir Frederick Madden's documents regarding Perkin Warbeck, Archaeologia, vol. xxvii, p. 153.)

Vergil wrote his work by express command of King Henry VII, the successor and bitter enemy of Richard. Hall copied from Vergil, but with his own additions gleaned from the malignant reports of the times. Grafton and Holinshed copied Hall giving as *facts*, however, much matter which Hall himself merely reported from hearsay or conjecture. All these chroniclers availed themselves largely of the graphic descriptions of Sir Thomas More without seeking to invalidate the inconsistencies of More's narrative by reference to contemporary writers. [More was only seven at the time of Richard's death. He had grown up in the household of Bishop Morton, Richard's most implacable enemy, and wrote his narrative when he was only an undersheriff of London. The unfinished and unpublished manuscript, which covers only a few months in 1483, was found after More's death. Authorities agree that Morton either wrote the history or supplied most of the information.]

The best materials for compiling the historical records of this period could only be gleaned from the most corrupt and prejudiced sources. The Tudor historians had either no means of access to contemporary documents or were unacquainted with the Croyland Chronicler, and with those other more concise narratives connected with Richard's time which were afterwards collected by John Stow and are now deposited in the Harleian library. These records were altogether unavailable to Shakespeare. The two university libraries were then almost the only repositories of books of erudition in the kingdom. The royal library, founded after the general dissolution of religious houses (from manuscripts collected out of the spoils of the monasteries) by Henry VIII, was exclusively for the use of the royal family and their instructors (Preface to the Catalogue of the Harl. MSS.).

Shakespeare, however, did not profess to be a historian. He was a dramatist. Unrestrained by history, he took his characters from the current fables of the days and 'adapted their depositions so as to give to such fictions a show of probability' (Whately on Shakespeare,

p. 20). As actor, manager, and poet, he had no time to seek out materials which were difficult of access. His object was emphatic recitation, distinction, and preservation of character, and the production of pictures which would rest on the mind. *Facts* well substantiated and chronological exactness are indispensable to the historian. Not so to the dramatist. He is licensed to substitute the *fable* for the reality and is privileged to select only the most striking features to illustrate the scenes he portrays. He must develop the plot by making each character support the part which he was supposed to have enacted when living.

Thus, it is apparent that, however pleasing, a historical play can scarcely be considered the most effective or surest mode of conveying historical instruction. It is most unwise to form an estimate of the character of Richard of Gloucester from such a source. Yet, Shakespeare's Richard III, by the acting of Garrick, Kemble, Cooke, Kean, and other great tragedians, has acquired a degree of popularity and been invested with a spirit and appearance of truth far beyond many other of the great dramatist's plays.

The leading events in the tragedy of Richard III, especially those connected with the depravity of his mind and the deformity of his person, are either closely copied from Holinshed or from Holinshed's authority on such points, Sir Thomas More. Many passages are merely changed from the quaint prose version of the chroniclers themselves to Shakespeare's melodious verse. It would be premature here to extract these samples, as they chiefly relate to portions of Richard's life not yet considered in these memoirs. It is apparent, however, that the prejudices entertained against Richard III in Shakespeare's time led to his being charged by the dramatist in his earlier days with crimes in which, from Richard's youthful age, he could not have participated.

Shakespeare's interest — drama — not history

The career of Richard, Duke of Gloucester, was too rich in variety of subject, too fertile in harrowing scenes, to be overlooked by the dramatist. Shakespeare's royal mistress, Queen Elizabeth, distinguished him with her favour and patronage. She rejoiced at the public debasement of a monarch whose ruin had elevated her grandsire, Henry VII, to the crown and laid the foundation of that dynasty of which she was so bright an ornament.

Queen Elizabeth distinguished Shakespeare with her favour. Her successor, King James, with his own hand honoured the great dramatist with a letter of thanks for the compliment paid in Macbeth to the royal family of the Stuarts (Symmon's Life of Shakespeare, p. x). 'It is evident from the conduct of Shakespeare', says Lord Orford, 'that the House of Tudor retained all their Lancastrian prejudices even in the reign of Queen Elizabeth'. (*Hist. Doubts*, p. 114.) Malone, also, says of Shakespeare's Richard III, 'The play was patronised by the queen on the throne, who probably was not a little pleased at seeing King Henry VII placed in the only favourable light in which he could have been exhibited on the scene'. (*Courtenay's Commentaries*, vol. ii, p. 116.)

Courtenay adds (vol. i, p. 8), 'either he (Shakespeare) or his more ancient author has taken such liberties with facts and dates, and has omissions so important, as to make the pieces, however, admirable as a drama, quite unsuitable as a medium of instruction to the English youth'. Shakespeare's chronological errors must be attributed to the dramatic spirit in which he wrote. He thought as a dramatist and made mere matter of fact subservient to the powerful delineation of character. Furthermore, he had access only to incorrect authorities. These were the causes of his depicting Richard of Gloucester unfaithfully, according to genuine historical record.

All who desire that truth and not fiction should characterise the national archives of England must lament that Shakespeare selected Richard III, the last monarch of the chivalrous Plantagenets, to display his great powers as a dramatist. As Sir Walter Scott observed (*Rob Roy*, vol. i, p. 231), the 'Lancastrian partialities of Shakespeare, and a certain knack of embodying them, have turned history upside down, or rather inside out'.

Chapter IX

EDWARD IV ACCEPTS LOUIS XI'S BRIBE; CLARENCE EXECUTED

Richard's extensive powers in the north

From 1472, when Richard, Duke of Gloucester, assumed the vice-regal command of the northern parts of the kingdom, he appears to have devoted himself with energy and zeal to the wants of the district entrusted to his government.

He seems to have taken little or no part in political affairs, as far at least as relates to his brother's court and general administration. He directed his attention, rather, towards healing the divisions that had long distracted that part of King Edward's dominions. It was the abode of the Cliffords, the Percys, the Nevilles, the Montagues — the rallying point of the Lancastrian nobles. He worked to render his brother's government popular and acceptable even to the enemies of their House of York by the justice, vigour, and clemency with which he presided over the northern parts of England.

Richard was justiciary of North Wales, warden of the west marches of Scotland, keeper of all the king's forests beyond Trent, chief seneschel or steward of the duchy of Lancaster in the northern parts, and Lord Admiral and Lord High Constable of England. He was also proprietor, in right of the Lady Anne Neville, his wife, of half of the enormous possessions of her late father, the Earl of Warwick, which were increased tenfold by the gifts of the King.

Richard's honourable conduct and high character — northern historians

Richard's career, then, from the probable period of his marriage in 1472, must be chiefly sought in the records of local historians. It is happy for this Prince, in rescuing his memory from the sweeping charges that after times have brought against him, that documents still exist among the municipal and collegiate records of many ancient places and provincial towns associating his name and his acts with these localities. These records render untenable the tradition that incorporates him with all the proceedings of his royal brother's courts. The records exhibit Richard's talents and virtues in a clear and indisputable form and bear testimony to his wisdom and ability for government.

'The employment of this duke', observes the historian of Durham (Surtee's *Hist. of Durham*, p. 67) 'was, for the most part, in the north; and there lay his appenage and patrimony, with a great estate of the duchess, his wife, of which the seignory of Penrith, in Cumberland, was part, where he much resided, and built or repaired most of the castles, all that northern side generally acknowledging and honouring his magnificent deportment'.

But it was not alone the restoration of castles that occupied Richard's attention, zeal, and munificence. To his honour let it be recorded that religion and the worship of God in temples consecrated to His service was fully as much the object of his active zeal and attention. Whitaker states, in his interesting History of Richmond-shire, that that county abounds with memorials of this Prince's bounty to chantries and religious houses (Vol. i, p. 99).

Any evidence that bears testimony to the conduct and character of Richard of Gloucester during that period is invaluable. The historian of Durham was well qualified to judge and to ascertain by diligent local research the important truths which he asserts and substantiates by indisputable records concerning this Prince.

'He was at least', says Surtees (*Hist. Durham*, p. 66), 'whilst Duke of Gloucester, popular in the north, where he was best known'. . . . 'He followed the fortunes of his brother Edward with unshaken fidelity through many a bloody field; and when the title of York was established, his conduct won the affection of those northern counties in which, from the united influence of the great houses of Percy, Neville, and Clifford, the influence of the Lancastrian interest had been most prevalent'. How different is this portrait of Richard from that which is ordinarily given of him. How dis-similar was the active, useful, peaceable life which he really led, when reposing for a brief interval from the warlike duties of his martial profession from that 'malicious and wrothful' career, unqualified by any one redeeming point, usually attributed to this Prince.

Innumerable instances may be gathered from the local and provincial histories already referred to, and from other works, of Richard's attention to his domestic duties, his kindness to his attendants, his prudence and economy in the regulation of his household, and his bounty and munificence to the church. These, together with his justice to the poor and his hospitality to the rich, endeared him to all ranks.

'It is plain', observes Drake in his valuable History of York (Eboracum, p. 123), 'that Richard, represented as a monster of mankind by most, was not so esteemed in his lifetime in these northern parts'.

There is a document extant which shows Richard's generosity and kindness of heart towards his kindred. It illustrates, by a pleasing example, the nature of that influence which he possessed over the King and the manner in which he exercised it to soften his royal brother's revengeful spirit and to preserve for the male line of the House of Neville a remnant at least of that vast inheritance which had been, by the attainder of their race, alienated from them. On February 23, 1475, an act was passed (Rot. Parl., vol. vi, p. 124) which recites that the King, considering the treasons and other offences committed by John Neville, late Marquis Montague, had intended by the authority of the present parliament to have attainted him and his heirs for ever, 'which to do, he, at the humble request and prayer of his right dear brother, Richard, Duke of Gloucester, and other lords of his blood, as of other his lords, spareth and will no further proceed in that behalf'.

Richard and the Countess of Warwick

This legislative enactment tends to exonerate Richard from those mercenary, malicious, and covetous feelings usually attributed to him. It likewise weakens the imputation cast upon this Prince by Rous (Hist. Reg. Anglica, p. 215), but evidently without authority (Horace Walpole's *Historic Doubts*, p. 111), that he 'imprisoned for life the Countess of Warwick, who had fled to him for refuge'. The probability is rather that he aided to restore her to liberty and to release her from the religious sanctuary which she had been compelled to adopt upon her own and her husband's attainder.

The Paston Letters, dated 1473 (vol. ii, p. 145), state that 'the Countess of Warwick is out of Beaulieu sanctuary, and that Sir James Tyrrel conveyeth her northwards: men say, by the king's assent; whereto some men say, that the Duke of Clarence liketh it not'. Thus, she was removed to her native county and restored to her kindred by the 'assent' of the King, although in avowed opposition to the wishes of the Duke of Clarence. The inference is that a third party petitioned for her release. Who so likely as Richard of Gloucester, who had recently been united to her youngest child?

There exists not a single record to fix upon Richard either severity or persecution towards the unfortunate Countess. Neither could she, by any possibility, have 'fled to him for refuge', as stated by Rous, for she was not at large at this period. Besides, the religious asylum which had protected her was far greater security than any protection that could have been given her by Richard.

The Countess of Warwick was released from sanctuary in 1473, openly and not covertly and with the express consent of the King. He provided suitable escort to ensure her safety during her progress northwards. It is important to point out that Sir James Tyrrel, though associated in after years with Richard, was at this time in the service of Edward IV, being master of the horse and a considerable officer of the crown (see Horace Walpole's reply to the president of the Society of Antiquaries, published in the Archaeologia for 1770). Tyrrel was then not in the slightest degree under the control of the Duke of Gloucester or connected with his household.

Richard's intercession for Montague's children, mentioned above, in conjunction with the other facts, warrants the supposition that he also exerted himself to soften the condition of the Countess by restoring her to her kindred and to liberty, although he had no power to reinvest her either with lands or possessions.

Popularity of Richard in northern counties

One thing, at all events, is apparent. Richard exercised his vast power for the benefits of the community at large, and he won universal popularity throughout a district embracing the most turbulent portion of King Edward's dominions. He evidenced active zeal and well-tempered judgment in defending the oppressed and advocating justice, without any respect to persons and without recourse to those severities which were common to the fierce and unsettled times in which he lived. On this point all the northern historians are fully agreed. Their local testimony is amply corroborated by various public documents connected with the acts which thus tend to relieve Gloucester's memory from the unjust imputations which have so long obtained concerning him.

Edward Plantagenet born at Middleham Castle

In the year 1473, Richard's and Anne's happiness was rendered more complete by the birth of an heir to their vast possessions. 'Edward, the eldest son of Richard, Duke of Gloucester, was born at Middleham, near Richmond, 1473' (King's *Vale Royal*, p. 33). This infant scion of a noble race appears to have passed not merely his infancy but the chief portion of his life in this favourite abode of his parents.

Richard accompanies King Edward
— war with France

But peace and its accompanying blessings were not destined for any length of time to smile on Richard's career. From his very childhood, the royal Edward felt and duly appreciated his brother's peculiar talents for aiding him, either by policy or generalship, in the more stormy paths of life.

Edward IV had never forgiven Louis XI for aiding the Duke of Clarence and the Earl of Warwick in their too successful rebellion. He felt that the insurrection which drove him from his kingdom, and which had almost cost him his life, was fomented by the French King. King Edward, still brooding over the injuries he had received from the French monarch and thirsting for revenge, worked toward settling the quarrel between Clarence and Gloucester, 'lest their disputes might interrupt his designs with regard to France' (*Chron. Croy.*, p. 557).

It was at this critical juncture, and immediately following the termination of his domestic troubles, that Edward was solicited by his brother-in-law, Charles, Duke of Burgundy, to return in kind the assistance given Edward towards regaining the throne of England. Charles asked Edward to aid him in making war on Louis XI, whose crafty policy had disgusted all the adjacent principalities, but especially those of Burgundy and Bretagne.

Edward seized with avidity the occasion he had so long desired of retaliating on the French monarch. He cemented an amicable truce with Scotland by betrothing his second daughter, the Princess Cecily of York, to the Duke of Rothsay, the heir apparent of Scotland's crown. Edward then summoned the Dukes of Clarence and Gloucester and all the chivalry of England to aid him in carrying warfare into France, under the plea of regaining the lost possessions in that kingdom.

In June 1475, King Edward proceeded to Sandwich with the flower of the English nobility. He landed at Calais with an army of 15,000 archers on horseback and 1,500 men at arms. With his characteristic hardihood, he had, on his embarkation, dispatched a herald to demand of Louis the crown of France.

Louis, however, with the keen subtlety that made him invariably overreach his enemies by attacking them on their weak points, was well aware of the impoverished state of the English treasury. He first corrupted the herald (Sandford's *Geneal. Hist. of England*, book v., p. 389). He then clandestinely bribed not only the immediate followers but the actual counsellors of the English monarch. They scrupled not to accept gifts and pensions and to barter their own and their sovereign's high military fame for the treasure Louis profusely distributed.

Richard's indignation at inglorious result

And who alone withstood this general defection from the hitherto proud and noble spirit of English knighthood? *Not* the King. He preferred a return to luxurious ease, with a pension. Edward consented to withdraw his army from France, and forthwith to return to England, on the immediate payment of 75,000 crowns, and 50,000 crowns as an annual tribute. To render more binding the treaty of peace between the two countries, it was ratified by an engagement entered into by the monarchs that the Dauphin of France should espouse the Princess Royal of England, as soon as the parties were of age to fulfill this part of the contract (Rymer, vol. xii, p. 14). *Not* the ministers of England. Even the Chancellor of the Realm, the Master of the Rolls, and the Lord Chamberlain scrupled not to accept the bribe which the latter, however, refused to acknowledge with a written document. *Not* the lordly peers and the proud barons, for the receipts for money and plate distributed to the most influential, says Philip de Comines (vol. ii, lib. vi, p. 6) are 'to be seen in the chamber of accounts at Paris!'

It was Richard, Duke of Gloucester, alone — the youngest Prince of the Plantagenet race and the one to whom, of all that race, covetousness and mercenary motives have been mostly imputed. He alone, of the three royal brothers — indeed, of all the noble and the brave in King Edward's court — withstood the subtlety of Louis. He disdained the gold that was to sell the honour of his country (Lord Bacon's Life of Hen. VII, p. 3), and refused to sacrifice, at the shrine of bribery and corruption, the renown and greatness of England's chivalry.

'Only the Duke of Gloucester stood aloof, off on the other side', observes the biographer of King Edward IV (Habington, p. 147), 'for honour frowned at the accord, and expressed much sorrow, as compassionating the glory of his nation blemished in it. He repeated his jealousy of the world's opinion, which necessarily must laugh at so chargeable a preparation to attempt nothing, and scorn either the wisdom or courage of the English, when they shall perceive them in so full numbers and so well armed to pass the sea, after a defiance sent and challenge to a crown, to return back without drawing a sword'.

But the single voice of Richard, Duke of Gloucester, however much it rebounded to his own credit, had no effect in weakening the French monarch's subtle policy. Nevertheless, Louis respected the feelings and honoured the principle (Philip de Comines, lib. vi, ch. 2) that made Gloucester reject those degrading mercenary overtures which were accepted by the royal Edward and his ministers and by his brother of Clarence. The crafty Louis well understood the influence which strong minds exercise over those of less powerful intellect. Despite Richard's avowed opposition to his insidious policy, he paid the young Duke the greatest respect, quickly perceiving the power he possessed over his royal brother and hoping to make it available in forwarding his own views (Hutton, p. 53).

But Gloucester, 'jealous of the honour of the English nation', (Bacon, Hen. VII, p. 2), was neither to be lured from his faith in his sovereign or duty to his country. Consequently, at the celebrated meeting at Picquiny, in which the two monarchs met personally to interchange friendly salutations after the amicable treaty that had been effected between them, the Duke of Gloucester was absent on the English side (Habington, Ed. IV, p. 155). On the other hand, when further opposition was fruitless, Richard is to be found watching over his brother's interests and witnessing the validity of those political agreements which were to cement this most extraordinary alliance.

The attestation of Lord Bacon, Richard's bitter calumniator, is perhaps the most valuable authority that could be adduced on this point. Lord Bacon was prone to magnify every evil report about Richard that malice had propagated to his discredit. 'At Picquiny, as upon all other occasions', says the learned chancellor (Lord Bacon's Hen. VII, p. 3), 'Richard, then Duke of Gloucester, stood ever upon the side of honour, raising his own reputation to the disadvantage of the king his brother, and drawing the eyes of all, especially the nobles and soldiers, upon himself'.

In less than two months, without loss of life, but with grievous loss of reputation, King Edward's army quietly prepared to return to England, without unsheathing the sword or bending the bow. Richard returned with King Edward to England on September 11, 1475. But the expenses attending this expedition could not be liquidated by the French King's profuseness to its leaders. Edward, though sanctioning the most severe measures, found it impossible to meet the difficulties resulting from his exhausted finances.

Causes of quarrel between King and Clarence

A statute was therefore passed in the following year, 1476, whereby it was enacted that all the royal patrimony, to whomsoever it had been granted, should be resumed and applied to the support of the crown (*Chron. Croy.* p. 559). This appears to have given great umbrage to the Duke of Clarence, whose sordid and avaricious disposition could ill brook the loss of any portion of his vast wealth (Dugdale, vol. ii, p. 164). He considered the Act of Resumption a personal affront since by it he lost many lands which he had previously obtained by royal grant '. . . and this' observes the chronicler of Croyland (p. 561), 'appears to have given rise to those dissensions between Edward and Clarence, which ended so fatally for the latter prince'.

'It was remarked', adds that historian, 'that the duke by degrees withdrew himself more and more from the royal presence, that he scarcely spoke a word in council, and would not willingly eat or drink in the king's house'. At length, he retired altogether from the court. Joining the Lady Isabel in the vicinity of Tewkesbury, he brooded over the discontent which he had so unwisely and intemperately displayed. However, the repose he had hoped to find in his domestic circle was destined to be of short duration. His wife, who had been some time in a declining state, died on December 22, 1476, within a brief period after the birth of their second son, Richard of Clarence, who soon followed her to the grave.

As was almost invariably the case with every illustrious personage who died suddenly or whose health gradually failed at this period of English history, the death of George's wife Isabel was attributed to poison. This conviction afforded fresh ground for the indulgence of George's impetuous temper and most injudicious conduct. He procured the illegal condemnation and execution of

Ankaret Twynho (Rot. Parl., vol. vi, p. 173), a female attendant of the deceased Lady Isabel, against whom no proof could be established. On this occasion, Edward's forebearance appears to have been severely tried. Still, Edward did forbear, although Clarence continued to excite and provoke him.

Not long after the death of the Duchess of Clarence, Charles, Duke of Burgundy, the husband of the Lady Margaret of York, was slain at the siege of Nanci, leaving as heiress to his vast possessions an only child, a daughter by a former marriage (*Chron. Croy.*, p. 561). George, Duke of Clarence, immediately sought the assistance of the Lady Margaret to aid him in furthering proposals of marriage with her richly endowed step-daughter [Halsted calls her 'daughter-in-law'.] But King Edward had too frequently experienced the unprincipled and treacherous conduct of his brother to countenance an alliance that might again have led to his aiming at the English Crown. Edward was unremitting in his efforts to promote a union between Maximilian, son of the Emperor of Austria, and the Princess of Burgundy, and eventually he was successful.

The anger of the Duke of Clarence against his royal brother now exceeded all bounds. Within a brief period he proceeded to the council-chamber and before the Lords there assembled in conference publicly accused the King of injustice and upbraided the conduct both of the monarch and his ministers.

Death of Clarence

The King, on receiving information of this outrage, commanded that Clarence be arrested and committed to the Tower. The monarch denounced Clarence's action 'as subversive of the law of the realm, and perilous to judges and juries' (*Chron. Croy.*, p. 561). The imprisonment of Clarence was shortly followed by his trial. The King, himself, appeared as a witness against his brother. Clarence was attainted and convicted of high treason (Rot. Parl., vol. vi, p. 143). 'The Duke was placed in confinement, and from that time never recovered his freedom', says the Croyland historian (*Chron. Croy.*, p. 561). 'What followed in the next parliament', he adds, 'the mind shuns to relate, so sad seemed the dispute between two brothers of so great ability; for no one argued against the duke but the king, no one answered the king but the duke'.

The accusations being deemed sufficient, sentence of death was pronounced against Clarence. Edward appears, however, to have hesitated in ordering his brother's execution, for the Chronicler states that 'judgment was deferred'. But the Commons, headed by their speaker, appeared at the bar of the House of Lords and prayed that the sentence might be carried into effect. The sentence was delivered to Clarence by Henry, Duke of Buckingham, who had been specially appointed, for the time being, to the office of high steward of England to pass upon him the awful judgment of the Peers and to superintend the accomplishment of the sentence. Accordingly, 'within ten days of his condemnation, Clarence was executed, whatever was the mode of death, secretly, within the Tower of London, on the 18th of February, 1478'. (*Chron. Croy.*, p. 561).

Richard blameless in dispute and brother's death

How or in what manner Clarence's death was effected will probably ever remain a mystery. His death forms one of the many accusations brought against Richard, Duke of Gloucester, although Richard was residing in the north during the entire period of the fatal dispute.

The contemporary narrator explicitly states that the trial of Clarence was public, the King sought and desired his condemnation, and his execution was not only sanctioned by the peers of the realm but also demanded by the speaker of the House of Commons.

There is not a single document that connects Richard with the quarrel, although the bill of attainder is still preserved and the Croyland writer appears to have been present at the trial. It was not until very many years after Richard's death that this serious crime was laid to his charge. Even the Tudor chroniclers, bitterly as they inveigh against him on most points, have not included this deadly act amongst the fearful crimes imputed to him. On the contrary, Hall, Holinshed, and Stow unite in saying he openly denounced the extreme rigour of the sentence. And Fabyan, Polydore Virgil, and indeed all the older as well as contemporary historians are silent regarding Gloucester's participation in any manner in the dispute.

Nearly the whole of these writers agree in ascribing the entire deed to the instigation and influence of the Queen and her aspiring and mercenary kindred. Of this fact there can be little doubt if we consider that the Queen and her followers (1) surrounded and had the greatest influence over the King, (2) were actively opposed to Clarence, and (3) were chiefly benefited by his death and attainder. Lord Rivers was so enriched by the execution of Clarence that in the grant which conveyed to him such vast wealth it was insinuated that

Clarence had made a nuncupative will in his favour (a will which is not written but is declared orally by the testator in his last illness). This grant is preserved in the Foedera, vol. xii, p. 95. Laing, in his comments upon it, says, 'The hypocritical language of this donation is curious, and seems to fasten the murder indisputably on Rivers. The grant insinuates that Clarence at his death made a nuncupative will in Rivers' favour; a proof that his conduct required exculpation' (Laing, *Appen. Hen. Hist. Engl.* vol. xii, p. 400).

In addition, the wardship and marriage of Clarence's heir, the infant Earl of Warwick, aged but three years, was granted to the Queen's son, the Marquis of Dorset — one of the most lucrative gifts the crown could bestow upon a subject. Completing the chain of evidence linking Clarence's death with the Queen and her kindred, the task of pronouncing judgment of death upon the royal prisoner devolved upon Henry Stafford, Duke of Buckingham, who was espoused to the Queen's sister, Lady Katherine Wydville.

Sir Thomas More is the first writer who intimates that the Duke of Gloucester acted with subtlety to Clarence, although even he admits that Richard protested against his execution. 'Some wise men', says More, 'also ween that his drift covertly conveyed, lacked not in helping forth his brother of Clarence to his death, *which he resisted openly*, howbeit somewhat (as men deemed) more faintly than he that were heartily minded to his weal' (More's Rych. III, p. 110). [Note how carefully More has almost concealed the single *fact* in this statement.]

Who, after reading this insiduous accusation, can fail to be struck with the chancellor's personal comment upon the report? It is more conclusive regarding the refutation of the charge than the most laboured efforts from a less virulent foe to disprove it: 'But of all this point', More comments, 'is there no certainty; and whoso divineth upon conjecture, may as well shoot too far as too short'. Yet upon this conjecture, upon the acknowledged uncertainty of this random accusation, has Richard of Gloucester been transmitted to posterity as the murderer of his brother. And this in defiance of innumerable testimonies from his bitterest enemies that he protested against so harsh a sentence, and likewise of positive proof that he benefited in no degree either by his brother's death or attainder.

But tales that savour of the marvellous or the horrible seldom lose by repetition — least of all when they are founded upon conjecture alone. More's insinuation that Richard's efforts to save Clarence were feeble and grounded on subtlety were magnified by Lord Chancellor Bacon into — 'that prince being the contriver of his brother's death' (Lord Bacon's *Hen. VII*, p. 2). Shakespeare improves on the tradition by representing Richard as the bearer of the warrant, nay, the associate of the murderers (*Richard III*, Act I, Scene III).

Sandford's *Genealogical History of the Kings of England* has been considered a standard authority for nearly two [now three] centuries. Yet, he completes the fearful picture by making Richard the actual perpetrator of the dark and terrible deed. 'After he had offered his mass penny in the Tower of London', says the Lancastrian herald, 'he was drowned in a butt of malmsey, his brother, the Duke of Gloucester, assisting thereat with his own proper hands' (Sandford, book v, p. 413).

Thus has Richard's character been gradually defamed. Horace, Lord Walpole, the keen examiner into the traditions of this period, concludes that 'the reign of Richard III has so degraded our annals by an intrusion of childish improbabilities, that it places that reign on a level with the story of Jack the Giant-Killer' (supplement to *Historic Doubts*, in Lord Orford's Works, vol. ii, p. 184). Foremost among these 'childish improbabilities' must be placed the report that Clarence was drowned in a butt of malmsey wine (Fabyan, p. 510, and Hall, p. 326). Dr. Lingard says, 'The manner of his death has never been ascertained, but a silly report was circulated that he had been drowned in a butt of malmsey; a tale which, in all probability, owed its origin to the duke's great partiality for that liquor'. Sharon Turner and Laing merely report the popular opinion, without attempting to refute so utterly incredible a tale.

Habington notes, pp. 190, 191, the following tradition well suited to the marvel-loving period of the 15th century, the age of necromancy: 'It is generally received among the vulgar and wants not the approbation of some chroniclers, that the chief ground of the King's assent to his death was the misinterpretation of a prophecy, which foretold that one, the first letter of whose name was 'G', should usurp the kingdom, and dispossess King Edward's children . . . this prophecy was alleged to be spoken by some of his servants, who by necromancy had understood this from the devil'. Shakespeare avails himself of this popular report. He incorporates it and the alleged mode of Clarence's death in those striking scenes which fix the murder of George, Duke of Clarence, upon Gloucester (See *Rich. III, Act I, Scenes I and IV*).

The expressive words of the Croyland chronicler, (p. 560) 'the king, however, was (as I think) very often repentant of the deed', fix the deed on his mandate. These words exonerate Richard equally with the other members of the House of York from tamely and inhumanly beholding the destruction of the ill-fated Clarence. There is not a single circumstance that gives any ground to warrant the assumption that Richard was implicated in anywise with the dissensions that led to his brother's arrest, or that he was even present at the trial that ended in Clarence's death. [Indeed, as already noted, Richard bitterly opposed Clarence's execution. Mancini says(p. 77) that after Clarence's death Richard rarely came to court. He reports the good reputation of Richard's public activities and his private life.]

Richard assists in marriage of infant nephew

Richard seems to have resided in the northern counties with little intermission during the three years between his return from France, 1475, and the execution of the Duke of Clarence, 1478. The only well-attested fact that connects the Duke of Gloucester with the court of Edward IV after that monarch's return from France was one which is peculiarly characteristic of the fraternal affection which united the two brothers. This public event was the solemnization of the marriage in 1477 of King Edward's second son, the infant Duke of York, with his cousin, the Lady Anne Mowbray, the heiress of the House of Norfolk. The bridegroom was but five, and the bride was under three years of age.

The active part taken in the ceremony by Richard of Gloucester is quite consistent with the warm feeling and affectionate energy which he invariably displayed upon all matters connected with the interests of his family. He attended as chief mourner the obsequies of his deceased father. He followed his brother into exile and poverty. He accompanied his young sister on her state progress, preparatory to her marriage. He was the chief mediator in reconciling his elder brothers when hostilely arrayed against each other. He attested the betrothal of his niece to the dauphin of France, although opposed to the treaty that led to the contract. On the present occasion, he is found supporting his infant nephew in a marriage sanctioned by the church and earnestly desired by the King.

This marriage occurred on January 15, 1477, about a month after the demise of the Lady Isabel and at the identical period when Clarence had ascribed her death to sorcery practised by the Queen consort. Every branch of the House of York was assembled on the joyful occasion, with the exception of the discontented Clarence.

Richard appears to have returned to the north after the festive scene which induced his visit to the court of Edward IV. Various important documents are extant which fix his residence at Middleham during the ensuing year. His occupation there forms a striking contrast to the unnatural dissensions between his elder brothers which reached their climax during this period. This fact is invaluable in disproving Richard's participation in the dispute. It also indicates how different was the bent of his mind from that mischievous spirit with which it has so long been the fashion to invest him.

Richard founds and endows the Collegiate Church at Middleham

Richard's strong attachment to Middleham has been noted. He evinced this in the most laudable and praiseworthy manner when it became his own baronial hall. The great object which engaged his attention now was a desire to amplify the parish church of Middleham and to found and incorporate a college there for a dean and twelve secular priests.

Richard appears to have followed up the matter with his accustomed zeal, until he succeeded in obtaining from Parliament a licence to found and endow the college (*Cal. Rot. Pat.*, p. 322) at his own expense and at his sole cost. This first step towards the advancement of a project which he had so much laboured to effect received the sanction of the legislature on January 16, 1478 (Rot. Parl. vol. vi, p. 172).

The consent of the rector, William Beverley, was then obtained. Nothing can be couched in stronger language or give a more amiable view of the motive which influenced Richard or the light in which he was viewed by his northern partisans than the manner in which the instrument conveying the rector's comment is worded: 'Whereas, among other remedies, &c., the solemnities of mass are deservedly esteemed to be grateful to the Divine mercy manifested by the sacrifice of our Saviour for the salvation of the living and the repose of the dead; the petition lately exhibited to me on behalf of the most excellent prince, Richard, Duke of Gloucester, Lord of Middleham, contained that the said most excellent prince proposed and intended to amplify the said parish church of Middleham, to the praise of Almighty God, His most excellent mother, and all saints, and the continual increase of divine worship, and the same to endow with greater rights and possessions; and also to increase the number of ministers in the same, devoutly dwelling with God, if the said

Church were erected into a collegiate Church, by the most reverend father in God, Laurence Booth, Archbishop of York, primate of England, &c.' — See an Abstract of Beverley's *Consent*, in Whitaker's *Richmondshire*, vol. i, p. 335.

Richard's son created Earl of Salisbury

Richard continued in favour with the King, although as More asserted he 'resisted openly' the condemnation of his brother, George, Duke of Clarence. This is evidenced by a signal mark of favour conferred upon him within a few days of Clarence's secret execution: 'Edward Plantagenet, eldest son of Richard, Duke of Gloucester', was 'created Earl of Salisbury, to him and the heirs of his body', by patent dated February 15, 1478 (Rymer, Add. MSS., No. 4615, art. 5).

Thus, by a singular coincidence, the renowned titles of Earl of Salisbury and Earl of Warwick were revived at the same period. The title of Salisbury was bestowed by the King on Edward of Gloucester, February 15, 1478, as noted above, and that of Warwick was inherited by Edward of Clarence upon the execution of his parent on the 18th of the same February, 1478. Few tales of fiction could depict more disastrous fortunes than those of Edward, Prince of Wales, Edward, Earl of Warwick, and Edward, Earl of Salisbury, the eldest sons of Edward IV, George of Clarence, and Richard of Gloucester. These were the last male heirs of the royal line of Plantagenet, the very name of which was destined to pass away with these ill-starred and unfortunate princes.

Chapter X

RICHARD SUBDUES SCOTLAND; EDWARD IV DIES

Richard, Duke of Gloucester, occupies Barnard Castle

Among the very small portion of the Duke of Clarence's confiscated lands which were bestowed upon Richard of Gloucester after his brother's death was Barnard Castle, in the county of Durham. This superb building, the abode of the Lady Anne's maternal ancestors, seems henceforth to have shared with Middleham Castle the peculiar attention and interest of Richard. Barnard Castle received its name from Barnard de Baliol, who came into England with the Conqueror, and whose great grandson was afterwards King of Scotland. Edward I dethroned him and seized the manor and castle.

Richard's cognizance, The White Boar, still preserved in ruins

While the foundation of Barnard Castle was coeval with the Norman conquest, its renovation and embellishment were the work of Richard of Gloucester. Here may be found the earliest trace and perhaps the best preserved specimen of his badge, the boar. Surtees, in speaking of Barnard Castle, says, '. . . a beautiful mullioned window, hung on projecting corbeils, still exhibits withinside on the soffit of its arch the boar of Richard, with some elegant tracery, plainly marking the latest portion of the castle to be the work of Gloucester' (Surtees, p. 90).

The badge, impress, or cognizance, as certain heraldic figures in general use at this period of English history were styled, 'was an emblematical device', says Camden, 'by noble and learned personages to notify some particular conceit of their own'. They are altogether distinct from coats of arms, 'which were used to distinguish families, and usual among the nobility in wars, tilts, or tournaments', or from the crest, the highest armorial distinction, which was worn in the helmet by the knight, himself, as an especial mark of nobility (Camden's *Remains*, p. 447). The badge, in short, was the household or livery cognizance worn by the retainers of princes and powerful barons to declare visibly the liege lord to whose service they were attached.

Many of the most remarkable associations relating to feudal times are connected with this ancient appendage, including the very name of Plantagenet. This was derived from the cognizance of the progenitor of that chivalrous race of English monarchs, Geoffrey, Count of Anjou. He adopted a sprig of the Planta-genista (the yellow broom) as a symbol of humility when performing a pilgrimage to the Holy Land (Buck's Richard III, p. 6). 'The white boar was the badge of Richard, Duke of Gloucester, and was retained by him after he ascended the throne. His arms were sometimes supported by two of them. In Sandford's time, there remained over the library gate at Cambridge, carved in stone, a rose, supported on the sinister side by a boar, which boar, the same author informs us, Richard had found among the badges of the House of York, being of silver, with tusks and bristles of gold, inscribed 'Ex Honore de Windsor'. The badge of the white boar is said to have been derived from the honour of Windsor' (*Retros. Review*, 2nd Series, vol. ii, p. 156).

Brackenbury attached to Gloucester's service

Nothing is more remarkable in the study of history than the fact that the sincerity of even the most impartial writers becomes affected when their prejudices, whether religious or political, are called into play. How completely the false colouring thus given by them to persons or things perverts the truth which they seek to establish and from which, indeed, they have no intention of departing.

Richard III is not the only instance in our regal annals that could be adduced to corroborate this fact. Queen Mary, melancholy as was her reign, resulting from the bigotry of her ministers and the fury of religious persecution at that period, was far from being the cruel and unfeminine character usually described. On the contrary, she was mild and amiable in private life. Her letters and literary productions which are yet extant (see Hearne's *Syllogi Epistolarium* and Strype's *Hist. Memorials*) prove her to have been a right-minded and very learned woman. She was the victim of the unhappy times in which she flourished rather than the willing agent of those savage deeds which procured for her in after years the approbrious term of 'Bloody Mary', — an epithet resulting from the same factious spirit which bestowed on Gloucester the epithet of 'Crook-backed Richard'.

The family of Brackenbury was of very ancient date, having settled at Selaby, in the immediate vicinity of Barnard Castle, from the end of the twelfth century. One of the main bulwarks of the Castle is still designated as 'Brakenbury's Tower'. The Robert Brackenbury whose name is inseparably interwoven with that of Richard of Gloucester was a junior member of this ancient family. It is a fair inference that upon Richard fixing his abode at Barnard Castle, a cadet of the Brackenbury family should be numbered among his retainers as the vassal of his princely superior.

Richard of Gloucester appears to have possessed qualities that won the greatest confidence from those who surrounded him, and inspired the most devoted attachment in those on whom he bestowed his friendship. He distinguished Brackenbury with marks of the highest favour, and there is no existing document or even tradition to prove him undeserving of the Prince's regard. With firmness and fidelity Brackenbury followed Gloucester's fortunes to the very close of his life, even at the sacrifice of his own. Thus, Brackenbury's name suffered from being so intimately associated with a Prince whose testimonies of regard were interpreted into bribery for crime, and whose rewards for faithful services were considered as designating only his co-partners in guilt.

Characters of Edward IV and Richard contrasted

It is scarcely possible to imagine a stronger contrast to the active and praiseworthy career pursued by Richard, Duke of Gloucester, than was afforded by the inert and luxurious life led by King Edward IV. His indolence increased with his years, and his love of pleasure and personal gratification gained strength by excessive indulgence. The tribute-money continued to be regularly paid by Louis XI after the Treaty of Picquiny. These funds gave Edward ample means for indulging to satiety those enervating habits which weakened his talents for government fully as much as they paralyzed his naturally active and energetic character.

Secure, then, in the peaceful possession of his own dominion and undisturbed by foreign enemies, King Edward yielded himself wholly to a life of frivolous amusements and the unrestrained indulgence of the most dissolute habits, leaving the entire charge of his kingdom, as relates to military affairs, to Richard, Duke of Gloucester. 'The king', observes Lingard (p. 202), 'desired to live to the best advantage of his pleasure; Gloucester, of his honour'. Richard's increasing importance throughout the country at large, as the only Prince of the House of York capable by age or inclination for active exertion, kept pace with his popularity in the North. His unblemished reputation in public life and his submissive and consistent deportment to King Edward increased his influence with that monarch and strengthened the attachment which had ever bound the brothers to each other. As a natural result, Richard perpetually received fresh proofs of the King's confidence and affection.

In the 17th Edward IV, he was reappointed Great Chamberlain of England for life, which office it will be remembered he had relinquished in favour of the Duke of Clarence, by whose death it became vacant and was again in the gift of the crown. In the 18th Edward IV, he was constituted Admiral of England, Ireland, and Aquitaine, and in the 20th Edward IV, he was nominated Lieutenant-General of the kingdoms in consequence of threatened hostilities with Scotland.

Richard was likewise appointed (to quote the quaint language of the times) 'one of the triers of petitions' for England, Ireland, and Scotland, in the Parliament which met in the painted chamber at Westminster, January 16, 1478 (*Rot. Parl.*, vol. vi, p. 167), an appointment which attests Richard's judgment and integrity and is proof also that he was accustomed to conducting the actual business of the state. De Lolme's *Constitution of England* (p. 234) explains that 'In the beginning of the existence of the House of Commons, bills were presented to the king under the form of petitions. Those to which the king assented were registered among the rolls of Parliament, with his answer to them; and at the end of each parliament the judges formed them into statutes. Several abuses having crept into that method of proceeding, it was ordained that the judges should in future make the statute before the end of every session. Lastly, as even that became in process of time insufficient, the present method of framing bills was established; that is to say, both Houses now frame the statutes in the very form and words in which they are to stand when they have received the royal assent'.

Richard leases Crosby Place

The King's increasing indolence rendered the judicious advice and active assistance of his brother not merely essential to his own individual ease, but important to the internal government of the kingdom. Up to this period, however, no fixed abode in London appears to have been appointed to the Duke of Gloucester. At this early period of English history the abiding place of the great feudal lords was their baronial halls. They rarely visited the metropolis and when they did so it was with a great retinue and purely on matters of state. Such business included attending the great councils of the nation, assisting at the coronation of their monarchs, allaying civil commotions and affording support or offering opposition to the reigning sovereign and his ministers.

At this time (about 1475), Richard occupied a newly erected mansion late belonging to Sir John Crosby, an alderman of London, from whose widow the Prince probably leased it. Erected in a style of princely grandeur, it was completed both within and without with that gorgeous splendour which peculiarly characterized the buildings of the 15th century. Crosby Place, with its embowered oriels, superb hall, and matchless roof is famed as perpetuating in this present day the only specimen now remaining in the metropolis of the domestic architecture of the middle ages. It is as interesting from its association with the last monarch of the Plantagenet race as is Barnard Castle, the abode of Richard of Gloucester in early and less troubled times, from the preservation in that Castle of his household cognizance, 'the bristled boar'.

Records relating to Richard

These habitations, and provincial records of his laudable proceedings in the northern counties previously related, constitute almost the only traces of Richard's private life after his marriage. His public acts, however, are most numerous. They are registered in the archives of the land and establish his reputation as a warrior and yet more his character as a patriot and his dignified conduct as a Prince of the blood royal of England. He was still in the prime of life, for he had not attained his twenty-sixth year on the death of Clarence (February 18, 1478).

Richard of Gloucester merited in its fullest sense the eulogium extorted by a sense of justice even from the prejudiced pen of Lord Bacon: 'a prince in military virtue approved, jealous of the honour of the English nation; and likewise a good law-maker for the ease and solace of the common people' (Bacon's *Life of Hen. VII*, p. 2). 'The northern parts were not only affectionate to the House of York, but particularly had been devoted to King Richard III' (Ibid., p. 17). Such, indeed, was the character which he bore universally in the extensive district in which his career as Duke of Gloucester must chiefly be sought for and judged, and where so many records yet exist (Drake's *Eboracum*, p. 117) to bear testimony of his bounty, his generosity, and his justice.

Records relating to Richard's wife and son

It is much to be lamented that so little is known of the childhood of Richard's son, Edward, Earl of Salisbury, and so little preserved of the Lady Anne, Richard's wife. However, the same dearth of material for biographical notice will be found in the case of all the consorts of the illustrious men who flourished at that period.

It appears probable that the Lady Anne suffered from the same ill health and inherited the same fragile constitution that carried the Lady Isobel to an early grave. Both sisters appear to have died of decline. In both instances, their wasting away and gradual decay were attributed, but without foundation, to poison.

The young Earl of Salisbury may not have been Richard's only legitimate child, but only the eldest and sole surviving son. This surmise is not based on conjecture. On the creation of the young Edward as Earl of Salisbury, the letters patent (Cal. Rot. Pat., p. 322), which yet exist, distinctly term him 'the *eldest* son of Richard, Duke of Gloucester'. In the Harl. MSS., 433, fol. 242, a very curious document is preserved in which Richard himself styles the young prince 'Edward, *his first begotten son*'. In a collection of ordinances which, at a later period of his life he issued for the regulation of his household in the North, one of the leading items is this (ibid., p. 269): That 'my Lord of Lincoln', his favourite nephew (son of Elizabeth, Duchess of Suffolk, the eldest surviving sister of King Edward IV and Richard, Duke of Gloucester) and 'my Lord Morley', probably his son's preceptor, 'be at one breakfast' and '*the children together* at one breakfast'. He also afterwards implies the high rank of the parties thus specified by commanding that no livery exceed his (Gloucester's) limitation, 'but only to my lord and *the children*'.

James, King of Scotland, breaks truce with England

It was fortunate for the honour of the kingdom and the tranquility of the Yorkist dynasty that the active habits of Richard of Gloucester were so singularly opposed to the supineness of King Edward. For his ancient enemy, Louis XI, was no indifferent spectator of a state of things which his tribute money had effected and the payment of which he meant to continue until such time as he considered it convenient to throw off the mask.

The King of Scotland was less scrupulous in preserving even an appearance of faith. He openly showed his intention of annulling the alliance with England which had been cemented by the betrothal of the heir of his crown with the Princess Cecily of York. Constant outrages were perpetrated by the Scottish borderers on the English frontiers for which neither redress nor compensation could be obtained. The rich dowry promised with the English princess on her union with the Duke of Rothsey was regularly paid by instalments beforehand, as had been agreed at the time of the contract. Still, year after year rolled on, and the articles of marriage were not fulfilled. Nor did James return the money received as the pledge of King Edward's sincerity as had been stipulated in the event of non-fulfilment of the marriage.

Edward declares war — appoints Richard Lieutenant-General

In 1478, the sums hitherto paid by England were discontinued but without producing the desired effect on the treacherous Scottish King. The exasperation of Edward IV at what he designated James' 'meanness of conduct and breach of faith' (Lingard, vol. v, p. 230) was heightened by the artful representation of the Duke of Albany, King James' brother, who had been exiled from his native Scotland because of his ambitious and rebellious conduct and now sought the assistance of England in restoring him to his country and his honours (Feodera, vol. xii, p. 173).

Accordingly, King Edward proclaimed war against Scotland and entrusted the command of the expedition to the Duke of Gloucester. 'This prince', observes Habington in his *Historie of Edward IV* (p. 223), 'had now no competitor in greatness both of judgment and power'. His royal brother was so subdued by his inert habits that he was well content to leave to others that vengeance which he had determined to inflict. 'Willing to decline labour', adds his biographer (Ibid.), 'he waived the expedition', thus proving the truth of a previous quotation from this same author 'that the king desired to live to the best advantage of his pleasure; Gloucester, of his honour'.

The successful result of Richard's mission presents a marked contrast to the inglorious peace purchased by France and displays in a remarkable manner the different sentiments which influenced the two brothers when called upon to uphold the honour of their country.

Both in England and Scotland the warlike preparations were on an extensive scale. King James resolved on heading his own troops. The wording of the patent which conferred upon Richard the sole command of the English army attests the confidence reposed in him by the King, as well as the popularity of the Prince himself. The letter recites 'that notwithstanding the truce which had lately been concluded with James, King of Scotland, he was again about to wage war; and that the King, not only on account of his consanguinity and fidelity, but also by reason of his approved prowess and other virtues, appointed his brother Richard, Duke of Gloucester, his lieutenant-general, during his own absence, to oppose, if they (the Scotch) should enter the English territory' (Feodera, vol. xxi, p. 115).

The expenses of assembling an army sufficiently powerful to invade Scotland and compel King James to make restitution for his breach of faith were enormous. King Edward devised the most despotic and novel measures for exacting sums of money from his subjects. The most obnoxious levy, and the one which bore heaviest on the whole country, was the method of exacting large sums by means of what was termed a 'benevolence' (Cont. Croy., pp. 558, 563). This consisted of plate and money demanded from the people as a gift or extorted from them on various pretexts without legislative authority. By this means, his agents gathered vast sums to replenish the regal coffers at the expense of his impoverished subjects.

Richard besieges Berwick
— marches to Edinburgh

Richard had secured the English frontiers from all hostile invasion by the efficient state to which he had brought the walls and fortresses on the border country (Issue Roll of Exchequer, pp. 499, 501).

All preliminaries were at length completed for invading Scotland, and in June 1482 the Duke of Gloucester laid siege to the town and castle of Berwick, justly termed the key of Scotland. He was accompanied by an army of nearly 23,000 men, including the most renowned English warriors, leading officers of the royal household, the King's own physician, and the King's treasurer — evidence of the King's support of his brother's honour, dignity, and safety.

The Castle of Berwick, then the strongest fort in the North, was commanded by the valiant Earl of Borthwick, who made such determined resistance that Gloucester speedily foresaw the length of time it would take to subdue the Castle. Having forced the town to capitulate, Richard lodged a small but determined band within it. He then resolved, with his accustomed energy, to penetrate instantly to the Scottish capital, surprise King James, and secure full indemnification for the contempt shown to England and her sovereign. He left Lord Stanley and 4,000 men-at-arms to continue the siege of Berwick Castle and entered Scotland with the main body of the English army.

Striking terror into the inhabitants in the line of his march by setting fire to such towns and villages as resisted his progress, he marched direct to Edinburgh. King James had taken refuge within Edinburgh Castle upon hearing of the Duke of Gloucester's approach. To the honour of Richard it must be recorded that he saved Edinburgh from pillage and destruction. Habington says (p. 204) 'his entry was only a spectacle of glory, the people applauding the mercy of an enemy who presented them with a triumph, not a battle; and welcomed him as a prince who took arms not for pecy (probably specie, an abbreviation of the old French word 'espece', or a corruption of the ancient Latin term 'pecuniosus', of or belonging to money — Bayley, vol. i) or malice, but for the safety of a neighboring kingdom'.

Richard agrees to cessation of hostilities on most honourable terms

The nobles of Scotland had as a body deserted their sovereign, who was deservedly unpopular with his subjects, and sent a message to the Duke of Gloucester imploring him to suspend arms. They offered him full restitution on every point, even to the immediate solemnization of the marriage between the Duke of Rothsay and the Princess Cecily, second daughter of King Edward IV.

Gloucester's reply 'that he came to right the honour of his country, often violated by the Scots', was worthy of him and so, also, were the terms which he submitted to them. These comprised restoration of the money paid by King Edward; capitulation of Berwick Castle, so dear to the Scotch from being an ancient appurtenance to their crown and representing the portal of their land; and recall and restoration of the Duke of Albany. Richard would not compromise the honour of his niece by accepting an extorted consent to her union with the young Duke of Rothsay. The marriage, he said, must be left to King Edward's future consideration, but the sums paid for her dowry must be refunded without delay.

No argument could weaken Gloucester's resolution. Therefore, a day was appointed for the restitution of all money lent by King Edward; a pledge was given for a reparation of all damage done the English by any inroad of the Scottish borderers; and Berwick was ceded to England with a covenant 'by no act hereafter to labour the reduction of it' (Habington, p. 205).

Richard receives thanks of King and Parliament

'Thus, having avenged the indignity shown to his niece, upheld the regality of his sovereign, defended his country from insult and wrong, and been the medium of effecting a reconciliation between the Duke of Albany and his misguided brother, Gloucester quitted Edinburgh in triumph; and with all increase of glory to the English name (and by consequence to his own), he returned to Berwick, which, according to the former agreement, had been yielded to Lord Stanley' (Habington, p. 206). 'Thence', continues Habington, 'in all solemnity of greatness he came toward London, to yield an account of his prosperous enterprise; and to show how much more nobly he in this expedition against Scotland had managed the peace for the honour of the English nation, than his brother had in his undertaking against France . . . ' (p. 207).

Richard was welcomed by King Edward — as, indeed, he justly merited — with the warmest affection. Having received, with his compeers, the thanks of the Houses of Parliament, the royal approbation was publicly given to Richard's wise and vigorous measures which had ended in reducing Berwick and humbling the Scots. Satisfied with the energy of Gloucester's proceeding and pleased with the ample revenge taken on his faithless ally, King Edward disguised his anxiety at the vast expense and strove to appease the discontent of his impoverished subjects by the most sumptuous entertainment and gorgeous festivities.

James Gairdner : This campaign augmented and confirmed Richard's reputation as a successful warrior. Despite the cost 'it was still a great achievement, and gave England a most important advantage in case of further hostilities. And not only by this, but by his rule over the West Marches, of which he was Warden, Richard earned for himself such golden opinions that the Parliament which met in January (1483) was not slow to recognize his merits. As Warden, he had acquitted himself so ably that he had brought a whole district, about thirty miles long, of what had formerly been debatable land, into acknowledged subjugation to the King of England; in reward for which service it was decreed, by a most extraordinary enactment, that the Wardenship of the West Marches should belong to him and the heirs male of his body forever. . . . In fact, the good rule of Gloucester on the borders, *notwithstanding his unpopularity afterwards as King Richard III*, was remembered long after his day as a very model of efficiency'.

'At this time, therefore, *whatever may have been thought* of his *character by close observers*, no man stood in higher honour than Richard throughout the kingdom generally'. (The underscored comments show Gairdner's bias against Richard — he cannot resist making these invidious observations.) (*History of the Life and Reign of Richard The Third*, rev. ed., Cambridge University Press, 1898, pp. 41, 42.)

Louis XI violates treaty of Picquiny

Little time, however, was allowed for feasting and pageants or for redeeming, by the blessings of peace and prosperity, the devastating effects of war. Louis XI had been the secret agent in fomenting discord between England and Scotland. Now an unlooked-for event afforded him the means, so long desired, of casting off the English yoke and ridding himself of the detestable tribute which necessity alone had induced him to pay.

Mary, Duchess of Burgundy, died within four years of her marriage with the Archduke Maximilian of Austria, leaving two infant children, a son and a daughter. The prospect of annexing to France a portion of the rich provinces of Burgundy by affiancing the Dauphin to the orphan Princess of that wealthy principality was far more tempting to the French monarch than the empty honour that would have accrued to his heir by the existing alliance with the Princess Royal of England, Elizabeth of York (see Chapter IX). Louis was never over-scrupulous in the measures he adopted for compassing his views. He considered faith and treaties as mere political agents — never as the pledge of kingly honour.

The infant Margaret was delivered to commissioners appointed by the French monarch. King Edward had not merely to endure the mortification of seeing the annulment of his long-cherished plans for the aggrandizement of his eldest daughter. At the same time, the tribute-money ceased to be paid. The serious deprivation this entailed because of Edward's extravagant habits increased his bitterness and mortification. He now saw fully the value of Gloucester's protest at Picquiny and how easily and completely he had been duped by Louis XI.

Edward IV resolves to invade France — impending death

No sooner was the French monarch's breach of faith communicated to Edward IV than he resolved on being avenged and humbling Louis as severely as he had the Scotch people and their ruler. Summoning the lords of his Council, Edward made known his injuries and his daughter's wrongs. The whole court — indeed the whole kingdom — were loud in their call for war and in requiring instant preparations to be made for invading France. The great feudal lords, retiring to their ancient halls, summoned their vassals and retainers. All who held lands by military tenure hastened to assemble the archers and knights by which they were bound to the service of the King. Parliament voted subsidies; the church levied considerable sums; and the tocsin of war, as if by universal consent, sounded throughout the land.

But Louis XI was again saved from a renewal of those desolating wars which had ever impoverished the French nation by one of those solemn decrees which prove the fallacy of human designs through the uncertain tenure of human life. King Edward, although in the prime of manhood, had prematurely accelerated old age by the luxurious habits in which he indulged. An illness, at first considered unimportant, soon began to assume an alarming appearance, and the monarch speedily felt that his dissolution was approaching. The period allotted him to prepare for the last solemn scene was very short. His attention, from the commencement of danger, was exclusively devoted to those religious duties which he had so fearfully neglected. He endeavoured to make reparations for the severe exactions with which he had grievously oppressed his subjects to enrich the royal coffers and gratify his personal enjoyments.

Paul Murray Kendall : Kendall notes (p. 155) that Edward IV was now concerned with the peaceful succession of his son. One of those who might threaten the succession was Henry Tydder or Tudor, who called himself the Earl of Richmond. He was a Lancastrian who obtained refuge at the court of Francis, Duke of Brittany (*Richard the Third*, Allen & Unwin Ltd., London, 1955. *All Citations are to this Edition*).

Halsted : On his *mother's* side, Henry's great-great-grandfather was John of Gaunt, fourth son of Edward III. Gaunt's mistress, Catherine Swynford, bore him four children. Gaunt married her after their respective spouses had died. Richard II legitimised Gaunt's bastards and gave them the name of Beaufort. In 1407, Gaunt's son, Henry IV, half brother to the Beauforts, confirmed their patent of legitimacy with the limiting phrase *excepta dignitate regali*. John Beaufort, the eldest of the four children Catherine Swynford bore Gaunt, became the Marquis of Somerset. His granddaughter, Margaret Beaufort, married Edmund Tudor, Earl of Richmond. Her only child, Henry Tudor, was born on January 28, 1457.

On his *father's* side, Henry's ancestry was equally flawed. His great-grandfather had been butler to the Bishop of Bangor. Henry's grandfather, Owen Tudor, had held a menial position in the household of Henry V's widow, Queen Katherine, but managed to effect a liaison with her. Their children were Jasper, Edmund, and Owen. When Henry VI's council discovered this union in 1437, it imprisoned Owen. He claimed to have been married to the Queen, but was unable to supply proof. Henry Tudor's father, as we have noted, was Edmund. Thus, Henry had no real claim to the throne. His lineage was flawed on both his maternal and paternal sides.

Gairdner : But the dying Edward IV was more concerned with the discord in his own court, aggravated by the greed of the Woodvilles and by Edward's debauchery. 'In the full prospect of death Edward had called before him those lords whom he knew to be at variance, especially the Marquis of Dorset and Lord Hastings, and implored them for the sake of his children and for the peace of the kingdom, to

109

forget their old quarrels and live thenceforward in amity. The lords were deeply touched by this appeal, and gave each other their hands in the presence of the dying man, making formal protestations of mutual forgiveness and reconciliation. Nevertheless, no sooner was the breath out of Edward's body than symptoms of the old suspicions began to show themselves' (pp. 44, 45).

Edward IV's death

Edward IV's disorder, an intermittent fever, produced by a surfeit (Habington, p. 223), but probably accelerated by agitation arising from the French monarch's perfidy and his own short-sightedness, terminated his life at the palace of Westminster on April 9, 1483, in the 41st year of his age and in the 21st of his reign. There was insufficient time to summon the young Prince of Wales from Ludlow, where he was residing, or to enable Richard, Duke of Gloucester, who had returned to his military duties in the north, to attend on the deathbed of a brother whom he had ever so faithfully served and to whom he was warmly attached.

King Edward's ancestors and progeny

By his Queen, Elizabeth Woodville, King Edward had a numerous progeny, of whom two sons and five daughters alone survived their father, the remainder dying in childhood, viz.:

1. Edward, Prince of Wales, afterwards Edward V, born November 4, 1470.
2. Richard, Duke of York, born May 28, 1474.
3. George, Duke of Bedford, died an infant.
4. Elizabeth, Princess Royal born February 11, 1466, betrothed to the Dauphin of France, but eventually married to Henry VII.
5. Cecily, affianced to James, Prince of Scotland, but afterwards married first to the Lord Viscount Welles, secondly to a person named Kyme, in Lincolnshire.
6. Anne, espoused Thomas Howard, Duke of Norfolk.
7. Mary, betrothed to the King of Denmark, but died in childhood.
8. Margaret, born 1472, died in her infancy.

9. Katherine, married to William Courtney, Earl of Devon.
10. Bridget, youngest child, born 1480, became a nun at Dartford. — Sandford, Geneal. Hist., book v., p. 393.

Of Edward's ancestors, Richard, Duke of Cambridge, the grandsire of Edward IV and Richard III, was beheaded at Southampton, August 6, 1415. Richard, Duke of York, their father, was beheaded on Wakefield Green, December 30, 1460.

Humphrey, Duke of Gloucester, youngest brother of King Henry V, was 'for his virtuous endowments surnamed *the Good*; and for his justice, *Father of His Country*'. In the first year of his infant nephew, King Henry VI, Parliament made him Protector of England during the King's minority. But 'by the envy of Margaret of Anjou, his nephew's Queen', he was murdered at Bury St Edmund's, A.D. 1446 (Sandford's Geneal. Hist., book iv, p. 308). Richard, Duke of Gloucester, youngest brother of the succeeding monarch, Edward IV, was the next Prince who bore that ill-omened title. In the first year of the reign of King Edward V, his nephew, 'he received the same power as was conferred on Humphrey, Duke of Gloucester, during the minority of Henry VI with the title of Protector' (Chron. Croy., p. 566).

King Edward's character

Edward IV presents one of the most deplorable instances regal annals can furnish of brilliant talents being sacrificed to trifling enjoyments. The glory of this monarch's character terminated with those brilliant actions that twice secured him the throne. The noble and princely qualities which gave such promise of future excellence on his accession at the young age of eighteen were lost in the selfishness, indolence, and frivolity that marked his maturer years and tarnished his eventful reign — perhaps the most striking in English annals. He supinely abandoned himself to unworthy excesses and relinquished the government, all but nominally, to his more right thinking and more nobly disposed brother, Richard, Duke of Gloucester.

111

Chapter XI

RICHARD APPOINTED PROTECTOR

Duke of Gloucester in north at brother's decease

Richard, Duke of Gloucester, was with the army in the marches of Scotland preparing to move the soldiery for the contemplated invasion of France when he received the news of the death of his brother, King Edward IV, on April 9, 1483. Almost the last act performed by the deceased King had been to assure to Richard by the authority of Parliament (*Rot. Parl.*, vi. p. 204) a broad extent of territory and increase of authority in the north, where Richard was already so popular. This fact reflects the absence of all jealousy on the King's part and the deserts of a Prince who could be thus fearlessly entrusted with almost unlimited power.

Rapacity of the Wydvilles

The amicable terms on which the two brothers had ever continued may in great measure be attributed to the pacific conduct which Richard observed towards the Queen, Elizabeth Wydville, and her relatives. In all likelihood, his prudence preserved him from the violent death of Clarence and Warwick's untimely fate. Nevertheless, Richard knew the undue influence exercised by the royal Elizabeth and the house of Wydville over the council and actions of the King. Richard shared the indignation of the ancient nobility at the elevation of a race who had no claim for preferment but that of consanguinity to the Queen. They had been raised to the highest offices in the state and permitted to occupy the chief seat in the council chamber. He also viewed with distrust and misgiving the blind policy of his royal brother. The King had removed the heir apparent, Edward, from all intercourse with his royal kindred and placed him under the direct tuition and immediate influence of his mother's family, in a remote part of the kingdom.

Richard was the sole surviving brother of Edward IV, and first Prince of the House of York, with the exception of the youthful offspring of that King. Richard's position became difficult and, judging from the fate of the Princes who had been similarly placed in the past, beset with danger also. Relinquishing plans for invading France, he hastily prepared to quit the north and assume that lead in the direction of public affairs, which his nephew's minority had imposed upon him.

Richard takes oath of allegiance to Edward IV's son

Richard wrote to the Queen, promising 'advent, homage, fealty, and all devoir to the King and his lord, eldest son of his deceased brother and of the said Queen' (*Chron. Croy.*, p. 565). Proceeding to York with a retinue of 600 knights and esquires 'all attired in deep mourning' (Ibid.), he commanded the obsequies of the deceased King to be performed at the cathedral with the splendour due to his regal station and assisted at the ceremony 'with tears' (Ibid.). He then constrained all the nobility of that district, as the late King's viceroy in the north, 'to take the oath of fealty to the King's son, he himself setting them the example by swearing the first of all' (Ibid. and Francis Drake's *Eboracum*: or the *History and Antiquities of the City of York*; William Bowyer, London, 1736, p. 111).

Edward V proclaimed King

The funeral of the deceased Edward IV was sumptuous, befitting the splendour and magnificence which had characterized his life. He was interred at Windsor in a chapel which he had erected, and his eldest son, aged twelve years and five months, was forthwith proclaimed his successor as King Edward V. (Edward, Prince of Wales, was born in the Sanctuary at Westminster, November 4, 1470; proclaimed King, April 11, 1483.)

The youthful monarch was residing at Ludlow when his father died, under the immediate charge and tutelage of his maternal uncle, Lord Rivers, and the monarch's half brother, Lord Richard Grey. Intelligence was forthwith sent to him of the demise of Edward IV, accompanied by letters from the Queen to her son urging his immediate return to London.

The widowed Queen of Edward IV, Elizabeth Wydville, had two sons by her first husband, Sir John Grey of Groby. The elder son was Sir Thomas Grey, created by her royal consort, in the eleventh year of his reign, Earl of Huntingdon, and four years later, Marquis of Dorset. He had been appointed governor of the Tower by Edward IV, who had bestowed upon him the marriage and wardship of Edward, Earl of Warwick, son of the late Duke of Clarence. The younger son was Lord Richard Grey, an appointed counsellor of the young Prince of Wales and associated with Lord Rivers in the important charge of his personal safety. Of the Queen's brothers, only two survived at the death of Edward IV, viz., Anthony, Earl Rivers, governor of Prince Edward's household, and Lionel Wydville, Bishop of Salisbury. (See *Dugdale's Bar.*, vol. ii, p. 719; *Cal. Rot.* p. 313.)

Note : Halsted is in error. The Queen's brother, Sir Edward Woodville, was also alive. Kendall (pp. 168, 178) notes that, on April 29, 1483, the day before the Queen fled to sanctuary, Sir Edward Woodville and his fleet sailed with a portion of the royal treasure in the Tower. When all but two ships of this fleet declared for the Protector and Council, Sir Edward and his adherents fled to Henry Tudor with the treasure he had taken from the Tower.

Edward IV's will — Richard to be Protector

During the lifetime of Edward IV, the court was divided into two distinct parties — (1) the Queen's relatives and supporters, together with those who coveted honour and official distinction without claim of high birth or lineage and (2) the ancient nobility and proud kindred of the House of York, attached either to the King's household or his administration. A perpetual rivalry and constant collision of interests existed between these two parties, so jealously opposed to each other.

The King, on his death-bed, foreseeing the disastrous consequences which were likely to arise from his son's minority and the prospect of a regency — that fruitful source of intrigue and evil ambition — used his expiring efforts to effect a reconciliation between the factious opponents (More, p. 13). He is believed to have nominated the Duke of Gloucester as Protector (Drake's Eboracum, p. 111) and guardian during the young Edward's nonage. 'The nobles at London and in the south parts speedily call the duke home by their .

114

private letters and free approbation to assume the protection of the kingdom and the princes committed unto him by the King. "Rex Edwardus IV filios suos Richardo Duci Glocestriae, in tutelam moriens tradidito", as Polydor testifieth'. (King Edward IV, on his death-bed, gave over his sons to Richard, Duke of Gloucester, for care and education — George Buck, *The History of Richard The Third*, W. Wilson, London, 1647.)

Gairdner: '. . . it was the will of the deceased King himself that after his death the care of his son's person and kingdom should be transferred to Richard Duke of Gloucester. This confidence may seem extraordinary . . . but as the fact is distinctly recorded by two well-informed writers of that day (Bernard André [Henry's official biographer] in Memorials of Henry VII, p. 23, and Polydore Vergil [Henry's official historian], p. 539), who are by no means friendly to Richard, there cannot be a doubt that such was Edward's real intention. . . . The Queen and her adherents had always been disliked by the old nobility, and it is probable that Richard was the man who seemed to him most likely to be able to keep the peace between two opposite factions. . . .

As Richard was in the North when his brother died, he could not have been called upon to take any part in these declarations of amity and goodwill; but there is no appearance (notwithstanding what we read in Shakespeare) that he had hitherto shared very strongly the common dislike of Queen Elizabeth Woodville and her relations. He had shown himself all along the zealous champion of his brother's rights, and . . . (Edward IV) had greater confidence in him than anyone else. . . . He believed that in committing to his brother the care of his family and kingdom during the minority, he was taking the best means that he could devise to avoid dissensions. . . . He most probably died in the hope that the Queen's relations would have been content to exercise hereafter a subordinate authority under the control of Richard as protector of the kingdom'. (pp. 44, 45.)

Early Chroniclers. André (*Vita Henrici* VII, p. 23), Vergil (*Anglicae Historia*, p. 685), and Molinet (*Chroniques*, ii, 377) state that Edward IV entrusted the care of his children and his kingdom to Richard. Mancini (p. 132) says that Edward probably appointed Richard Protector.

State of affairs at accession of Edward V

The two dissenting parties united in testifying their affection and respect for the memory of Edward IV by co-operating at the solemnization of the last sad rites. Very brief, however, was the unanimity thus formally displayed. Immediately after the funeral, the council assembled and fixed May 4, 1483, as the day whereon Prince Edward should receive the ensigns of his coronation. The Queen's ambitious views are made known by her desire that the young King should be conducted to London with a powerful army, commanded by her brother and son. The Chronicler of Croyland states (p. 564) that the more prudent of the council thought the custody of the King's person, until he became of age, ought not to be entrusted 'to the uncles and brothers on the mother's side; which they considered could not be prevented if they were permitted to attend the coronation otherwise than with a moderate number of followers'.

Little knowledge, indeed, of the condition of England at the accession of Edward V is necessary to perceive that physical strength was the chief agent employed to acquire and maintain authority and that justice was measured out in proportion to the force which could command it. The council, therefore, limited the retinue of the young Prince to 2,000 horsemen — 'A retinue not exceeding two thousand, which number was satisfactory to Lord Hastings, because he calculated that the Dukes of Gloucester and Buckingham, on whom he chiefly confided, would not bring with them a less number'. (Chron. Croy., p. 565.)

Alfred O. Legge. Lord Rivers had almost limitless power at Edward IV's death. He had control of Edward V, access to the royal treasury in the Tower, and supreme command of South Wales and the royal forces there. He need only summon the army in the King's name and march to London. Here he could join with his nephew, the Marquis of Dorset, Governor of the Tower of London and military commander of London. Thus the wisdom of limiting Lord Rivers' force is evident. (*The Unpopular King*, Ward and Downey, London, 1885, vol. I, p. 190.)

Croyland Chronicler. The more prudent counsellors thought the young King should be removed entirely from the sway of his maternal relations. This statement is noteworthy because the writer was himself a member of the council and a friend of the dead King and his family. Hastings, the Lord Chamberlain, threatened to retire to Calais, of which he was the governor, when the Queen Dowager asked for a strong force to escort the young King. With this threat of civil war, she gave way and agreed to limit her force to 2,000 horsemen (pp. 564, 5, as cited by Gairdner, pp. 46, 47).

Dominic Mancini. When King Edward IV went to France in 1475, the nominal head of state was the young Prince of Wales, but the Queen, Elizabeth Woodville, ruled. The Woodvilles probably intended to follow this pattern (Calendar of Patent Rolls, 1467-77, 534-5; Rymer, Foedera xii. 13; British Museum, MS Cotton, Vespasion C. xiv, f.272 vo, p. 140. See *The Usurpation of Richard III*, ed. C.A.J. Armstrong, Oxford, 1936, p. 140).

Richard's honourable conduct

Such was the state of affairs when Edward V left Ludlow for London on April 24, 1483, just a fortnight after his royal father's death. Richard, Duke of Gloucester, had been in no position to take any part either in the resistance made to the Queen's assumed authority or to the decisive measures adopted by the council. He had passed the interval thus occupied in dissensions at court and divisions in the cabinet in travelling from the Scottish borders to York, in commanding requiems to be solemnised there and in the large towns (Harl. MSS. 433, fol. 176) for the repose of the soul of Edward IV, and in exacting allegiance from all under his dominion to Edward V.

Richard's conduct was open and honourable throughout, consistent in every respect with the deference and love he had invariably shown to his royal brother, and such as was best calculated to insure the peaceful succession of his nephew to the throne. There was no undue asumption of power; no assembling, of which he had the entire control, to enforce his authority as nearest of kin to the royal minor; no tarrying in his viceregal territories to ascertain the feeling of the populace or to induce the most remote suspicion that he contemplated usurpation of the sceptre. Richard had long possessed the sole command of one-half of the kingdom and had dissipated in the north many of the factions which had disturbed the peace of the realm. He was Lord High Admiral and Chief Constable of England, and Lieutenant General of the land forces. His administration in these different capacities, maritime, civil, and military, were allowed by all to have been just, equitable, and prudent.

Legge. If Richard, Duke of Gloucester, had intended to seize power, he would have rushed to London or prevented Edward V from entering London. He did neither. Instead, he solemnized requiems in every large town on his route. His actions indicate he only intended to secure the protectorship during Edward V's minority and to prevent the Woodvilles from seizing power. To carry out the

117

responsibilities imposed by his brother's will, Richard had to obtain custody of the young Edward (vol. I, pp. 191, 192).

Gairdner. Richard's journey southwards was not very expeditious (pp. 48, 49).

Richard discovers plot — hastens southward

At York, however, the aspect of affairs assumed a very different hue. Richard received intelligence from the Duke of Buckingham and Lord Hastings concerning a deep plot formed by the Wydvilles to achieve the total overthrow of his protectorate and his claims to the regency. In the light of this plot, strong measures were immediately necessary.

Accordingly, Richard quitted York for Northampton so as to intercept the royal progress. '. . . when the Duke of Gloucester reached Northampton, there came there, to do him reverence, Anthony Earl Rivers, the King's uncle, and Sir Richard Grey, the King's uterine brother, and others sent by the King his nephew, that they might submit all things to be done to his decision'. (Chron. Croy., p. 565.) In the evening, Richard and his associates were joined by Henry, Duke of Buckingham, accompanied by 300 horsemen.

Only four days remained before the time appointed by the council for the coronation of Edward V, May 4, 1483. Edward was already at Stony Stratford, 13 miles advanced toward London, whither they intended 'on the morrow to follow the kyng, and bee with hym early ere he departed' (More, p. 28).

Markham. Edward IV's will entrusted his kingdom during the minority and the care of his son solely to Richard (André, p. 23; Vergil, pp. 530, 171, 173, Eng. trans.). Richard proclaimed his nephew King and proceeded to London to assume the responsibilities his brother had imposed upon him. He was accompanied only by 600 gentlemen in deep mourning.

In sharp contrast, the Woodvilles conspired to ignore Edward IV's wishes by excluding Richard and using force to retain the power they had exercised through the Queen:

Rivers left Ludlow with 2,000 men and arms on April 24 (Rous, p. 212; Croy. Chron., p. 564).

Dorset equipped a naval force to command the channel and seized treasure in the Tower.

Council orders were issued in Rivers' and Dorset's names as uterine uncle and uterine brother. Richard was excluded — his name was not mentioned.

These acts prove the Woodvilles' treasonable intentions. They also planned Richard's death according to Rous (p. 213) and the Croyland monk (p. 565). See *Richard III: His Life & Character*, Smith, Elder, and Co., London, 1906, pp. 89, 90.

Mancini. The council considered the question of government during the minority. One view was that Richard, Duke of Gloucester had the right to govern because of the specific directions in Edward IV's will and the law. Others held that Richard should be the head among several persons who would govern. Hastings informed Richard of these contrasting views. He added he, Hastings, was in danger because of his friendship with Richard. Richard then wrote to the council stating he had been loyal to Edward IV and would be also loyal to his brother's children. He asked the councillors to consider his rights in governing to which he was entitled by law and, specifically, by his brother's will. A contrary decision would be harmful. The people, who had previously favored Richard because they believed in his integrity, now openly supported him. The council, however, voted for the alternative view (pp. 87-91).

Paul Murray Kendall. The Woodvilles were aiming to crown Edward V immediately and govern in his name. Richard was being systematically excluded from carrying out the responsibilities of Protector imposed on him by Edward's father, Edward IV. Therefore, Richard had to obtain custody of the young King (p. 164).

Treacherous actions of the Wydvilles

The Marquis of Dorset had taken possession of the King's treasure (More, p. 27) and had already commenced equipping a naval force, although Richard as Admiral of England, had the entire control over the maritime affairs of the country. This information explained the subtle part acted by Lord Rivers in sending the young King to Stony Stratford, a day's journey in advance of his uncle — although Richard was hourly expected at Northampton — and thus withdrawing Edward on the very verge of his coronation from all contact with his father's brother. Richard and Buckingham and their most chosen friends spent a great part of the night in council, reviewing the extraordinary actions of the Queen's family in London and the sinister conduct of Earl Rivers in greeting Richard, Duke of Gloucester, unaccompanied by the young King.

Legge. Gloucester, Buckingham, and Hastings were not engaged in a private plot. More (p. 41) says 'the two Dukes *with a few of their most privy friends*, set them down in council, wherein they spent a great part of the night'. Sharon Turner (vol. iii, p. 427) says the conference at Northampton 'was a serious discussion of their party on the measures proper to be taken . . . ; whether the Queen's family should exclude or be excluded from the regency or government, and whether this should be determined by an appeal to open war, or by their use of the opportunities that lay before them'. (Vol. I, pp. 194, 195.)

Conspiracy to kill Richard
— imprisonment of Rivers and Grey

The reason for Richard's next actions is explained by Rous: 'They were accused of having compassed the death of the protector', he says (p. 212). Rous based his statement not on public report or casual hints from nameless eavesdroppers but on no less an authority than the Earl of Northumberland! He was 'their chief accuser' (p. 214).

On April 30, 1483, before the day had dawned, or Richard's rivals were stirring, every avenue of the city was guarded, and horsemen stationed on the high road to intercept all communications with the King and his escort. All the lords departed Northampton together, but when they had nearly approached Stony Stratford, Earl Rivers and his chief associates were suddenly arrested, by command of Richard, Duke of Gloucester.

Continuing their route, Richard, Buckingham, and their companions proceeded with all speed to Stony Stratford. Here the wily scheme of the young King's attendants for hurrying him to London, and separating him from his uncle of Gloucester became still more evident, for 'they founde the kinge with his companie readye to leape on horsebacke' (More, p. 26). Richard arrested Sir Thomas Vaughan, the King's chamberlain; Dr. Alcock, Bishop of Worcester, his chief preceptor; and other of his personal advisers. The Duke was convinced that the young monarch, now in his thirteenth year, was a party to the deception sought to be practiced upon him, in sending the Lord Rivers to Northampton ostensibly to submit 'all things to his decision', but in reality to gain time and to blind Richard to the scheme at which his royal nephew seems to have connived. This is made apparent by the following remarkable passage with which the Croyland historian ends his brief account of these most singular proceedings:

'The Duke of Gloucester, who was the chief of this faction', (here he plainly intimates that the Duke did not act merely on his own responsibility), 'made no obeisance to the prince, by uncovering, bowing, or otherwise. He merely said that he would take heed for his safety, since he knew that those who were about him conspired against his honour and his life. This done, he caused proclamation to be made, that all the King's servants should forthwith withdraw themselves from the town, and not approach those places whereunto the King should remove, under pain of death. These things were done at Stony Stratford the 31st April, 1483'. (Chron. Croy., p. 565.)

Richard had only 600 of his own retainers, plus Buckingham's 300 horsemen, or 900 in all. Nevertheless, the 2,000 horsemen appointed to guard their Prince did not oppose Richard's orders to stay Edward V's progress and to disperse his attendants. The young Edward expressed his ignorance of the news about the Marquis of Dorset who 'hadde entered into the Tower of London, and thence taken out the kynge's treasure, and sent menne to sea' (More, p. 26).

Upon their return to Northampton from Stony Stratford, Richard sent the Lord Rivers, the Lord Richard Grey, and Sir Thomas Vaughan to Pomfret Castle and other fortresses in 'the North parts' (Rous, p. 212). He then took upon himself 'the order and governance of the young King' (Chron. Croy., p. 565; More, p. 28), whom the said lords, his counsellors, had sought to mislead, and over whom they had obtained such dangerous ascendancy.

Gairdner. Apparently the Woodvilles decided to govern by force until their control had been secured by the crowning of Edward V. They fixed an early date for the coronation, attempted to bring a large body of armed followers to London, and were racing to London with the young King. The Marquis of Dorset violated his office as Constable of the Tower by rifling the royal treasure, taking arms, and outfitting a naval force. When the Woodville baggage was taken at Stony Stratford, large quantities of arms were found and seized. More speaks lightly of this discovery. But the common people believed the Lords Rivers and Grey had treasonable intentions and that 'it were alms to hang them' (pp. 53, 54).

121

Hastings approves Richard's actions

Richard then sent a messenger to the assembled lords in London informing them, through the Lord Chamberlain Hastings, of the decisive measures he had taken, which were fully approved by that most devoted partisan of the late King. Richard likewise wrote to the leading nobles of the realm, explaining the motives by which he had been actuated, viz. 'that it neyther was reason, nor in any wise to be suffered, that the young king, their master and kinsman, should be in the hands and custody of his mother's kindred; sequestered in manner from theye companie and attendance' (More, p. 19) the which 'quod he, is neither honourable to hys majestie, nor unto us'. (Ibid.) Richard, nevertheless, is represented as treating the young monarch with honour and reverence, and as behaving to his captive friends with courtesy and kindness (Ibid., p. 28).

Gairdner. '. . . the lords of the council met, and Hastings, who was informed how matters really stood, gave an exact account of what had happened. He explained that nothing had been done or meditated against the royal person; that Rivers and the others had been arrested on account of a conspiracy against the Dukes of Gloucester and Buckingham; that their arrest was ordered for the security of those noblemen, not with any design against the King, and that they were kept in confinement only till the matter should be properly investigated. Finally, he said that the two dukes were coming up to London for the coronation, so that they might soon be expected to answer for themselves, and that any disturbance would only tend to delay that event. These representations, becoming public, soon allayed the excitement and prevented any violent outbreak'. (p.52)

Kendall. Hastings sent a message to Richard, May 1, 1483, that his actions were approved and that the Woodvilles were not a threat now (p. 180).

Edward V not an infant

Here it is important to show that Edward V was not at his accession a mere infant — a babe in loose robes — as shown in many a fanciful engraving. He was in his thirteenth year when he was proclaimed King, certainly old enough to exercise judgment and competent to discriminate in most matters in which he was personally concerned.

He had been early prepared by able preceptors for that position to which probably he would one day be elevated. Henry V limited Henry VI's guardianship to the age of sixteen. Richard II was two years younger than Edward V when he was crowned King and was only fourteen when he dispersed the infuriated mob assembled by Wat Tyler.

The young King seems to have been tender, affectionate, and docile, but void of energy, of 'a weak and sickly disposition' (Buck, lib. iii, p. 85), meek rather than courageous, and studious rather than enterprising (More, p. 27). Thus, the reign of Edward V bid fair to revive those fearful calamities which had characterized the reign of Edward II. England would have to contend with the intrigues of the Queen mother, a factious administration, an irritated and discontented nobility, and the ascendancy exercised over a too yielding disposition by unpopular and unworthy favourites.

Richard was ardently devoted to his country and politically, if not personally, opposed to the Queen and her kindred. His objective was to save the one from the threatened evils likely to ensue from the uncontrolled ambition of the other. But he acted towards the young Prince, his nephew, with the greatest tenderness and compassion (Lingard, vol. v., p. 240).

The Queen and Dorset take sanctuary in Westminster

On May 1, 1483, the night following the capture of Lords Rivers and Grey, rumours reached London of the King being in the hands of the Dukes of Gloucester and Buckingham. Queen Elizabeth betook herself to the Sanctuary at Westminster with her children. 'You might have seen, on that morning, the fautors of one and the other party, some truly, others feignedly, as doubtful of the events, adhering to this or that side: for some congregated and held their assemblages at Westminster, in the Queen's name: others at London, under the shadow of Lord Hastings' (Chron. Croy., p. 566). Hastings was the leading adviser of the late king, Edward IV, and was the member of his council most opposed to the Queen and her kindred.

The Marquis of Dorset, awed by the decisive actions of Richard, Duke of Gloucester, abandoned the Tower and the unjustifiable assumption of authority which he had exercised there as its governor. He fled for safety to Westminster where his mother, the Queen, had already sought refuge.

Richard escorts Edward V in state to London

'After the lapse of a few days', continues the annalist (Chron. Croy., p. 566) 'the aforesaid dukes (Gloucester and Buckingham) brought the new king to London', conveying him thither with every testimony of respect. On May 4, 1483, the day originally fixed for his coronation, the youthful prince entered the metropolis, escorted by Gloucester, Buckingham, and a suitable retinue. They were all habited in deep mourning, except the monarch himself (More, p. 34), who was clothed in his kingly mantle of blue velvet. The civic authorities and 500 citizens sumptuously attired (Buck, lib: i., p. 11) met the royal cavalcade a short distance from the city.

The King was conducted to the bishop's palace at St. Paul's where he was lodged with regal state and etiquette. On the way, he was followed by the civic authorities and citizens and preceded by the Duke of Gloucester, who rode uncovered before his nephew and, in passing along, said with a loud voice to the people, 'Behold your prince and sovereign'. At the bishop's palace, Gloucester compelled the lords spiritual and temporal, and the mayor and aldermen of the city of London, to take the oath of fealty to their lawful and legitimate sovereign (Chron. Croy., p. 566), which 'as the best presage of future prosperity, they did most willingly'. (Ibid.)

Perfect tranquility was the consequence of this unanimous feeling. The legislature and municipal authorities fully cooperated with Richard in carrying out measures which restored confidence and allayed the feverish excitement of the populace. 'The laws were administered', says Rous (p. 212), 'money coined, and all things pertaining to the royal dignity were performed in the young king's name . . .'.

Edward takes regal abode in Tower

The Protector speedily assembled a general council, since some legally constituted executive power was essential, not merely up to the young King's coronation but until he became old enough to govern on his own responsibility. 'This council assembled daily at the bishop's palace, because there the young Edward was sojourning; but as this imposed upon the prince unnecessary restraint, it was suggested that he should be removed to some more free place of abode' (Chron. Croy., p. 566). Various dwellings were proposed, and the Tower was finally chosen.

Prejudice has been unduly exercised against this decision of the council because the Tower of London is better known now as a state prison than as the ancient palace of the English sovereigns, which it really was during the middle ages (see Bayley's *History of the Tower*). In Edward V's day, the Tower was the King's palace, which guarded alike the treasure of the kingdom and the person of its monarch whenever his safety was likely to be endangered. Henry III first made the Tower the regal abode and dwelt there almost exclusively. Every succeeding monarch to the time of Edward V lived there occasionally, since the unsettled state of the kingdom made a fortified abode indispensable for the King's security.

The council's selection of the Tower was justified by precedent since the Tower had been, by ancient usage, the abiding place of English monarchs before their coronation. 'It had for a long while been the custom of the king or queen to take up their residence at the Tower for a short time previous to their coronations, and thence they generally proceeded in state through the city, to be crowned at Westminster' (Bayley's *History of the Tower*, vol. ii, p. 263).

Richard's actions produce tranquility

The wavering conduct of Rotherham, Archbishop of York and Lord Chancellor, greatly increased the fears of the populace. On learning of the arrest of the Lords Rivers and Grey, 'he tooke the great seal with him, and came yet before day unto the queen', delivering unto her hands this important badge for the 'use and behoof' of her son (More, p. 31). Repenting his imprudence in giving the signet of state to the Queen, 'to whom the custody thereof nothing pertained without expecial commandment of the king' (Ibid.), Rotherham secretly sent for the seal again on the next day and brought it with him to the council chamber.

Gairdner. The Woodvilles' cause had collapsed, but no blood had been spilled. A reign of peace and prosperity appeared to have started — Chron. Croy., p. 566 (p. 57).

Council and senate unanimously choose Richard 'Protector and Defender of the Realm'

The first act of the council was to appoint the Duke of Gloucester

Protector of the King and his realm. More (p. 34) says he was 'the only man chose and thought most mete'. The Chronicler of Croyland (p. 566), corroborating this fact, adds that 'Richard received the same power as was conferred on Humphrey Duke of Gloucester during the minority of Henry VI, with the title of Protector'. He adds, 'this authority he used by the consent and good pleasure of all the lords . . . '. A new parliament was summoned for the 25th of the ensuing month (June), as shown by an ancient document preserved in the Lambeth register (Royal Wills, p. 347).

On May 16, Rotherham, Archbishop of York, was deprived of his office as Lord Chancellor, after being severely reproved for having delivered up the greal seal to the Queen, causing alarm in the city. Dr. Russell, late privy seal and Bishop of Lincoln, was appointed Lord Chancellor in his place — 'a wise manne and a good and of much experience', testifies More (p. 35), 'and one of the best learned men, undoubtedly, that England had in hys time'. Some new counsellors were appointed, replacing other lords, but Lord Hastings (late chamberlain of the household), Lord Stanley, the Bishop of Ely (John Morton), and other personal friends of the deceased monarch, Edward IV, kept still 'theyr offices that they had before' (Ibid.).

The youthful Edward issued various grants, the functions of government were orderly and wisely executed, and the feast of St. John the Baptist (June 22, 1483) was fixed as the day whereon the King's coronation was to take place without fail. On May 19, the Duke of Gloucester conducted the new monarch to Westminster for presentation to the estates in parliament assembled.

Edward delivered a speech from the throne (Sharon Turner, vol. iii, p. 419), claiming their fealty and asserting his royal prerogatives and right of succession. (Cott. MSS., Vitel. E. 10.) He eulogized 'the right noble and famous prince the Duke of Gloucester, his uncle, protector of the realm, in whose great prudence, wisdom, and fortunes restyth at this season the execution of the defence of his realm'. Noticing the dangers to be feared from the opposing party, he urged 'thys hygh court of Parliament' to confirm the Duke of Gloucester in the protectorate, to which he had been previously nominated by the council of state. 'The power and authority of my Lord Protector is so behoffull and of reason to be asserted and established by the authority of this hygh court, that among all of the causes of the assemblyng of the parliament in thys time of the year, thys is the greatest and most necessary to be affirmed' (Ibid.).

Richard, Duke of Gloucester, had no competitor for the office of Lord Protector. He wisely desired, however, that the kingly authority which had temporarily devolved upon him should be confirmed beyond all controversy by legislative enactment. His title to be so confirmed was admitted by all parties. As stated in the speech from the throne, he was 'next in perfect age of the blood royal to be tutor and protector' (Ibid.). His unblemished character up to this point is demonstrated by the unanimous action of the legislature in ratifying his protectorate and proposing him to the young monarch as an example of mature wisdom, felicity, and experience (Ibid.).

The sole guardianship of Edward V having been committed to his charge by the Parliament, Richard henceforth issued the viceregal mandates under the title of 'Duke of Gloucester, brother and uncle of kings, protector and defender of the realm, great chamberlayne, constable and lord high admiral of England' (Chron. Croy., p. 566; Feodera, xii, p. 184; and Drake's Eboracum, p. 115). In doing so, Richard adhered to the precedent afforded by Humphrey, Duke of Gloucester, uncle of Henry VI, who held the same power in Henry's reign and whose protectorate was the example given when the same power was conferred upon Richard, uncle of Edward V. Humphrey, after his nomination to the protectorate, used the titles 'Humphrey, by the grace of God son, brother, and uncle to kings, Duke of Gloucester, Earl of Henault, & c., Lord of Friesland, Great Chamberlain of the Kingdom of England, Protector and Defender of the said Kingdom and Church of England' (Sandford, book iv, p. 308).

Richard of Gloucester was now in effect the ruler of the kingdom — its sovereign all but in title. The Chronicler of Croyland says (p. 566) that Richard's power 'used by the consent and good pleasure of all the lords' was such 'that it empowered him to command and forbid in everything like another king'.

Gairdner: As noted earlier in this Chapter, Gairdner (pp. 44, 45) states 'it was the will of the deceased king himself that after his death the care of his son's person and kingdom should be transferred to Richard Duke of Gloucester'.

More, though hostile to Richard, says that on Edward V's arrival in London, there was no one more popular than Richard. The council formally proclaimed him Protector and Defender of the Realm (p. 55).

Kendall. Richard summoned his deceased brother's advisers to his first council, including Woodville supporters. The council confirmed Richard as Protector of the King and kingdom, as Edward IV had directed in his will (pp. 184, 185).

Buckingham and Northumberland alerted Richard of plot

Edward V appears, by his signature to certain instruments (Harl. MSS. 435, p. 221) to have moved from the bishop's palace at St. Paul's to the regal apartments occupied by his predecessors in the Tower between May 9 and May 19, 1483. During this brief period, Edward made some weighty appointments, the most remarkable being the nomination of the Duke of Buckingham to high military commands in South Wales and the adjoining English counties (*Rymer's Add. MSS.*, 4616, art. 6). This appointment, and the Earl of Northumberland's investiture with corresponding authority in the north (Drake's *Eboracum*, p. 111), indicates that these two lords had informed Richard of the alleged plot for his destruction which is detailed by all contemporary writers, and had been speedily recompensed with such high offices.

Richard's appointment effects wishes of Edward IV and council

Richard's power was the result of no illegal measures he pursued but was the voluntary gift first of the privy council and finally of the whole legislature itself assembled in Parliament. And, as we have seen, it carried out the wish of his deceased brother, King Edward IV. The council of state convened for this purpose, before the dissolution of the old Parliament and the assembling of the new one, was sufficiently powerful to have resisted the Duke's assumption of the high office of Protector if the council thought Richard had unjustifiably and unlawfully seized that office. The young King was securely lodged in his royal citadel. He had been placed there expressly to permit free discussion, so that his person was no longer subject to his uncle's detention when Parliament confirmed Richard in the protectorate.

Richard had no army in London or resources either civil or military sufficient to intimidate his opponents, even had he evinced such a disposition to violence. He based his claims on ancient usage and on a character free from stain and reproach. The favourable decision of the solemn assembly of the land, which met to consider investing the brother of King Edward IV with the sole guardianship of Edward's heir and successor, was unanimous. It attests their belief of the just, prudent, and upright manner in which, as quaintly expressed in the language of that day, 'my said lord protector will acquit himself of the tutel and oversight of the king's most royal person during his years of tenderness' (Cott. MSS. Vitel. E. fol. 10).

Thus, we have the most convincing proof of the injustice which has been exercised for 500 years against the character, actions, and motives of Richard, Duke of Gloucester, up to the critical period when by universal consent he was entrusted with the helm of state and appointed 'protector and defender of the realm'.

Chapter XII

EDWARD IV'S OFFSPRING ILLEGITIMATE; RICHARD PROCLAIMED KING

Richard enters upon duties of Protectorate

The eyes of the whole nation were now fixed upon Richard, Duke of Gloucester. In the face of political convulsion, he had secured the tranquil accession of Edward V, quelled the divisions in the late King's council, revived the people's sinking spirits, and restored faith and confidence in the government. And he had achieved all this without striking a blow, without causing the death of one human being or engaging in acts of cruelty, vengeance, or retaliation. 'Without any slaughter, or the shedding of as much blood as would issue from a cut finger'. (Chron. Croy., p. 566.)

Civil war would have ensued had no legitimate claimant for the protectorate existed. Otherwise, the succession of insults inflicted by the Wydville family upon the ancient nobility of the realm would have rendered an appeal to the sword unavoidable. The fear of this impending collision probably led to Richard's being unanimously confirmed in the protectorate by the friends of both parties.

There is nothing to indicate that Richard had formed any design to usurp the throne. Nor is there any indication that he contemplated the death of Lord Rivers and Grey, who had been arrested at Stony Stratford (see Chapter XI), until he had investigated the reports about them. 'They were accused of having conspired the death of the protector'. (Rous, *Hist. Reg.* Ang., p. 217.) The conduct of the Duke of Gloucester thus far, considering the temper and character of the times, was irreproachable. His actions were not conducted in the dark but openly, before the gaze of the people. (Polydore Vergil, lib. i, p. 11; More, p. 29.)

Demoralization of the realm at this corrupt period

Succeeding ages have dwelt on this epoch as one of the most corrupt in English history, and justly so. 'The state of things and the dispositions of men were such', writes Sir Thomas More (p. 64), 'that a man could not tell whom he might trust or whom he might fear'. 'Every man doubts the other' (Excerpt. Hist., p. 17). From the period of the birth of Richard of Gloucester to his elevation to the protectorate, the worst passions had disgraced the highest in rank and station.

The Duke of Gloucester well remembered that the leading members of the very council who were now associated with him in governing the realm were those peers and prelates who had been bribed by the wily monarch of France, Louis XI. '. . . Dr. Rotherham, bishop of Lincoln, lord chancellor of England, and Dr Morton, bishop of Ely, master of the rolls, with other noblemen and councillors of special credit with the King, had 2,000 crowns apiece per annum' (Buck, lib. 1, p. 29). Richard also knew that their unanimity in raising him to be 'defender of the realm' arose more from hatred of the Queen Mother, Elizabeth Wydville, and her family than from respect to him or devotion to their youthful sovereign.

A pleasing contrast — Cecily, Duchess of York

As a pleasing contrast to this melancholy picture, Cecily, Duchess of York — mother of Edward IV and Richard — remained in the high esteem of the populace. On reaching London, Richard had gone at once to her abode, Baynard's Castle, and continued there for some days. Cecily had recently become a member of the Benedictine order (Cott. MSS., Vitel. L. fo. 17). Her religious vows would seem a sufficient surety that she would not lend herself to any projects for disinheriting her grandchild or for unjustly elevating her son to the throne.

The threat of the Wydvilles

The death of the Duke of Clarence, promoted as it had been by the Queen, Elizabeth Wydville, and her brother, Lord Rivers, still rankled deeply and painfully in the heart of every member of the House of York. Richard, Duke of Gloucester, and his mother, Lady Cecily, knew that if the aspiring and unscrupulous Wydvilles could secure the ear of the new King, Edward V, Richard himself, would speedily fall a victim to their hatred and ambition.

Thus, upon the demise of Edward IV and the accession of Edward V, a struggle for preeminence arose between the young monarch's royal kindred and his maternal relatives. The natural consequence was that the Protector was supported in his resolute measures by every branch of his own princely house, but chiefly by his mother, whose heart had ever inclined to Richard, the youngest but most judicious of her sons.

Dean Hook : 'No one can read attentively this portion of history, comparing the tradition with the authentic documents, without seeing that the blame of the quarrel between him (Richard) and the late King's family, in the first instance, attaches to the Queen and her relatives. Richard was, in all probability, prepared to treat that weak and wayward woman with respect; to place her at the head of her son's Court; and to be satisfied for himself with the substance of authority, with the trappings of royalty. But he found that she and her party were plotting against his authority, his liberty, perhaps his life. Richard was not the man to submit patiently to this state of things. If the Queen's party were not annihilated, nothing less than the annihilation of Richard would satisfy their ambition or silence their fears . . . '. *Lives of the Archbishops*, vol. v, p. 367, as quoted by Legge, vol. I, p. 204.

Gairdner : '. . . although the Queen's influence was great with Edward himself, she was scarcely regarded with more respect by the nobility than the courtesans by whom she was dishonored. To the last she and her family were regarded as upstarts, and their interference in public affairs was generally resented. . . . Even Henry VII, who afterwards became King and married her eldest daughter, found it advisable to shut up his mother-in-law in a monastery, and had not the slightest scruple in taking her property away from her (Polydore Vergil, 571, Hall, 431). The fact is confirmed by her will, which contains the following clause: 'Item, where I have no worldly goods to do the Queen's Grace, my daughter, a pleasure with, neither to reward any of my children according to my heart and mind, I beseech Almighty God to bless her Grace, with all her noble issue, and with as good a heart and mind as is to me possible I give her Grace my blessing and all the foresaid my children'. The will is dated April 10, 1492. Royal Wills, p. 350'. (p. 70.)

Divisions in the council

The month of May, 1483, glided on more tranquilly towards its close than the portentous events which heralded its dawn. Richard presided with his characteristic energy at the helm of state. Three groups of nobles assisted him.

First, the following were servants of the late Edward IV and were also his executors: Hastings, lord chamberlain to Edward IV; Stanley, lord steward of the late King's household; Rotherham, Archbishop of York; and John Morton, Bishop of Ely.

Second, · Richard's special adherents included the following: Buckingham, created Constable of the Duchy of Lancaster; Northumberland, Warden of the North; Howard, seneschal of the Duchy of Lancaster; and Lovel, Chief Butler of England.

Third, the neutral parties were: Bourchier, Archbishop of Canterbury; Russel, Bishop of Lincoln and the new Lord Chancellor; and Gunthorp, Dean of Wells, his successor in the office of Privy Seal.

The new acts of the young Edward V were attested at Westminster as well as at the Tower. This fact proves that he was under no undue restraint, but that he occasionally joined his council at Westminster, or was visited by its members at his apartments in the Tower.

The advisers of Edward's administration had all united in opposing the Queen and her family when they had reason to dread their aiming at the regency. They had joyfully elevated Richard to the guardianship of the King in order to crush his rivals. But in so doing they had not designed to invest this Prince with the absolute power conferred on him, 'commanding and forbidding in every thing like another king!' (Chron. Croy., p. 566.)

The first sympton of discontent, says the Chronicler of Croyland (p. 566), arose from 'the detention of the King's relatives in prison, and the protector not having sufficiently provided for the honour and security of the Queen'. This disunion was reflected by the secret meetings in the Protector's London abode, Crosby Place, in Bishopsgate Street. Sometimes, these meetings were held at the same time when members of the council favourable to the young King and his mother were officially assembled elsewhere. Lord Stanley 'said unto Lord Hastings, that he much misliked these two several councils; for while we (quod he) talk of one matter in the tone place, little wot we whereof they talk in the tother place' (More, p. 67).

Turner and Legge : Sharon Turner and Alfred O. Legge quote official documents to show that Edward V was not in confinement. *Royal Grants* lists visits by him to Bishop's Palace on May 4, 1483, to the Tower on May 19, and again to the Bishop's Palace, June 13, where he met his brother, the Duke of York (Legge, vol. I, p. 213).

Preparations for Edward V's coronation

Nevertheless, the important affairs of state progressed without serious interruption, and the month of June, 1483, was ushered in by active preparations for Edward V's coronation. This ceremonial was officially announced as definitively fixed for June 22. Letters were addressed to numerous persons in the King's name charging them 'to be prepared to receive the order of knighthood at his coronation, which he intended to solemize at Westminster on the 22nd of the same month' (*Feodera*, vol. xii, p. 185). Costly robes were ordered for the young King's coronation.

The appointed time 'then so near approached that the pageants and subtleties were in making day and night at Westminster . . . ' (More, p. 76). Subtleties or sotilties were paste moulded into the form of figures, animals, etc., and grouped so as to represent some scriptural or political device. Richard, Duke of Gloucester, summoned knights from all parts of the realm. The Duchess of Gloucester 'reached the metropolis on the aforesaid 5th instant' (*Excerpt. Hist.*, p. 17), and joined her husband at Crosby Place.

Richard's difficult position
— aims at long protectorate

The difficulties of Richard's position daily increased, and he feared to release Lord Rivers and Grey. Yet he knew that each day's captivity alienated the young King's affection farther from himself. He also knew that the high dignity of Protector of the realm always lapsed after the coronation of the monarch. This had been the case in all minorities preceding that of Edward V. Also, the legislature, in nominating Richard as Protector, expressly restricted him to 'the same power as was conferred on Humphrey Duke of Gloucester during the minority of Henry VI' (Chron. Croy., p. 566).

The disastrous fate of that noble Prince was too recent to be forgotten. Richard well knew the history of the Lancastrian monarch, Henry VI, whom Richard's brother, Edward IV, had deposed. Henry was crowned in his eighth year, with the express design of terminating the office and power of his uncle, Humphrey, also Duke of Gloucester and Lord Protector. Richard knew the murder of that Duke of Gloucester in 1447 resulted from the jealous and determined malice of his political enemies — principally, Henry VI's Queen Margaret of Anjou and the faction led by Bishop Beaufort.

Another Duke of Gloucester, Thomas of Woodstock, uncle of Richard II, had been murdered in 1397. The young King had treacherously inviegled the Duke from his castle at Pleshy and had him murdered for having opposed his wishes when the King was a minor (Froissart, lib. iv, c. 86.92). Also Thomas Le Despencer, Earl of Gloucester, closely allied to the House of York was beheaded at Bristol by command of Henry IV in 1399, the first year of his usurpation (Heylyn, p. 330).

The prospect that awaited Richard of sinking into a mere lord of council, after having ruled for some months as Protector of the realm could easily result in his falling a victim to the same dangerous elevation which had proved the death-warrant of preceding Dukes of Gloucester.

Turner, Legge, Gairdner : As we have seen, Richard knew that two other Dukes of Gloucester, in his same position and also uncles of the reigning King had been killed. His position and tenure were not as secure as that of his father and grandfather, who had been Regents and Protectors. Richard had been made Protector because, says Sir Thomas More (p. 486), 'not only as the King's uncle and the next Prince of the blood, and a person fit for that trust as of eminent wit and courage, but as one that was most loyal and loving to the King, and likely to prove the most faithful in that station'. But he held by an uncertain tenure an office which simply gave him precedence among the lords of the council. Some of the council opposed continuation of the protectorship, and it might end with the approaching coronation of Edward V. The Parliament would have to confirm Richard's authority for the period until Edward V would be competent to rule. The Houses of Parliament were therefore summoned to meet on June 25, 1483, three days after the scheduled coronation day, to confirm the protectorship (Turner, vol. iii, p. 436; Legge, vol. I, pp. 205, 209; Gairdner, p. 64). See Turner's *History of England during the Middle Ages*, 4 vols., the Longman Group Ltd., successors to Longman, Rees, Orme, Brown, and Green, London, 1830.

Gairdner : 'His (Richard's) power as protector was in a critical condition, a party in the council being clearly opposed to its continuance, and the coronation day was approaching, when, according to the precedent of Henry VI's time, it ought to terminate. But as Parliament was to meet immediately after, Richard proposed to obtain from the lords there assembled a confirmation of his authority until the time that his nephew should be competent to rule in person. This apparently was the utmost of what he ventured at present to put forward, and the Chancellor prepared a speech for the opening of Parliament declaring that the confirmation of the protectorship was the main object of their being called together'.

Richard writes to city of York

On June 8, 1483, Richard renewed his former connection with the city of York by writing to the city authorities. He was warmly and firmly beloved in the North, which had for nearly ten years been under his immediate jurisdiction. The letter which he has been charged with writing 'artfully, to curry favor' was an official answer to an earnest appeal from the mayor and commonalty of the city of York.

Conspiracy for Richard's destruction

Scarcely had Richard's pacific letter of June 8 been transmitted than some intimation of approaching danger appears to have reached his ear. No details remain of the exact nature and extent of this threatened evil. It appears certain, however, that it was some plot for Richard's destruction, from a second letter he addressed to the citizens of York on June 10, 1483:

'The Duke of Gloucester, brother and uncle of king's, Protector and Defender, Great Chamberlain, Constable, and Admiral of England. Right trusty and well-beloved, we greet you well. And as you love the weal of us, and the weal and surety of your own self, we heartily pray you to come unto us in London in all the diligence ye can possible, after the sight hereof, with as many as ye can make defensibly arrayed, there to aid and assist us against the queen, her bloody adherents and affinity, which have entended, and do daily entend to murder and utterly destroy us, and our cousin the Duke of Buckingham, and the old royal blood of this realm, and as is now openly known, by her subtle and damnable ways forecasted the same, and also the final destruction and disherison of you, and all other the inheritors and men of honour, as well of the north parts as other countries that belong unto us, as our trusty servant this bearer shall more at large shew you; to whom we pray you to give credence; and as ever we may do for you, in time coming, fail not, but haste you to us. Given under our signet at London the 10th of June. To our trusty and well-beloved the Mayor, Aldermen, Sheriffs and Ckommonalty of the City of York'. (Drake's *Eboracum*, p. 111.)

It seems certain that this fresh outbreak decided the fate of the prisoners in the North. The bearer of the above letter, Sir Richard Ratcliffe, was charged by Richard with commands to the Earl of Northumberland to proceed to the castle of Pontefract to preside at the trial of Lord Rivers (Rous, *Hist. Reg. Ang.*, 214). Ratcliffe also carried a warrant for the immediate execution of Grey, Vaughan, and Hurst (Drake's *Eboracum*, p. 111). The following day, June 11, Richard addressed an earnest appeal for support to his kinsman, Lord Neville.

Up to this period, no accusation of homicide, either as Prince or Protector, has been laid to Richard's charge by contemporary writers. This fact is remarkable considering that he lived in an epoch noted for summary vengeance and utter disregard of human life (Turner's *Middle Ages*, vol. iv, p. 398).

The reason for Richard's appeals soon became evident. William Catesby, a close friend of Lord Hastings, had discovered and reported the designs of Hastings, Stanley, Rotherham, and Morton. Catesby, in his double capacity of friend and betrayer, appears indeed to have possessed himself of some treasonable plans and schemes that involved the destruction of Richard.

Gairdner : 'It must not, however, be too readily presumed that there was no foundation at all for Richard's charge of conspiracy against the Queen and her relations. Polydore Vergil, a writer who cannot be suspected of any design to palliate the protector's misdeeds, expressly states that an act of sudden violence was at this time contemplated in order to liberate the young king from his uncle's control'. (p. 61)

'. . . it appears by the York City Records (Davies' York Records, p. 154) that writs of *supersedeas* had been issued to prevent its (Parliament) assembling. . . . The chief object . . . for which Parliament was originally summoned was to preserve Richard in his office of protector — an office which, without special safeguards, was always held by a rather uncertain tenure, and which if the precedent of Henry VI's minority had been followed, would have ceased upon the king's coronation. It is quite conceivable, therefore, that the issue of the *supersedeas* was designed to defeat this object, that is to say, to prevent Richard being confirmed in the office of protector, and so to terminate his power. . . . The *supersedeas* could not have been received in every borough and county; and this in itself affords reason for believing that the design to set aside the meeting of Parliament was that of Richard's enemies'. (pp. 84, 86, 87)

Markham : Rastell says (p. 80) a plot was formed to seize the Protector and kill him (p. 98).

Kendall : The council decided that the policy of extending the protectorship during Edward V's minority would be the principal reason for summoning Parliament to meet. Richard followed orderly procedures of justice in summoning the Lords and Commons to confer this authority on him. No one else could lawfully do so, since Edward V was a minor (pp. 197, 198).

Arrest and execution of conspirators

Accordingly, on Friday, June 13, 'the protector having with singular cunning devided the council, so that part should sit at Westminster and part at the Tower, where the king was, Hastings, coming to the Tower to the council, was by his command beheaded. Thomas, Archbishop of York, and John, Bishop of Ely, although on account of their order their lives were spared, were imprisoned in separate castles in Wales'. Such is the brief account given by the faithful historian of that time (Chron. Croy., p. 566).

Sir Thomas More, in the spirit of romance which pervades his work, embellishes this portion of his narrative by a display of his oratorical powers. But these descriptions can no longer pass for authentic history. His discrepancies have been examined and exposed by many writers of repute. See Walpole's *Historic Doubts*, 47; Laing (in Henry), xii, p. 415; together with Carte, Rapin, Lingard, Turner and many others.

One of More's more absurd word pictures, powerfully employed by Shakespeare, follows:
'Then said the Protector, "Ye shall all see in what wise that sorceress (the Queen), and that other witch of her counsel, Shore's wife, with their affinity, have by their sorcery and witchcraft wasted my body". And therewith he plucked up his doublet sleeve to his elbow upon his

left arm, where he shewed a werish, withered arm and small, as it was never other'. (More, p. 72.) (More does not explain how a Prince, who was distinguished as the ablest general of his time, a time noted for ponderous armour and weapons of almost gigantic size, could have had 'a werish withered arm'. Nor does he explain how a Prince of Richard's prominence could have reached the age of 30 without his associates knowing he had a withered arm.)

Hastings seems to have admitted that Lords Rivers and Grey were concerned in some league to get rid of the Protector. More states (p. 74) that these nobles 'were by his (Hasting's) assent before devised to be beheaded at Pontefract this self-same day . . . '.

The news of Hastings' execution and the imprisonment of the bishops, Lord Stanley, and others 'suspected to be against the Protector', quickly spread throughout London and caused extreme consternation. But Richard, anticipating this reaction, sent a herald within two hours through the city 'in the king's name', proclaiming the fact that 'Hastings, with divers other of his traitorous purpose, had before conspired that same day to have slain the Lord Protector and the Lord Buckingham sitting in the council; and after to have taken upon them to rule the king and the realm at pleasure, and thereby to pil and spoil whom they list uncontroulled'. (More, p. 80).

More's information was derived from Bishop Morton himself, who was implicated in the plot and one of the conspirators accused and imprisoned for it. This accounts for More's marvellous tales and for his concealing facts that would possibly justify the Protector's prompt and stern decision. 'The artificial glare with which the whole is surrounded generates a suspicion that some treason was detected and punished, — a conspiracy in which Morton had participated with Hastings, and was therefore desirous to remove from view'. — See Laing (Appendix to Henry), vol. xii, p. 417.

Gairdner : Gairdner admits that More's informant, John Morton, took a leading part against Richard and therefore is a prejudiced source. But he clings to tradition, saying 'we have every reason to believe that the facts (Morton's tales) are strictly true', because Morton was an eye witness. Gairdner's faith in More's integrity is shaken, however, when More undertakes to tell us of Hastings' dreams (p. 67).

Gairdner and Kendall : Gairdner and Kendall agree that Hastings broke with Richard because of his power as Protector — not from any suspicion that Richard planned to take the crown. Apparently, Richard presented such strong evidence of Hastings' plot against Richard, after the execution, that the council decreed that the young Duke of York must be taken from sanctuary.

Richard had no withered arm, so he could not have accused the Queen and Jane Shore of having withered it by sorcery. Why did Morton substitute the charge of sorcery for the real reason? Perhaps because Morton was heavily involved in the plot against Richard. No mention of sorcery is made by *The Great Chronicle*, Fabyan, the *Croyland Chronicle*, or Mancini. Stowe's sources said Richard was 'comely'. Contemporary descriptions by persons who knew Richard well, and the portraits in the Royal Collection at Windsor, prove that Richard had no noticeable bodily deformity. Shakespeare's monster was based on the tales of the late Tudor chronicles.

In summary, Richard's bitterest enemy, John Morton, was More's informant. Morton's story, however, is disproved by contemporary sources (Kendall, pp. 459, 465, 470-472; Gairdner, p. 62).

Mancini : A Silesian noble, Nicholas von Poppelau, spent ten days in Richard's household in May, 1484, and spoke alone with Richard. Poppelau says that Richard was taller and thinner than himself, and he does not mention any deformity. He concludes that Richard had 'auch ein grosses Herz' — also a great heart. (p. 163)

Young Duke of York withdrawn from sanctuary

Richard was, in some degree, justified in striving to obtain possession of the King's brother, the infant Duke of York, as heir presumptive to the crown (More, p. 43). The King desired, as was natural, the companionship of his brother (Chron. Croy., p. 566). Also a report had been circulated that it was intended to send the young Prince out of the kingdom (More, p. 36). Richard knew that Marquis Dorset, Lord Lyle, and Sir Edward Grey, his young nephews' maternal relatives, had already effected their escape (Rous. *Hist. Reg.* Ang., p. 212), although Lionel Wydville, Bishop of Salisbury, remained in sanctuary to counsel and aid his royal sister.

The strongest test and greatest surety for the lawfulness of Richard's proceedings up to this time rests upon this fact — he was supported in his design by the heads of the church and the chief officers of the crown, 'my Lord Cardinale, my Lord Chancellor, and other many lords temporal' (Stallworth Letters, *Ex. Hist.*, p. 15).

More's elaborate account of the transaction, and the long orations of the Queen and Cardinal Bourchier, have long been considered as the effusions of More's fertile imagination (Lingard, vol. v, p. 244). The simple statement of the Croyland Chronicler, the soundest authority of that day, probably embraces the entire facts of the proceeding: 'On Monday, the 16th of June, the Cardinal-Archbishop of Canterbury, with many others, entered the sanctuary at Westminster for the purpose of inducing the Queen to consent to her son, Richard Duke of York, coming to the Tower for the consolation of the king his brother. To this she assented, and he was accordingly conducted thither by the archbishop'.

Fabyan's account is even more laconic. Simon Stallworth was one of the officers of the Lord Chancellor into whose hands, he states, the young duke was placed. Consequently, had personal violence been intended, he must have known it. He relates there were 'at Westminster great plenty of armed men', the natural consequence of the troubled state of the metropolis. But he in no way couples this with what he terms 'the deliverance of the Duke of York', and he mentions the princely reception given to the royal child.

The silence of the Croyland Chronicler, Fabyan, and Stallworth exonerates Richard from the alleged violence imputed to him by More. The City Chronicler confirms two assertions of Sir Thomas More which tell greatly in the Protector's favour. *First*, Cardinal Bourchier, the Archbishop of Canterbury, pledged his life for the young Prince's safety (More, p. 79), so implicitly did he rely on the honour and integrity of Richard, Duke of Gloucester. *Second*, Richard pledged that if their royal parent would voluntarily quit the sanctuary, her sons should not be separated from her. But Fabyan adds 'the queen, for all fair promises to her made, kept her and her daughters within the foresaid sanctuary' (Fabyan, p. 513).

Execution of Lord Rivers

Richard's dispatch forwarded to York by Sir Thomas Radcliffe on June 10, 1483, did not reach that city for five days. On June 19, its contents were acted upon by a proclamation (Drake's Eboracum, p. 111) requiring as many armed men as could be raised to assemble at Pontefract by June 22. On June 23 (ten days after Hastings' execution), Lord Rivers was removed from his prison at Sheriff-Hutton. He was tried and executed there Wednesday, June 25, by the Earl of Northumberland, who acted both as judge and accuser (Rous, *Hist. Reg. Angl.*, p. 213).

However harsh this proceeding may appear, it is clear that this unfortunate nobleman was himself satisfied that his sentence conformed with the proceedings of the age and had been merited by his own conduct. He had confidence also in the Protector's justice, as shown by the following conclusion to his will dated at Sheriff-Hutton, June 23, 1483: 'Over this I beseech humbly my Lord of Gloucester . . . to comfort, help, and assist, as supervisor (for very trust) of this testament, that mine executors may with his pleasure fulfill this my last will'.

Lord Rivers, although learned and chivalrous, was by no means free from the vices which characterized his family and the times in which he lived. He was universally unpopular, from the selfish and covetous ambition which marked his political conduct during the ascendancy of his royal sister. He was the cause of King Edward's committing to the Tower his 'beloved servant' Lord Hastings. He persuaded the Queen to insist on the Duke of Clarence's execution (see Feodera, xii, p. 95).

He grasped at every profitable or powerful appointment in King Edward's gift. He would doubtless have sacrificed the Duke of Gloucester to his insatiable ambition. But that Prince, learning of Rivers' designs, felt justified in committing him to prison and commanding his execution.

Markham : Rivers, Grey and Vaughan were beheaded on June 25, 1483. Richard not only pardoned but rewarded Stanley, placed Morton in the custody of the Duke of Buckingham, and permitted Archbishop Rotherham to return to his diocese (pp. 99, 100).

Kendall : Kendall speaks harshly of the characters of Anthony Woodville's (Lord Rivers') father, mother, and brother Lionel. But he reserves his harshest adjectives for the Queen, Elizabeth Woodville — mean, stupid, and cruel (p. 213).

Arrest of Jane Shore

Immediately after Lord Hastings' execution, June 13, 1483, Edward IV's favorite mistress, Jane Shore, was arrested. After Edward's death she had been living in the same unlawful manner (More, p. 80) with Hastings up to his execution. She was arrested on suspicion of being implicated in the same conspiracy against Richard for which Hastings had been executed. But it was her immorality, not her political offences, on which she was accused. Dr. Kempe, the Bishop of London, sentenced her to perform open penance (as a harlot, with a lighted taper in the streets) on the Sunday following Hastings' execution. Her saddened look, subdued manner, and rare beauty excited general commiseration.

Gairdner : '. . . there can hardly be a doubt that she was employed as a political agent and go-between by the Hastings and Woodville party'. (p. 69)

Dr. Shaw's sermon

'Bastard Slips Shall Never Take Deep Root' : On Sunday, June 22, 1483, Dr. Raaf Shaw, an eminent ecclesiastic and brother of the Lord Mayor, Sir Edmund Shaw, advocated the Duke of Gloucester's claims publicly from the pulpit. He ascended St. Paul's Cross, in St. Paul's churchyard, 'the Lord Protector, the Duke of Buckingham, and other lords being present' (Fabyan, p. 514) and selected his text from the Book of Wisdom (ch. iv, v. 3) ' "Spuria vitulimina non agent radices altas''; that is to say, Bastard slips shall never take deep root' (More, p. 100). He 'there showed openly that the children of King Edward IV were not legitimate, nor rightful inheritors of the crown', because of a previous contract of marriage by Edward. He concluded by pointing out the preferable title of the Lord Protector, disanulling that of the young king and urged the immediate election of Richard as the rightful heir to the throne (Fabyan, p. 514).

Distortion of the Sermon : Dr. Shaw's sermon was later distorted and greatly exaggerated, making Richard perform a part better suited to a strolling player: 'Now was it before devised, that in the speaking of these words, the Protector should have come in among the people to the sermon, to the end that those words, meeting with his presence, might have been taken among the hearers as though the Holy Ghost had put them in the preacher's mouth, and should have moved the people even there to cry "King Richard! King Richard!" that it might have been after said that he was specially chosen by God, and in manner by miracle. But this device quailed either by the Protector's negligence, or the preacher's over-much diligence'. (More, p. 102.)

Further Distortion — Alleged Charge Against Richard's Mother : The distortions of a later time even have Richard act in so revolting a manner as that of instructing (Ibid., 99) the preacher to impugn the reputation of his own mother, fixing the stain of illegitimacy on all her sons but himself, her youngest and eleventh child! Horace Walpole says 'The tale of Richard's aspersing the chastity of his own mother is incredible; it appearing that he lived with her in perfect harmony, and lodged with her in her palace at that very time' (*Historic Doubts*, p. 125. See *Archaeologia*, xiii, p. 7 and *Historic Doubts*, p. 42). Monstrous indeed is the charge, a fitting accompaniment to the common story of Clarence's death in a butt of malmsey and Richard's 'werish and withered arm'.

All reply to this gross accusation against the Protector may be summed up in the simple fact that all contemporary writers are silent on the matter. They make no allusion whatever to Lady Cecily or the unnatural and uncalled-for part said to have been acted by her son. It is later chroniclers who create the distortion.

The prior of Croyland wrote his *Chronicle* in 1484.

Rous of Warwick wrote his *History* in 1487.

Fabyan's *Chronicle* was compiled about 1490.

Sir Thomas More wrote his *Life of Richard III* in 1508, (Kendall says 1513).

Polydore Vergil was sent to England by Pope Innocent VIII to collect Papal tribute in 1500. He commenced his history shortly after his establishment at the English court and completed it in 1517.

The Prior of Croyland and Rous of Warwick seem to have considered Dr. Shaw's sermon too unimportant to call forth remark. Sir Thomas More was the next writer in chronological order and the first who relates the calumny. More not only certifies that Richard was acquitted of all share in the transaction but also lays the entire blame on Dr. Shaw.

Who, then, was it who affixed on the Protector the infamy of aspersions on Lady Cecily's honour? It is Polydore Vergil, Henry VII's annalist, who compiled his history under the auspices of Richard III's bitter rival. From this corrupted source sprang those calumnies which for ages have supplied the stream of history. But, Polydore Vergil was not contemporary with that time, as was the Croyland doctor. He wrote what he had heard at the court of Richard's enemy, Henry VII, many years after Richard's death, whereas the Croyland chronicler testified that which he had seen and known during Richard III's reign.

Vergil undertook his history at a period when one of those very children — Elizabeth of York — whose illegitimacy Parliament had confirmed in *Titulus Regius* (*Rot. Parl.* 6, 240) — was Queen of England and mother of the heir apparent. Vergil wrote after Henry VII had commanded the obnoxious statute expunged from the rolls. 'The statute was abrogated in Parliament, taken off the rolls, and destroyed; and those possessed of copies were directed, under the penalty of fine and imprisonment, to deliver them to the chancellor, "so that all things said or remembered in the bill and act be for ever out of remembrance and forgotten" ' (See Henry, vol. xii, App. p. 409; Carte, vol. ii, p. 824). Fabyan, however, was uninfluenced by the political changes which made it expedient in Polydore Vergil to remove the stigma of illegitimacy from the queen consort, and fix the imputation on the children of the deceased Duchess of York.

(Cecily, Duchess of York, survived her illustrious consort, Richard, Duke of York, thirty-five years. After outliving her royal sons, Edward IV and Richard III, she died in retirement at her castle of Berkhampstead in 1495 — 10th Henry VII. She was buried by the side of her husband in the collegiate church of Fotheringhay, Sandford, book v. p. 369.)

Legge : To divert attention from the fact of Edward IV's invalid marriage — the basis for Richard's claim to the throne — the historians charged Richard with questioning his mother's chastity (vol. I, p. 263).

Illegality of Edward IV's marriage

Dr. Shaw's sermon was based on the testimony of Robert Stillington, Bishop of Bath and Wells. Stillington had informed the Protector that Edward IV's marriage with Elizabeth Wydville was not valid (*Rot Parl.*, vol. vi, 241), as he had before been secretly married to the Lady Eleanor Butler (Milles's *Cat. of Honour*, p. 743). She was the daughter of a great peer, John Talbot, Earl of Shrewsbury, and the widow of Lord Butler. She was 'a lady of very eminent beauty and answerable virtue, to whom the king was contracted, married, and had a child by her' (Buck, lib. iv, p. 122).

Sir Thomas More substitutes the name of Elizabeth Lucy for that of Eleanor Butler. Elizabeth Lucy was King Edward IV's mistress and mother of his illegitimate son Arthur Lord Lisle whereas Eleanor

Butler was the King's espoused wife (see More, p. 96). 'This contract was made in the hands of the bishop, who said that afterwards he married them, no person being present but they twayne and he, the king charging him strictly not to reveal it' (Phil. de Com., lib. v, p. 151).

Edward's mother, Cecily, Duchess of York, had tried unsuccessfully by entreaties and remonstrances (More, p. 93) to prevent the second marriage entered into by her son in direct violation of a sacramental oath and in open defiance of the law, ecclesiastical as well as civil (Buck, lib. iv, p. 119). Buck states the announcement of the king's second marriage 'cast the Lady Elianora Butler into so perplext a melancholy, that she spent herself in a solitary life ever after' (Lib. iv, p. 122). She did not long survive Edward IV's infidelity. Retiring into a monastery, she devoted herself to religion. She died on July 30, 1466 and was buried in the Carmelites' church at Norwich.

Legge : A contract of marriage was valid, before the Reformation, without further church or civil ceremony. Consent was the essence and was as binding as a marriage ceremony (vol. I, pp. 259, 264, 268, and Gibson's *Codex*).

Gairdner : If, indeed, Bishop Stillington's imprisonment (March-June 1478) was at all connected with this disclosure, it is by no means improbable that Clarence did endeavor to make use of it to the queen's prejudice, for the time corresponds very closely with the date of his attainder, and nothing could better explain the necessity felt by Edward of putting his brother to death (February 18, 1478) in spite of apparent reluctance, than the fact that Clarence had got possession of such a secret.

'Another point, which is perhaps rather an evidence of the truth of the story, is the care afterwards taken to suppress and to pervert it. When Henry VII became king, and married the daughter of Edward IV and Elizabeth Woodville, any allusion to the pre-contract was treated as disloyal. The petition to Richard to assume the crown was declared to be so scandalous that every copy of it was ordered by Parliament to be destroyed. The allegations contained in it were misrepresented; the pre-contract was said to have been with Elizabeth Lucy, one of Edward's mistresses, instead of with Lady Eleanor Butler, and the name of the latter lady was omitted from the story. Thus, in Sir Thomas More's history, a courtesan of obscure birth is made to take the place of an earl's daughter as the person to whom Edward was first betrothed; and such is the version of the story that has been current nearly ever since. It was only after the lapse of a century and a quarter that Sir George Buck discovered the true tenor of the parliamentary petition in the MS. history of Croyland; and again, after another like period had passed away, the truth received ample confirmation by the discovery of the very Roll of Parliament on which the petition was engrossed. Fortunately, notwithstanding the subsequent statute, all the copies had not been destroyed'. (pp. 91, 92.)

Kendall : Kendall says that only the Croyland Chronicle, of all the narrative sources, accurately tells about Edward IV's pre-contract with Lady Eleanor Butler. The story of the pre-contract is contained in a bill (*Titulus Regius*) enacted by Richard's Parliament of January, 1484 (*Rot. Parl.* 6, 240), confirming the parliamentary petition adopted by the informal Parliament on June 25, 1483. Kendall believes that the inaccuracies in Mancini's manuscript are due to his thinking that Richard sought the throne from the outset. Kendall disagrees. He believes that Richard did not seek men's opinion on this possibility until Tuesday or Wednesday, June 17-18, 1483.

Henry Tudor issued a warrant for Stillington's arrest on August 22, 1485, immediately after the battle. Although later pardoned, he was kept in a cell at Windsor Castle after espousing Lambert Simnel's cause in 1487, and died four years later. As noted above, Henry had his first Parliament enact a bill ordering all copies of the *Titulus Regius* to be destroyed.

Nothing is said of Lady Eleanor Butler or Stillington by either More or Vergil. The true story was not uncovered until the seventeenth century when Buck told the accurate account of the Croyland Chronicle and a copy of the *Titulus Regius* was found.

Richard genuinely believed Stillington's revelation that Edward IV had made a pre-contract of marriage with Lady Eleanor Butler. Henry VII and the Tudor historians evidently also believed it. Henry imprisoned Bishop Stillington and did everything he could to destroy all evidence of the pre-contract. And all the Tudor historians falsified or suppressed the story. These later actions indicate that Richard had good reason to believe Stillington's story. When the inner council heard of Stillington's revelation they also believed it. They decided that Richard was entitled to the throne (pp. 219, 468-470, 473-477).

(Readers interested in a detailed discussion of the canon law and common law aspects of the pre-contract should read 'The Pre-Contract and its Effect on the Succession in 1483', by Mary

O'Regan, in *The Ricardian*, a publication of the Richard III Society, Vol. IV, No. 54, September 1976, pp. 2-7.)

Parliament formally deposes Edward V

We should discard the irreconcilable discrepancies of a later period, and adhere scrupulously to the coeval accounts transmitted by Fabyan and the Prior of Croyland. The change of government which elevated Richard of Gloucester, and excluded his nephews from the throne may be thus briefly summed up in the concise words of Fabyan, the city chronicler:

'Then upon the Tuesday following Dr. Shaw's address (June 24, 1483), an assembly of the commons of the city was appointed at the Guildhall, where the Lord of Buckingham in the presence of the mayor and commonalty rehearsed the right and title that the Lord Protector had to be preferred before his nephews, the sons of his brother King Edward, to the right of the crown of England. The which process was so eloquent-wise shewed, and uttered without any impediment', he adds, thus implying that he was present, and heard the discourse, — 'and that of a long while with so sugred words of exhortation and according sentence, that many wise man that day marvelled and commended him for the good ordering of his words, but not for the intent and purpose, the which thereupon ensued' (Fabyan, p. 514).

On the following day, Wednesday, June 25, 1483, Parliament had been legally convened (*Royal Wills*, p. 347) by Edward V. A supplicatory scroll was presented to the three estates assembled at Westminster (Rot. Parl., vol. vi, p. 240), although not 'in form of parliament'. 'From which I should infer that the parliament was summoned, but that it was not opened in due form; Richard not choosing to do it as Protector, because he meant to be king, and for the same reason determining that Edward should not meet it' (Turner, vol. iii, p. 458).

'There was shown then, by way of petition, on a roll of parchment, that King Edward's sons were bastards, alleging that he had entered into a precontract with Dame Alionora Butler, before he married Queen Elizabeth; and, moreover, that the blood of his other brother, George Duke of Clarence, was attainted, so that no certain and incorrupt lineal blood of Richard Duke of York could be found but in the person of Richard Duke of Gloucester. Wherefore it was besought him on behalf of the lords and commons of the realm, that

148

he would take upon him his right' (*Chron. Croy.*, p. 566). Such is the clear and explicit account of the contemporary historian.

'Whereupon the lords and commons, with one universal negative voice, refused the sons of King Edward' (Buck, lib. i, p. 20), not for any ill-will or malice, but for their disabilities and incapacities, the opinions of those times holding them not legitimate. For these and other causes the barons and prelates unanimously cast their election upon the Protector'. (Ibid., lib. i, p. 20; More, p. 110.)

Parliament tenders the crown to Richard

The Three Estates Petition Richard : Importuning the Duke of Buckingham to be their speaker, the chief lords, with other grave and learned persons, had audience granted to them at the Lady Cecily's mansion in the great chamber at Baynard's Castle, then Yorke House. There, they addressed themselves to the Lord Protector. After rehearsing the disabilities of Edward V and reciting the superiority of his own title, they petitioned him to assume the crown.

The result of this solemn invitation is thus narrated in the parliamentary report which attests this remarkable fact: 'Previously to his coronation, a roll containing certain articles was presented to him on behalf of the three estates of the realm, by many lords spiritual and temporal, and other nobles and commons in great multitude, whereunto he, for the public weal and tranquility of the land, benignly assented'. (*Rot. Parl.*, vol. vi, p. 240.)

Parliament's Action Exonerates Richard of Two Charges : This parliamentary report corroborates the plain account by the contemporary chroniclers, both as regards (1) the cause that led to Richard of Gloucester being elected King and (2) the mode of proceedings observed on the occasion. It exonerates this Prince altogether from two of the odious charges brought against him by subsequent historians.

First, Parliament's action in deposing Edward V because of illegitimacy and tendering the crown to the next Prince of incorrupt lineal blood, Richard of Gloucester, disproves his alleged unnatural and offensive conduct to his mother, the Lady Cecily. Not only did he select her mansion, Baynard's Castle, for the audience that was to invest him with the kingly authority, but his alleged aspersion of his mother's character was totally uncalled for.

Valid grounds existed for displacing and excluding his brother's children without calumny or injustice to her. 'The doubts on the validity of Edward's marriage were better grounds for Richard's proceedings than aspersion of his mother's honour. On that invalidity he claimed the crown and obtained it; and with such universal concurrence, that the nation undoubtedly was on his side'. (Walpole, *Historic Doubts*, p. 40.)

Second, in a legal and constitutional sense, Richard has been undeservedly stigmatized. He neither seized the crown by violence, nor retained it by open rebellion in defiance of the laws of the land.

The heir of Edward IV was set aside by constitutional authority on an impediment which would equally have excluded him from inheritance in domestic life. Richard, having been unanimously elected (Rot. Parl., vol. vi, p. 240) by the three estates of the realm, took upon him the proffered dignity by their common consent.

Legal and Constitutional Basis for Richard's Acceptance : 'The jurisprudence of England', says Archdeacon Paley, 'is composed of ancient usages, acts of parliament, and the decisions of the courts of law; those, then, are the sources whence the nature and limits of her constitution are to be deduced, and the authorities to which appeals must be made in all cases of doubt'.

Hereditary succession to the crown at this period of English history was but feebly recognized. The grand fundamental maxim upon which the *jus coronae* or right of succession to the throne of Britain depends, Sir Wm. Blackstone takes to be this: The crown is, by common law and constitutional custom, hereditary, and this in a manner peculiar to itself: But the right of inheritance may from time to time be changed or limited by act of parliament, under which limitations the crown still continues hereditary.

'We must not judge of those times by the present. Neither the crown nor the great men were restrained by sober established forms and proceedings as they are at present; and from the death of Edward III force alone had dictated. Henry IV had stepped into the throne contrary to all justice. A title so defective had opened a door to attempts as violent; and the various innovations introduced in the latter years of Henry VI had annihilated all ideas of order. Richard Duke of York had been declared successor to the crown during the life of Henry and of his son Prince Edward, and, as appears by the Parliamentary History, though not noticed by our careless historians, was even appointed Prince of Wales'. (Walpole, *Historic Doubts*, p. 30.)

If the throne becomes vacant or empty, whether by abdication or by failure of all heirs, the two houses of Parliament may, it is said by Blackstone, dispose of it. The right of Parliament to depose one monarch and elevate another had been admitted, not only in the previous reign of Edward IV, but also in the case of Edward III and Henry IV — examples grounded on far less valid pretences than that which led to the deposition of Henry VI and Edward V.

Crown Legally Preferred to Richard : Thus, the crown assumed by the Protector was not a crown of usurpation but one that, having become void by alleged failure of legitimate heirs, was legally proferred to him. Richard of Gloucester could hardly have resisted an appeal and throne which under such circumstances he was unanimously called upon to fill.

Rotuli Parliamentorum (Rolls of Parliament) : On Wednesday, June 25 1483, the parliamentary assembly drew up 'An Act for the Settlement of the Crown upon the King and his issue, with a recapitulation of the Title', stating in part: 'Therefore, at the request, and by assent of the Three Estates of this Realm, that is to say, the Lords Spiritual and Temporal, and Commons of this land, assembled in this present Parliament, by authority of the same, be it pronounced, decreed, and declared, that our said Sovereign Lord the King was, and is, very and undoubted King of England . . . '. (pp. 241, 2) (spelling modernized)

Richard, Duke of Gloucester, proclaimed King Richard III

Richard was petitioned to ascend a throne which had been previously declared vacant. Assenting, therefore, to a choice freely made by the constituted authorities of the realm, he assumed the proferred sovereignty on Thursday, June 26, 1483.

'The said Protector', says Fabyan (p. 514), 'taking then upon him as king and governor of the realm, went with great pomp unto Westminster, and there took possession of the same. Where he, being set in the great hall in the seat royal . . . after the royal oath there taken, called before him the judges of the law, exhorting them to administer the laws and execute judgment, as the first consideration befitting a king'.

He then addressed the assembled barons, clergy, and citizens, pronouncing a free pardon for all offences against himself and ordering a proclamation to be openly made of a general amnesty throughout the land — (More, p. 125).

Having thus taken possession of the regal dignity amidst the acclamations of the multitude, Richard proceeded in due state to Westminster Abbey. There, he performed the usual ceremonies of ascending and offering at St. Edward's shrine. He was met at the church door by the leading ecclesiastics, the monks singing 'Te Deum laudamus', while the sceptre of King Edward was delivered to him by the abbot — (Buck, lib. i, p. 24). From thence he rode solemnly to St. Paul's, 'assisted by well near all the lords spiritual and temporal of this realm, and was received there with procession, with great congratulation and acclamation of all the people in every place and by the way, that the king was in that day' (Kennet, vol. i, note to p. 522).

After the customary oblations and recognition in the metropolitan cathedral, the Protector 'was conveyed unto the King's palace within Westminster and there lodged until his coronation', (Buck, lib. i, p. 24). That same day he was 'proclaimed king throughout the city, by the name and style of Richard III' (Fabyan, p. 515).

Richard's coronation, July 6, occurred just two months and twenty-seven days after the death of his brother, Edward IV, on April 9, 1483. That monarch's hapless child, Edward V, had succeeded to a crown which he was destined never to wear. His name, however, survives on the regnal annals of England as the second monarch of the Yorkist dynasty and the last Edward of the Plantagenet race.

Gairdner : 'Such were the mode and circumstances of Richard III's usurpation. A usurpation it certainly was in fact, and so it has always been regarded. So, too, it was considered at the time, even by writers as moderate as well affected to the House of York as the continuator of Croyland. Yet, in point of form, one might almost look upon it as a constitutional election, if election could be considered a constitutional principle in those days. Indeed, it was rather a declaration of inherent right to the crown, first by the council of the realm, then by the city, and afterwards by Parliament, — proceedings much more regular and punctilious than had been observed in the case of Edward IV . . . we must at least acknowledge that the usurpation was one in which the nation, at first, tacitly concurred. The unpopularity of the Woodvilles, and the evils already experienced since the death of Edward IV may have made the termination of the minority seem a real blessing'. (pp. 95, 6)

Did Richard have prior designs on the crown?

Kendall : Mancini and Tudor writers like More and Vergil make the basic assumption that Richard began to seek the throne as soon as he reached London. This assumption may account for their important error in chronology — that Richard secured little York *before* executing Hastings as the last remaining obstacle to the crown.

Is this assumption true? Richard believed in the truth of the precontract. But, as noted above, Kendall believes that Richard did not actively consider assuming the throne, on the basis of Stillington's revelations, until about Tuesday or Wednesday, June 17-18, 1483. He did not have a preconceived plan to assume the throne. It was the fast developing events of May and June, 1483, that thrust Richard upon the throne (pp. 219, 469, 470, 473-477).

Chapter XIII

LEGITIMACY OF RICHARD'S CORONATION: PROGRESS NORTH

Commencement of Richard's Reign

Richard Receives Great Seal at Baynard's Castle : Richard III ascended the throne of England on June 26, 1483, aged thirty years and eight months (Sir Harris Nicolas, *Chronology of History*, p. 326). The last known signature of Edward V is dated June 17, and the first instrument attested by Richard after his accession is dated June 27. On the same date, the Bishop of Lincoln, who was reappointed Chancellor, delivered the great seal to the King at Baynard's Castle, the dwelling place of his mother, Lady Cecily, Duchess of York (Foedera xii, p. 189). This fact, among others, seems decisively to disprove the charge that Richard impugned the character of his mother and that she had openly expressed indignation at her son's unfilial conduct.

Conciliatory Actions of Wydville and Hastings Followers : What did the followers of Elizabeth Wydville and Lord Hastings do? Lord Lyle was the brother-in-law of Edward IV's widowed Queen and therefore the uncle of Lord Richard Grey, recently executed at Pontefract, and the Marquis of Dorset (Dugdale, Bar., vol. i, p. 719). Although he had openly opposed the elevation of the Duke of Gloucester to the protectorate, he now espoused Richard's cause (Stallworth Letters, Excerpt. Hist., fo. 15). Also, the followers of the late Lord Hastings entered the Duke of Buckingham's service. These actions show that at least a portion of the deposed Edward V's kindred were satisfied with the justice of Richard's conduct, and that Hastings' adherents, so far from resenting his execution, actually joined with one of the two Dukes who are charged with having unjustly compassed Lord Hastings' death.

Conspiracy against Richard : Another fact affords evidence that the

154

armed men sent for from York were indeed required for the safety of Richard and London and were not sent for under a false plea to seize the crown. 'It is thought', writes Stallworth to Sir William Stoner, after describing the disturbed state of the city, 'there shall be 20,000 of my Lord Protector's and my Lord Buckingham's men in London this week, to what intent I know not, but to keep the peace' (*Excerpt. Hist.*, p. 560). Yet, Stallworth's letter is dated June 21, 1483, the day previous to Dr. Shaw's sermon — *before* any attempt had been made to promote Richard's accession or to oppose his nephew's coronation. Thus, it is evident that London's disturbed state did not arise from revolt instigated by the Protector. Stallworth's letter expressly mentions preparations for Edward's coronation — a fact at variance with the supposition that Richard had planned for weeks to dispossess Edward of the crown.

Stallworth's testimony is confirmed by Fabyan : 'Soon after, for fear of the queen's blood, and other, which he had in jealousy, he sent for a strength of men out of the North, the which came shortly to London a little before his coronation, and mustered in the Moorfields, well upon 4,000 men'. (p. 516) These two accounts, one written by an officer in the Lord Chancellor's household and the other by a contemporary London citizen, confirm the truth of Richard's assertions to the citizens of York that a conspiracy had been formed to compass his destruction. Polydore Vergil (p. 540) distinctly asserts that Lord Hastings speedily repented his support of Richard and that he privately convoked a meeting of Edward IV's closest friends to discuss the most expedient course for the future.

Did the young princes remain in Richard's household?

Davies' York Records of The XVth Century : 'The Harleian MS. No. 433, contains the copy of a document, which affords some curious information. . . . It is styled, "The Ordinance made by the King's good grace for such number of persons as shall be in the North as the King's house-hold, and to begin the 23rd day of July, anno 2ndo. (1484)" . . . the children (are to be) together at one breakfast'. Their high rank is shown by the order that no livery is to exceed the allowance 'but only to my lord (Lincoln?) and the children'. — fo. 269 . . . 'The Earl of Warwick was probably one of the children whom the ordinance directs to be together at one breakfast. May not the others have been some of the offspring of Edward IV?' (p. 212, note.)

Richard a legitimate sovereign — not a usurper

Richard of Gloucester was now King of England — King by the unanimous consent of the nation and the unanimous choice of the nobles, the clergy, and the people (*Chron. Croy.*, p. 567). But for almost 500 years he has been designated as an usurper. Was he?

Richard neither deposed Edward V, nor forcibly seized the throne. The regal dignity was tendered to him voluntarily and peaceably by the Lords and Commons, whose responsibility it was to examine into the just pretentions of the new sovereign before he was irrevocably annointed ruler of the kingdom.

Here are the words of a modern eminent writer, who minutely examined every available document involved: 'Instead of a perjured traitor, we recognize the legitimate sovereign of England; instead of a violent usurpation, we discover an accession, irregular according to modern usage, but established without violence on a legal title' (Laing, App. to Henry, vol. xii, p. 414).

Whatever difference of opinion may prevail about the alleged disability of Edward V, there can exist none as to his having been dethroned by the 'lords and commons of the realm' (Chron. Croy., p. 567). 'The power and jurisdiction of parliament', says Sir Edward Coke, 'is so transcendent and absolute, that it cannot be confined either for causes or persons within any bounds. It can regulate or new model the succession to the crown. It can change and create afresh even the constitution of the kingdom, and of parliaments themselves' (Coke, quoted by Guthrie, p. 26).

But the laws of inheritance cannot be infringed, even by Parliament, without raising a sense of injustice. Thus, the odium which has ever attached to Richard's memory as King may by traced to two factors:

(1) The early suppression by Henry VII of the *Titulus Regius* — the statute which attested the disqualification of Edward V and stated Richard's just claim to the crown.
(2) Insufficient attention to the fact that the young Prince was rejected by his subjects on the ground of disqualification alone, and his uncle elected to the throne in his place because that throne was about to be vacated.

'Henry's policy in suppressing that statute affords additional proof of Edward's marriage with Elenor Butler', observes Mr. Laing, who adds: 'The statute would have been destroyed without the ceremony of being reversed, but an act was necessary to indemnify those to whose custody the rolls were intrusted' (See *Year Book*, Hilary Term, 1 Hen. VII). The statute was abrogated without recital in order to conceal its purport and obliterate, if possible, the facts it attested; and a proposal for reading it — that Stillington, bishop of Bath, might be responsible for its falsehood — was overruled and stifled by the king's immediate declaration of pardon'. (Ibid.) 'Its falsehood', continues Mr. Laing, 'would have merited and demanded detection, not concealment; and Stillington, whose evidence had formerly established the marriage, was, if perjured, an object of punishment, not of pardon' (Laing's *Dissertation*, Appendix to Henry's *England*, vol. xii, p. 409).

The peers and prelates of England were aggrieved at fealty having been exacted for a Prince (Edward V) who had no legal claims to their oath of allegiance. This conviction greatly supported and confirmed the Lord Protector's cause when the matter was formally submitted to them. 'He then brought in instruments, authentick doctors, proctors, and notaries of the law, with depositions of divers witnesses, testifying King Edward's children to be bastards' (Grafton, *Cont.* More, p. 153).

Much sympathy has been elicited for the calamities of the young Prince, the victim of error not his own. Yet, his deposition and the elevation of his uncle to the throne was not the act of the Lord Protector — it was the decree of Parliament and the people. The constituted authorities elected Edward V's uncle their King from their conviction that what Parliament had sanctioned under false premises Parliament had a right to nullify for legitimate cause. Thus, one deduction can alone be made regarding King Richard — *instead of usurping the crown it was settled upon him by due process of the Lords and Commons of the Kingdom.*

Kendall : Kendall cites Polydore Vergil, the official Tudor historian, to prove that Richard III was not overly ambitious and that he made a sincere effort to consult the Lords and Commons: '. . . not withstanding that many of his friends urged him to utter himself plainly and to dispatch at once that which remained, yet, lest his doings might easily be misliked, his desire was that the people earnestly be dealt with, and the whole matter be referred to the determination of others'. (Kendall pp. 223-225; *Anglicae Historiae*, ed. H. Ellis, Camden Society, 1844.)

Richard's election analogous to 1688 dynasty change

'The great regularity with which the coronation was prepared and conducted', observes Lord Orford (Horace Walpole), 'and the extra-ordinary concourse of the nobility at it, have not at all the air of an unwelcome reception, accomplished merely by violence; on the contrary, it bore great resemblance to a much later event, which, being the last of the kind, we term "the Revolution" '. And a revolution truly it was, although not a usurpation.

Consider that Richard's accession was accomplished —

without bloodshed,

without the aid of an armed force,

after a fortnight of calm and deliberate preparations for solemnizing the ceremony,

with the most minute attention to regal splendor and court etiquette, and

with the observance of proper ecclesiastical and judicial forms.

Thus, every reflective person will ask the same question Lord Orford asks in concluding his examination into Richard's coronation: 'Has this the air of a forced and precipitate election? or does it not indicate a voluntary concurrence in the nobility?' (*Historic Doubts*, p. 17.)

The circumstances of Richard's election were indeed singularly analogous to those which took place on the change of dynasty in 1688. Upon that great occasion, states Blackstone, 'the lords and commons, by their own authority, and upon the summons of the Prince of Orange, afterwards King William, met in a convention, and therein disposed of the crown and kingdom' (Blackstone's Commentaries, vol. i, p. 152).

Blackstone says that this assembling proceeded upon a conviction that the throne was vacant. 'In such a case', he says, 'as the palpable vacancy of the throne, it follows *ex necessitate rei* that the form of the royal writs must be laid aside, otherwise no parliament can ever meet again'. (Ibid.)

And he puts the possible case of the failure of the whole royal line, which would indisputably vacate the throne: 'In this situation', he says, 'it seems reasonable to presume that the body of the nation, consisting of lords and commons, would have a right to meet and settle the government, otherwise there must be no government at all'.

'The three estates of nobility, clergy, and people, which called Richard to the crown, and whose act was confirmed by the subsequent parliament, trod the same steps as the convention did, which elected the Prince of Orange; both setting aside an illegal pretender, the legitimacy of whose birth was called in question: in both instances it was a free election' (*Historic Doubts*, p. 45).

It was upon the principle stated by Blackstone that the conventions of 1483 and 1688 both proceeded:

Both presumed the throne to be vacant — the former because of the illegitimacy of Edward IV's children, the latter because of James II's abdication;

both met without writ, as they must do if they assembled at all, because of the vacancy of the throne;

both declared the throne to be vacant;

both tendered the crown to sovereigns selected by themselves; and

both procured a subsequent parliamentary ratification of their proceedings.

So far, therefore, as relates to strict legal form, the proceedings on the election of Richard III were exactly similar to those adopted on the transfer of the throne from James II to William and Mary.

Coronation preparations

Richard Exacts Oath of Allegiance : The nobles, the clergy, the citizens, and the people at large hailed the accession of Richard III with as much unanimity as if Edward V had died a natural death and the crown had, of necessity, reverted to his uncle. The preparations and festivities so nearly completed for the deposed monarch were in readiness for the immediate enthronement of his uncle. Richard assembled the lords of the council and the great officers of state, and on June 27 the day for the coronation of himself and his Queen was fixed. On June 28, instructions were despatched to Lord Mountjoy and others, the governors of Calais and Guisnes, commanding them to make known to the garrisons of these important fortresses 'the verry sure and true title which our sovereign lord that now is, King Richard III, hath and had to their fealty' (Harl. MSS. 433, fol. 238) and to exact from them anew the oath of allegiance which had become void by the dethronement of his nephew.

Richard's Unwise Leniency in Pardoning His Dangerous Enemies : Richard presided in person at the judicial courts, declaring it to be 'the chiefest duty of a king to minister to the laws' (More, p. 244). He withdrew his personal enemies from sanctuary that he might openly pardon their offences before the people (Ibid.).

On July 4, 1483, Richard proceeded in state to the Tower (*Harl. MSS.* No. 293, fol. 208) by water, accompanied by Anne. Here, he released Lord Stanley from confinement, pardoning his reputed connection with the conspiracy of Lord Hastings. With a generosity not in accord with the evil deeds imputed to him, and with complete disregard to personal danger, Richard sought to bury the past and make Lord Stanley his friend by appointing him lord steward of his household (Grafton, p. 799). Richard likewise freed the Archbishop of York and confirmed him in his primacy (Buck, lib. i, p. 26). Again with unwise leniency, at odds with his alleged cruelty, Richard liberated another dangerous enemy, John Morton, Bishop of Ely, who had conspired for Richard's destruction. Morton was committed to the charge of the Duke of Buckingham, to be under nominal restraint until he showed less violent opposition to the newly-elected King.

State Progress Through The City : On July 5, 1483, Richard and his Queen rode from the Tower through the city in great state (Buck, lib. i, p. 26), attended by all the chief officers of the crown, the lord mayor, the civic authorities, and the leading nobility and commons, sumptuously arrayed. During the procession not the slightest disturbance occurred nor did the populace show any disapproval of Richard's accession.

Coronation of King Richard III and Queen Anne

A Magnificent Ceremony : A more peaceful or tranquil accession can scarcely be adduced from the regnal annals of England than that of Richard III. But if Richard's peaceful accession excites wonder, still greater astonishment must be felt at the unanimity which prevailed at his coronation. This celebration was perhaps the most magnificent ceremonial on record. It was remarkable for the vast attendance of the aristocracy, for the extraordinary magnificence displayed, and most of all for the participation of the influential leaders of both the Lancastrian and Yorkist factions.

Copies are still in existence of the oath of allegiance to Richard III taken by the lords spiritual and temporal (*Rymer's Add. MSS.*, 4616, art. 17, 18) and of the names of the persons whom Richard created knights on the Sunday before his coronation (Harl. MSS. 293, art. 208). Many other very minute particulars are preserved in the Heralds' College and in the Harleian manuscripts (Ibid. 433, art. 211) about the gorgeous ceremony *(Excerpta Historica,* p. 380).

On Sunday, July 6, 1483, King Richard and Queen Anne, with the great of the crown and preceded by trumpets, clarions, and heralds passed from the Tower, through the city, to Westminster Hall. Here, they were met by the priests, abbots, and bishops, with mitres and crosiers, who conducted them to the Abbey. The King, himself, was under a canopy borne by the Barons of the Cinque Ports. He was sumptuously habited in robes of purple velvet furred with ermine. His hose, coat, and surcoat were of crimson satin and his sabatons (shoes) were covered with crimson tissue cloth of gold.

The Queen's procession followed. She was under a gorgeous canopy corresponding with Richard's, but with the addition of a bell of gold at every corner. Like him, too, she was habited in robes of purple velvet, furred with ermine. Her shoes were of crimson tissue cloth of gold and her head was adorned with 'a circlet of gold, with many previous stones set therein'.

Evidence of Richard's Fairness : The coronation of King Richard III and Queen Anne is notable for much more than its grandeur and magnificence, which contemporary accounts state nothing could exceed. It is remarkable for the evidence it gives of Richard's fairness and impartiality and his great desire to bring together in amity the houses of York and Lancaster:

> In the King's procession, the Earl of Northumberland carried the pointless sword of mercy — Lord Stanley the mace of constable-ship. Northumberland had been a chief instrument in promoting Richard's elevation, while Stanley, the step-father of Henry Tudor, had just been released from imprisonment in the Tower for conspiring to destroy Richard.

> The Queen had at her right side a Princess of York (the Duchess of Suffolk, second daughter of Richard, Duke of York, and Lady Cecily) and at her left side a princess of Lancaster (Margaret Beaufort, mother of Henry Tudor and the great grand-daughter of John of Gaunt, Duke of Lancaster, fourth son of Edward III).

> In the Queen's procession, the Earl of Huntingdon bore the sceptre, and Lord Lyle (so created by Edward IV) bore the rod

with the dove. Huntingdon was betrothed to Lady Katherine Plantagenet, King Richard's illegitimate daughter, while Lyle was a Grey — brother by marriage to the widowed Queen, Elizabeth Wydville, and uncle to her sons by Lord Grey.

Bourchier Crowns Richard : Entering the west door of Westminster Abbey, Richard and Anne proceeded direct to their chairs of state. After resting until 'divers holy hymns were sung', they were solemnly annointed from a vessel of pure gold. Donning new robes of cloth of gold, they were both crowned with great solemnity by Cardinal Bourchier, Archbishop of Canterbury.

The Cardinal Archbishop then performed high mass and administered holy communion. Yet this venerable ecclesiastic, this high dignitary of the Church of Rome, the primate of all England, who thus absolved Richard from his sins was the same Lord Cardinal who had pledged 'his own body and soul' to the widowed Queen when receiving the young Duke of York from sanctuary scarcely three weeks before. Can there remain any longer a doubt that some just cause existed for young Edward's deposition, or that Richard's election to the throne was free and unbiased?

Bourchier's Action Indicates Justice of Richard's Claim to Throne : The character of Thomas Bourchier, Archbishop of Canterbury, and Cardinal of St. Cyrac, has never been impeached (*Historic Doubts*, p. 55). He was not raised to high office for the occasion or as reward for services to the Lord Protector. He had been a bishop almost forty years and primate of Canterbury even before the accession of the house of York.

Bourchier was venerable by age and eminent for his talents and virtues. He was lineally descended from Edward III, had annointed Edward IV King and invested him with the crown, and had twice sworn allegiance to his youthful heir, Edward V. Any remonstrance from Bourchier could scarcely go unheeded. Yet, Cardinal Bourchier, with the appeal to his God yet fresh upon his lips, that 'the estate as well as safety' of the young Princes should be required at his hands, consecrates Richard of Gloucester ruler of the kingdom and absolves him from all sin.

Factors Leading to Richard's Coronation: But one conclusion, surely, can result from this extraordinary proceeding, sanctioned as it was by the whole body of the clergy, by the judges, and by the knightly representatives of the people; viz. that the nobility met

Richard's claim to the throne at least halfway (*Historic Doubts*, p. 45). What were the factors that impelled them to crown Richard? *First*, they were convinced of the fact of Edward IV's previous marriage. *Second*, they hated and were jealous of the queen-mother's family, the Wydvilles. *Third*, they perceived the calamities that would probably ensue from Edward V's defective title during a long minority. 'And that the great wise man well perceived, when he sayde, "Veli regno cujus rex puer est", —Woe is that realme that hath a child to their king' (More, p. 113). *Fourth*, they hailed a legitimate plea for quietly deposing the youthful son of Elizabeth Wydville and elevating for their ruler one of the popular race of York. Richard's abilities and firmness had been tested. His military reputation would alike conduce to peace at home and, should the honour of the kingdom require it, command respect for the English arms abroad.

Coronation Ceremonies Continue : About 'four of the clock', Richard and his royal consort entered the hall and sat down to dinner accompanied by an immense assemblage of the nobility and the most illustrious ladies of England. The royal couple were waited upon by the noblest persons in the realm. At the second course, Sir Robert Dymoke, the King's champion, came riding into the hall 'his horse trapped with white silk and red, and himself in white harness', and inquired 'before all the people, if there by any man will say against King Richard III why he should not pretend to the crown; and anon all the people were at peace awhile'. Then making proclamation that 'whosoever should say that King Richard III was not lawfully king, he would fight with him with all utterance', the champion threw down his gauntlet for gage thereof, when all the people cried, King Richard! God save King Richard!'

Kendall : It was the most magnificent coronation ever held in Westminster Abbey, dwarfing the coronations of Edward IV and Henry VII. Almost the entire peerage attended, reflecting England's warm acceptance of Richard III (p. 231).

Wisdom and justice of Richard III's early measures

Proofs of Richard's Just, Equable, and Prudent Administration : King Richard speedily showed his capacity for government by the vigor and resolution which characterized the opening of his reign and by the wisdom of his measures. No testimony that could be given by historian or biographer, no panegyric by follower or friend, on Richard's talents, vigilance, and energy could so truly depict his actual character or the powers of his mind as the evidence of his own acts as Lord Protector and king. Fortunately, this evidence has been transmitted to posterity.

Amongst innumerable documents connected with the history of the Plantagenet monarchs there is preserved in the Harleian Library a most curious folio volume in manuscript. This volume contains a copious register of the grants and public documents during the reigns of Edward V and Richard III. It consists of no less than *two thousand three hundred and seventy-eight articles!* (See *Catalogue Harleian MSS.*, preface.)

These entries commemorate the proceedings of little more than two short years. Yet they abound in instances of Richard's generosity and benevolence, with proofs of his just, equable, and prudent administration.

King Richard first enjoined the judges in an eloquent address, to firmly and impartially administer justice. He told them of his resolve to go forthwith to the North 'to pacify that country, and to redress certain riots there lately done' (Fabyan, fol. 154). He mentioned his determination, in his intended progress through the kingdom, to examine personally into his subjects' wants. He would correct abuses and severely suppress all insubordination or disregard of the laws.

On July 9, three days after he was annointed King, Richard by letters patent appointed the 'right high and mighty prince, Edward, his first-begotten son' (*Harl. MSS.* 433, fol. 242) to be lieutenant of Ireland.

Richard's sense of justice is strikingly shown in the next instrument which passed the royal signet. Letters patent, bearing the date the 18th of July anno 1 mo. Richard III, were issued for payment 'due to divers persons for their services done to his dearest brother the late king, and to Edward bastard, late called Edward V'. (*Harl. MSS.* 433, fol. 233).

Richard's Generosity to Buckingham : Having arranged matters in London to promote the confidence and peaceable disposition of the citizens, King Richard and Queen Anne went to Greenwich and Windsor to arrange for their progress through the kingdom and to requite the services of his trusty friends. To the Duke of Buckingham, he gave the munificent recompense of all the manors, lordships, and lands of Humphrey de Bohun, Earl of Hereford, for 'the true, faithful, and laudable service which our said cousin hath, in many sundry wise, done to us, to our right singular will and pleasure' (*Harl. MSS.* 433, fol. 107).

Besides receiving many valuable donations, as 'a special gift' from the king, very speedily after the coronation ceremony Buckingham was successively created constable of England for life (*Rymer's Add. MSS.*, 4616, art. 23), confirmed in his former appointments of chief justice and chamberlain of North and South Wales (Ibid., art. 6), made steward of many valuable crown manors, and appointed governor of the royal castles in Wales (Ibid., art. 6).

In view of this written record of Richard's generosity to Buckingham, what becomes of Shakespeare's famous scene in which Richard angrily rejects Buckingham's request for reward?

Household Ordinance Reflects Richard's Principles of Order and Justice : In the midst of all this pressure of business involved in commencing a new reign, Richard did not neglect his domestic duties. With characteristic foresight and vigilance, he regulated his establishment at Middleham and provided for the rule and management of his young son's household there.

'This is the ordinance made by the king's good grace', states the ancient and curious manuscript (*Harl. MSS.* 433, fol. 265) which has thus perpetuated Richard's attention to the well-being of his family at his favorite Middleham, 'for such numbers of persons as shall be in the North as the king's household'. An attentive observance to the hours of God's service is the first thing enjoined. Then, the utmost care is given towards providing for the just and equitable government of the whole establishment, including the welfare of the humblest retainer. This ordinance, so notable in evidencing Richard's sound principles of order and justice, concludes with these remarkable words — 'that convenient fare be ordained for the household servants, and strangers to fare better than others' (Ibid., p. 269).

King Richard's progress through his dominions

Richard's Great Generosity to Hastings' Family : All preliminaries being arranged, King Richard commenced his royal progress, July 23, 1483, quitting Windsor for Reading. His stay here was marked by an act of liberality that is greatly at variance with the heartless spirit so universally imputed to him. He granted to Lord Hastings' widow, Katharine, his full and entire pardon for the offences of her recently executed lord. Richard released the title and estates from attainder and forfeiture, confirmed her son and the rest of her children in all their possessions, and promised 'to protect and defend the widow and to suffer none to do her wrong' (*Harl. MSS.* 433, p. 108).

Oxford Honours Richard : At the entrance to the city of Oxford, Richard was welcomed with great reverence by the chancellor and heads of the university. 'After they had expressed their love and duty to him, he was honourably and processionally received in Magdalen College by the founder, Bishop Waynflete, the president and scholars thereof, and lodged there that night' (Gutch's Hist. of Oxford, p. 638). Magdalen College is required by its statutes to entertain the Kings of England and their eldest sons, whenever they come to Oxford (Chalmers Hist. of Oxford, p. 211).

Oxford welcomed Richard with loyalty, respect, and affection. Every honour that could be paid to him by the university was abundantly shown. His visit to the university is perpetuated by its famed antiquary, Anthony Wood (Wood's Hist. and Antiq. of Oxon., vol. i, p. 233), as one of the most interesting and memorable scenes in the early history of this seat of learning.

Richard's Benevolence to Oxford and Cambridge : The day after his arrival, solemn disputations on moral philosophy and divinity were held in the hall, by command and at the desire of the King. Next day, King Richard and his noble retinue visited several colleges, 'scattering his benevolence very liberally to all that he heard dispute or make orations to him' (Gutch, p. 639). As he promised the scholars at his reception, he confirmed the privileges of the university granted by his predecessors. He showed his love for the town of Oxford, also, by releasing it from the usual crown fee due to each sovereign at his accession.

Richard III was a great benefactor to Cambridge also. In addition to other marks of royal favour, he endowed Queen's College. For the benefit of both Oxford and Cambridge, he caused an act to be made that strangers might bring printed books into England and sell them by retail. This was a matter of great importance to these seminaries of learning in the infancy of printing.

Most histories are filled with accounts of Richard's alleged depravity. Few notice the undeniable evidence of his bounty, his patronage of literature, and the high estimation in which he was evidently held by the learned and the good. Yet the golden opinions which he reaped during his stay at Oxford are registered in the college archives.

Richard's Liberality to Gloucester, Tewkesbury, and Worcester :
Gloucester received Richard with the utmost loyalty and affection.
This city, from which Richard derived his youthful title of duke, had
remained firm to King Edward and himself amidst all their reverses of
fortune. 'When Queen Margaret besieged the city of Gloucester with
the king's power, the citizens stood at defiance with her army, and
told her it was the Duke of Gloucester his town, who was with the
king, and for the king, and for him they would hold it'. (Buck, lib. iii,
p. 83; Fleetwood Chron., p. 26.)

Richard never forgot a kindness. True indeed, as asserted by his
bitter enemy Sir Thomas More, with 'large gifts he got him unstead-
fast friendship' (p. 9). But his grateful remembrance of former
benefits, his justice, and his munificence, even in this royal progress
alone, exemplify in a striking degree the additional evidence of More
that 'he was free of dyspence' and 'above his power liberal'. He most
abundantly rewarded Gloucester for the love its citizens had borne
him.

Tewkesbury, the scene of Richard's early military renown, was the
next station on his progress. Richard reached it on August 4, 1483,
visited the abbot, and bestowed large sums on Tewkesbury Abbey
(Harl. MSS. 433, p. 110).

Richard and his royal train next passed on to Worcester, whose
Bishop Alcock had attended Richard to Oxford (Gutch, p. 639) and
had accompanied him throughout his tour. This prelate, it will be
remembered, was one of the executors (Royal Wills, p. 347) of
Edward IV, and preceptor and president of the council to the
deposed Edward V (Sloane MSS., No. 3, 479). As such, he had been
arrested by the Lord Protector at Stony Stratford. Yet he is
chronicled as one of the four bishops who by their presence imparted
sanctity and added dignity to the new King's progress through his
dominions. Such support seems wholly incomprehensible if Richard
were the monster of depravity usually represented. This is the more
so as Dr. Alcock, the Bishop of Worcester, was highly celebrated in
his day for his virtues, his learning, and his piety.

Still more irreconcilable with the odious character so long affixed
to King Richard III is the popularity which greeted him wherever he
went. The city of Worcester, following the examples of London and
Gloucester, tendered him 'a benevolence' or sum of money to defray
his expenses. The severe imposition called 'benevolence' was a
despotic mode of raising money by exacting large sums as voluntary
gifts from the great body of the people. It was devised by Edward IV,
but Richard abolished benevolences (Harl. MSS. 980, art. 23).

Richard saw the evil of a tax which pressed so firmly on his subjects. He therefore thanked them for their liberality but in each case declined the money offered, stating that he 'would rather possess their hearts than their wealth' (Rous).

Richard the Victim of Prejudiced Writers : Such incidents tend to disprove the calumnies of a later age, based only on oral conjecture, originating in political rancor, and propagated by angry opponents and prejudiced writers. 'Every one that is acquainted with English history', says Drake, who rescued from obscurity so many original documents connected with Richard III, 'must know that there is hardly any part of it so dark as the short reign of this king: the Lancastrian party which destroyed and succeeded him took care to suppress his virtues, and to paint his vices in the most glaring colours' (p. 118). Drake's *Eboracum or History and Antiquities of York*, is a work of great research. It contains literally copies of all King Richard's letters and proclamations sent to the mayor and citizens of York, and the daily orders in council about the state of affairs to this King's death, extracted from the city registers.

Queen and Son Join Richard; They Proceed to York : From Worcester, the King proceeded to Warwick, Coventry, Leicester, Nottingham, and York. The Queen, with numerous retinue, joined him at Warwick, and their son, Edward, Earl of Salisbury, left Middleham on August 22 to join his royal parents prior to their triumphant entry into York.

Gairdner : 'Every step in his progress was signalised by gracious acts, which won him popularity. From Oxford he went to Woodstock, where, in compliance with a petition from the inhabitants of the adjoining district, he disafforested a considerable tract of land which his brother Edward had arbitrarily, and for his own pleasure, annexed to Whichwood Forest. The act was remembered to his credit after he was gone, even by one (Rous, p. 216) who did not love his memory' (p. 112).

'In the North, undoubtedly, and perhaps with the common people generally, Richard was at this time highly popular. Such at least was the opinion of Bishop Langton, who, in a private letter written while the king was at York, says of him: "He contents the people where he goes best that ever did prince; for many a poor man that hath suffered wrong many days have been relieved and helped by him and his commands in his progress. And in many great cities and towns were great sums of money given him which he hath refused. On my truth, I never liked the conditions of any prince so well as his. God hath sent him to us for the weal of us all". Sheppard's *Christchurch Letters*, 46' (p. 115).

Richard's son created Prince of Wales — reputed second coronation untrue

The royal party entered York in great state on August 29, 1483. York welcomed Richard with a display of enthusiasm and zealous attachment that fully confirms the accounts of local historians of the devotion with which Richard was beloved in the northern counties (Surtee's Durham, p. 60). The feeling was reciprocal. 'This place', says Drake, 'he seems to have paid an extraordinary regard to'.

On September 8, a second coronation was held in York Minster. On the same day, the King created his young son 'Prince of Wales and Earl of Chester', investing him 'by a golden rod, a coronet of gold, and other ensigns' (Foedera, vol. xii, p. 200).

Robert Davies : '. . . not the slightest ground is afforded for believing that there was a second coronation'. (*Extracts from the Municipal Records of the City of York*, App. p. 286.) Gairdner, p. 113, and Kendall, p. 258, agree with Davies.

Richard's splendid apparel — a defense

It is but justice here to clear Richard III of a charge which, unimportant in itself, helps to swell the catalog of offences which measure the ill-fame of this last Plantagenet king. Richard's splendid apparel has subjected him to reproach (Turner's *Middle Ages*, vol. iii, p. 479). But he was only acting in conformity with the age in which he lived. Nicolas, in refuting Sharon Turner's arguments, concludes there is not a single circumstance which justifies the opinion that Richard was more fond of splendor than his predecessors. 'These inferences', observes Nicolas, 'with respect to the character of Richard III, are, it is submitted, drawn from a mistaken estimate of evidence, rather than from erroneous data; and they *prove the necessity of an historian, not merely using research, but of being able to attach a proper value to his materials*'. (underscoring added)

'The grounds upon which the opinion of Richard's vanity is built are, the account of the articles delivered out of the wardrobe for his coronation; the descriptions of chroniclers of his pompous appearance on public occasions; and the clothes for which he sent from York. Viewed without reference to similar accounts, in previous and subsequent reigns, the conclusion is natural, that the sovereign to whom they relate was 'a vain coxcomb', especially if the opinion be correct, that that list was prepared by the monarch himself'.

'But when records of this nature are compared with others, and it becomes evident that the splendid dresses worn by Richard formed the general costume of persons of rank of the age; and when the minuteness of detail, which is ascribed to his own taste, is proved to be the usual form in which wardrobe keepers and their officers entered the articles intrusted to their custody, the error of supposing that the splendour or the accurate description of the robes are in any degree indicative of Richard the Third's character, is manifest'.

'A reference to these wardrobe accounts, or to any other list of apparel or jewels in the 14th or 15th and 16th centuries, will prove that there is not a single circumstance connected with Richard which justifies the opinion that he was more fond of splendour than his predecessors, much less that he was either "a fop" or "a coxcomb" ' (*Privy Purse Expenses of Elizabeth of York*, edited by Sir Harris Nicolas, p. 4).

Richard administers justice during his journey north

Richard devoted a considerable portion of his time to receiving petitions, redressing grievances, and administering justice. That he did so, and with strict impartiality, is proved by the local records that have perpetuated his progress from town to town during his journey to the north.

'Thanked be Jesu', writes the royal secretary, 'the king's grace is in good health, as is likewise the queen's grace, and in all their progress have been worshipfully received with pageants and other &c. &c., and his lords and judges in every place, sitting determining the complaints of poor folks, with due punition of offendors against his laws' (Drake, p. 116). The example set by King Henry I of making a progress into the remote parts of the land for the administration of justice, was followed by most of his successors (*Harl. MSS.* 980, fol. 34).

York's loyalty to Richard

King Richard closed his stay at York by confirming overtures of peace and amity with the courts of Spain (Feodera, xii, p. 200) and Scotland (Harl. MSS. 433, fol. 246). He also knighted his illegitimate son, Lord John Plantagenet, and conferred the same honour upon many northern gentlemen (Drake, 117).

On September 17, 1483, Richard sent for the mayor, the aldermen, and commons, and 'without any petition or asking', bestowed upon the city of York a charter of great value and importance. 'Richard's munificence to our city at this time', observes Drake (p. 117), 'whether it proceeded from gratitude or policy, was a truly royal gift. . . . I never found him, amongst all his other vices, taxed with covetousness, and he had many reasons, both on his own and his family's account, to induce him even to do more for a city which had always signalised itself in the interest of his house'.

'What opinion our citizens of York had of King Richard will best appear by their own records; in which they took care to register every particular letter and message they received from him. And as his fate drew nigh, they endeavoured to show their loyalty or their gratitude to this prince in the best manner they were able'.

So, he departed from York, carrying with him abundant proofs of the love of her citizens. That personal attachment was never diminished, never withdrawn — not even when calumny had blighted his fair fame and death had rendered him powerless to reward the fidelity with which his grateful northern subjects cherished the memory and upheld the reputation of their friend and benefactor, King Richard III.

171

Chapter XIV

THE TWO PRINCES
IN THE TOWER

For slander lives upon succession,
For ever hous'd where it once gets possession.

Shakespeare, *The Comedy of Errors*,
Act III, Scene 1.

PART 1: HALSTED'S VIEWS

Richard's acts of justice

King Richard, accompanied by Queen Anne and the Prince of Wales, recommenced his royal progress about September 15, 1483, proceeding directly from York to Pontefract. Here his action in ordering a portion of the garrison at Calais to be discharged implies that Richard's mind was thoroughly at ease before he left York.

The register that recorded Richard's acts at this period include numerous documents associated personally with him and various edicts that bear the sign manual and mark his progress from town to town. Yet not one entry can be produced that convicts King Richard of being 'dispitious (spiteful) and cruel' (More, p. 9). He was bountiful to the poor, indulgent to the rich, and generous in all his transactions.

To the widow of Earl Rivers, who had 'intended and compassed' his destruction, he ordered the payment of all duties accruing from the estates which had been settled on her as her jointure (*Harl. MSS.*, 433. fol. 166). He presented the Lady Hastings with the wardship and marriage of her son and entrusted her with the sole charge of his vast estates after removing the attainder (Ibid. fol. 27). But the most remarkable instance that could perhaps be adduced of Richard's kind and forgiving disposition was the commiseration he felt for the destitute state of the unfortunate Countess of Oxford. She was the wife of the bitterest enemy of Richard and his race. He settled on her a pension of 100 pounds a year during the exile of her lord, although

Oxford was openly and avowedly arrayed in hostility against Richard.

Unsatisfactory sources

The ultimate fate of Edward V and his younger brother, Richard, Duke of York, is completely veiled in mystery. Tradition has long fixed on their uncle the odium of their deaths. For this reason, the memory of Richard III has for many ages been a subject of universal horror and disgust.

Nevertheless, an examination of the sources which attribute terrible crimes to him reveals how vague and unsatisfactory they are. The alleged facts of the disappearance of the two Princes are interwoven with fable, errors in dates, and discrepancies in detail. More important, many if not most of the sources are corrupt — written by Richard's bitter enemies or based on information supplied by them. For 500 years this mystery has effectively baffled the labors of the antiquary, the historian, and the philosopher to unravel the tangled web of falsehood and deceit in which it is enveloped.

Halsted on other sources

The Croyland Chronicler : Judging from the testimony of the Croyland historian, the report which has so blackened King Richard's fame may be traced to the unstable and ambitious Duke of Buckingham. It cannot be denied that the words of the Croyland Chronicler regarding Buckingham are very remarkable. They tend more strongly to fix the report on that nobleman and his party than any allegation afterwards made against Richard III: 'Henry Duke of Buckingham, repenting the course of conduct he had adopted, would be their leader', are the words of the Chronicler. He immediately follows this statement by asserting that 'it was reported', as if in consequence of the change in Buckingham's views, 'that King Edward's sons were dead, but by what kind of violent death was unknown' (*Chron. Croy.*, p. 568).

Fabyan, the City Chronicler : Fabyan says, after describing the accession of the Lord Protector, 'King Edward V, with his brother the Duke of York, were put under sure keeping within the Tower in such wise that they never came abroad after' (Fabyan's Chron.,

p. 515). And again, 'the common fame went that King Richard put unto secret death the two sons of his brother' (Ibid., p. 516). *The New Chronicles of England and France*, ed. H. Ellis, London, 1811.

Rous : Rous of Warwick is the next contemporary authority. Although coeval with King Richard, he —like Fabyan — wrote the events which he records after Richard's death. 'The Duke of Gloucester, for his own promotion, took upon him to the disinheriting of his lord, King Edward V, and shortly imprisoned King Edward with his brother, whom he had obtained from Westminster, under promise of protection; so that it was afterwards known to very few what particular martyrdom they suffered' (Rous, *Hist. Reg. Ang.*, p. 213).

Rous, however, places the death of the Princes during the protectorate: 'Then ascended the royal throne of *the slain*, whose protector during their minority he should have been, the tyrant Richard'. This assertion is so utterly at variance with every contemporary account that it materially weakens the effect of his other assertions.

The fact that Rous dedicated his work to King Henry VII is alone sufficient to demonstrate his Lancastrian bias. In addition, proof exists that Rous's characterization of Richard *during* his reign was very different from that which he afterwards wrote for Richard's rival and successor. In the Rous Roll, which he left to posterity as a monument of the earls and town of Warwick, to which he was so much attached, here is the inscription in his own hand: 'The most mighty prince Richard by the grace of God King of England and of France and lord of Ireland . . . ruled his subjects in his realm full commendably, punishing offenders of his laws, especially extortioners and oppressors of his commons, and cherishing those that were virtuous, by the which discreet guiding he got great thanks of God and love of all his subjects, rich and poor, and great laud of the people of other lands about him' (From the original MS. roll, now in the College of Arms, published in Horace Walpole's works, vol. ii, p. 215).

Bernard André : Bernard André, Henry VII's biographer and poet laureate, states that 'Richard ordered the princes to be put to the sword' (Cott. MSS. Dom. A. xviii). If Richard had given such a positive order, that fact would have been known to the contemporary annalists. André could only narrate events of this period from hearsay. He was a Breton and did not reside in England until after the accession of Henry VII, to whose suite he was attached and whose fortunes he followed (*Memorials of King Henry VII*, ed. J. Gairdner, London, 1858)

Polydore Vergil : Vergil compiled his work under the immediate patronage and at the express desire of Henry VII. Churchill (p. 128) says 'Vergil was busy working on the reign of Henry VII as early as 1512 and as late as 1524'. Yet neither contemporary chroniclers nor those who wrote subsequently by Henry's express command, as Vergil did, give any firm account of the young Princes' fable. In fact Vergil says *it was generally reported and believed that the sons of Edward IV were still alive, having been conveyed secretly away, and obscurely concealed in some distant region* (Pol. Verg., p. 569).

John Stow : The antiquary, John Stow (The Annals of England, 1592), being required to give his opinion of the alleged murder affirmed it was never proved by any credible witness that King Richard was guilty of it.

Bacon : 'Neither wanted there even at that time (anno 1 Henry VII) secret rumours and whisperings, which afterwards gathered strength and turned to treat troubles, that the two young sons of King Edward IV, or one of them, which were said to be destroyed in the Tower, were not indeed murdered, but conveyed secretly away, and were yet living' (Bacon's *Henry VII*, p. 4). 'And all this time (anno 2 Henry VII) it was still whispered every where that at least one of the children of Edward IV was living' (Ibid. p. 19).

More's History of King Richard III

Since practically all subsequent accounts of the alleged murder of the young Prince, including Shakespeare's play, are based on More's account (p. 127), it is important to examine it closely:

More says that during the royal progress to Gloucester, King Richard's mind misgave him that 'men would not reckon that he could have right to the realm' so long as his nephews lived. Whereupon he sent John Green, 'whom he especially trusted', unto Sir Robert Brackenbury, the Constable of the Tower, with a letter 'and credence also' commanding him to put the two children to death. Green rejoined the King at Warwick, telling him that Brackenbury had refused to fulfil his commands.

Greatly displeased at this result, the King complained to the page in waiting that even those he had brought up and thought most devoted to his service had failed him and would do nothing for him. The page replied that there was a man upon a pallet in the outer chamber who, to do him pleasure, would think nothing too hard. He meant Sir James Tyrrel, 'a man of right goodlye personage, and, for nature's gifts, worthy to have served a better prince'. Richard, pleased with the page's suggestion and well aware that Tyrrel 'had strength and wit', and an ambitious spirit, took Tyrrel into his chamber and 'broke to him secretly his mind in this mischievous matter'.

Sir James undertook the revolting office. Whereupon on the morrow the King sent him 'to Brackenbury with a letter, by which he was commanded to deliver to Sir James all the keys of the Tower for one night, to the end that he might there accomplish the King's pleasure in such things as he had given him commandment'. . . . 'After which letter delivered and the keys received, Sir James appointed the night next ensuing' to destroy the Princes. 'To the execution thereof, he appointed Miles Forest', a known assassin, and John Dighton, his own groom, 'a big, broad, square, strong knave'.

All other persons being removed, the ruffians entered the chamber where the Princes were sleeping at midnight, when, wrapping them up in the bed-clothes, and keeping them down by force, they pressed the feather-bed and pillows hard upon their mouths, until they were stifled and expired. When thoroughly dead, they laid their bodies naked out upon the bed, and summoned Sir James Tyrrel to see them. He caused the murderers to bury them at the stair-foot, deep in the ground, under a great heap of stones. 'Then rode Sir James in great haste to the king, and showed him all the manner of the murder, who gave him great thanks, and, as some say, there made him a knight'. 'But it was rumoured', continues Sir Thomas More, 'that the king disapproved of their being buried in so vile a corner; whereupon they say that a priest of Sir Robert Brackenbury's took up the bodies again, and secretly interred them in such place as by the occasion of his death could never come to light'. See Halsted, vol. II, pp. 190-192, and *Sir Thomas More, Saint, 1478-1535*, ed. Richard S. Sylvester, vol. 3 Yale University Press, 1976.

Sir Thomas More himself seems to have felt doubtful of the facts he relates. He prefaces his account of the murder of the Princes by these remarkable words: 'whose death and final infortune hath notheless so far come in question, that some yet remain in doubt whether they were in Richard's days destroyed or no' (More, p. 126). Again, in detailing the tradition of their death, he admits that the reports were numerous and that even the most plausible rested on report alone. 'I shall rehearse you the dolorous end of those babes, not after every way that I have heard, but after that way that I have so heard by such men and by such means as me thinketh it were hard but it should be true'.

Internal evidence in More's History confirms Buck's assertion that it was written by John Morton. Morton had united with Hastings against Richard, as Lord Protector, and had goaded Buckingham to open rebellion. Morton deserted Buckingham, as soon as he had weaned him from the allegiance to Richard, and escaped to the Continent when Buckingham's rebellion failed. It must therefore be apparent that Morton is a highly prejudiced witness and that his testimony is unsatisfactory and unreliable.

Inconsistencies of More's Story : The more closely we examine More's story of the alleged murder of the young Princes, the more inconsistent it appears from the very beginning:

Richard had been proclaimed and annointed King with almost unparalleled unanimity. He had no reason to fear the claims of his nephews, who had been declared illegitimate.

If Richard had decided to murder the Princes, he would have done so before leaving the Tower for Greenwich and Windsor. Otherwise he would have to commit his order to paper and thus entrust a design so destructive to his reputation to a common messenger on the chance of its falling into his enemies hands.

Richard was a wise and cautious Prince, evidently striving for popularity and desirous, by his regal acts, to soften any feeling of discontent because of his accession. Would such a person be likely to lay himself open to a charge of murder, especially when the oath had scarcely faded from his lips by which he pledged himself to preserve the lives of the princes? 'He promised me, on his fidelity, laying his hand on mine, at Baynard's Castle, that the two young princes should live, and that he would so provide for them and so maintain them in honourable estate, that I and all the realm ought, and should be content' (Grafton, *Cont. More*, p. 154).

Would anyone with common foresight have risked two letters which might serve as positive proof of an act which would result in the hatred of his kindred and the detestation of the kingdom?

More says one letter was sent by an ordinary attendant, 'one John Green', to Brackenbury, commanding Sir Robert to 'put the two children to death'. The other letter, according to More, was sent by Sir James Tyrrel to Brackenbury, commanding him to deliver to Sir James the keys of the Tower that he might accomplish the very crime which Brackenbury had previously refused himself to perform. 'And has any trace of such a document been discovered?' asks the historian of the Tower. 'Never', he adds, 'it has been anxiously sought for, but sought in vain; and we may conclude that Sir Thomas More's is nothing but one of the passing tales of the day' (Bayley's *Hist. of the Tower*, part i, p. 64).

Was it probable that facts known to so many unprincipled men should never have been narrated until 1513, after a lapse of thirty years? Yet it was at this distance of time that More's history was written. Green, Brackenbury, Tyrrel and the page; Forest, Dighton, Slaughter, and the priest of the Tower — these individuals could have implicated or cleared King Richard if the accusation of murder had been made by his enemies during his lifetime.

Why didn't Henry VII, upon his accession, either expose the villainy or punish the reputed murderers of the two brothers of his betrothed Queen?

Why was no mention of the murder 'made in the very act of Parliament that attainted King Richard himself, and which, could it have been verified, would have been the most heinous aggravation of his crimes?' (Walpole, p. 59.)

Sir Thomas More says that King Richard took 'great displeasure' at Sir Robert Brackenbury's refusal to murder the two Princes. Is this borne out by Richard's subsequent conduct, as proved by existing records? Did he remove Brackenbury from the office of governor or otherwise show his anger against him? On the contrary, throughout the whole of his reign, Richard bestowed honors and emoluments upon Sir Robert. Brackenbury did serve Richard, but not as a midnight assassin in a secret chamber. When he received the call in August 1485, he rushed north to Bosworth and died fighting bravely — not for Henry but for Richard.

Tyrrel's Role : Sir James Tyrrel, the other leading personage in the reputed tragedy, has been even more obviously misrepresented than Sir Robert Brackenbury. Instead of being an obscure person who had to be recommended to Richard by a page in waiting, he was a great officer of the crown under Edward V and Richard III. His prowess had been rewarded by Richard possibly before the page was born. So far from Tyrrel being created a simple knight by King Richard for murdering his royal nephews, he bore that distinction full ten years previously.

At the identical period when, according to More's story, an obscure page advanced the interests of 'a man who lay without in the pallet chamber' (More, p. 128), the person in question — Tyrrel — was Master of the King's pages! As such, he held a position of great trust, personally attending King Richard and keeping guard in the outchamber as long as the monarch was stirring. As one of King Richard's bodyguards and counsellors (Harl. MSS. 433, fol. 40), 'Tyrrel's situation was not that in which Sir Thomas More represents him; he was of an ancient and high family, had long before received the honour of knighthood, and engaged the office of master of the horse'. In this capacity he walked at King Richard's coronation (Bayley's *Hist. of the Tower*, vol. i. p. 62; see also Walpole's Reply to Dr. Milles, *Archaeologia* for 1770).

Sir James Tyrrel, instead of being an object of execration, continued unblemished in reputation. He was honored and trusted, not only by Richard III, but by his rival, Henry VII. Henry appointed him Governor of Guisnes and nominated him, even after Warbeck's appearance and honorable reception at Paris, one of the royal commissioners for completing a treaty with France (Laing, in *Henry*, vol. xii, p. 446). Henry VII, although wanting to prove the fact of the murders, neither accuses Sir James of the act in his public declaration nor gives any foundation whatever throughout his reign for a rumor that rests on no other grounds than common report (see Bacon's *Henry VII*, p. 125; Walpole's *Hist. Doubts*, p. 57; Laing in *Henry*, vol. xii, p. 446).

Henry committed Tyrrel to the Tower in 1502, not to be examined on the death of the two Princes, but on the escape of their cousin, the persecuted Edmund, Duke of Suffolk. Edmund was the eldest surviving son of Elizabeth, Duchess of Suffolk, sister of Edward IV and Richard III. His elder brother, John, Earl of Lincoln, was slain in the battle of Stoke (1487) and had therefore been attainted in Parliament. Edmund, the second son, was entitled to the honors and estates on the death of his father, the Duke of Suffolk. But Henry VII, jealous of all kindred of the House of York, deprived Edmund most unjustly of his inheritance on the frivolous pretence of considering him the heir of his attainted brother, rather than the inheritor of his father's titles and possessions (Rot. Parl., vi, p. 474).

For aiding the flight of this unfortunate Prince, the eldest surviving nephew of Edward IV and Richard III, Henry VII executed Sir James

Tyrrel, Friday, May 6, 1502. Tyrrel's death proves his devotion to the House of York. It disproves, as far as recorded proofs of fidelity can disprove gossip and rumor, More's picture of Tyrrel as a hireling assassin a cool, calculating, heartless murderer. As for the unfortunate Edmund, he wandered for years over France and Germany in abject penury (Sandford, *Geneal. Hist.*, book v, p. 379).

Curious History of More's 'Confession' : There is one point on which the entire guilt or innocence of Richard III may be permitted to rest. More says that Tyrrel and Dighton made the confession so craftily put out by Henry VII, although not officially disclosed by his command. How was it then that More, bred to the law and familiar with judicial proceedings, did not use this proof of Richard's criminality and of Tyrrel's and Dighton's revolting conduct, not only as one of '*many reports*', but as affording *evidence of the FACT*?

'If Dighton and Tyrrel confessed the murder in the reign of Henry VII, how could even the outlines be a secret, and uncertain, in the reign of Henry VIII? Is it credible that they owned the fact, and concealed every one of the circumstances? If they related those circumstances, without which their confession could gain no manner of belief, could Sir Thomas More, Chancellor of Henry VIII, and educated in the house of the Prime Minister of Henry VII (John Morton) be ignorant of what it was so much the interest of Cardinal Morton to tell, and of Henry VII to have known and ascertained?' (Walpole's *Supplement of Hist. Doubts*, p. 215.)

Fabyan lived and wrote at the precise time when these events are said to have occurred. However, he neither records the examination nor the alleged confession, although he expressly mentions Tyrrel's imprisonment and execution for helping Suffolk to escape (p. 533).

On no other ground, then, than one of the passing tales of those days was Sir James Tyrrel alleged to have made a confession. And the alleged confession was never published or imputed to him until after he had excited Henry VII's jealousy and had been executed for reputed treason against the Tudor race and acknowledged fidelity to the house of York.

From Mere Report to Asserted Fact : The high reputation of Lord Chancellor More gave an interest and force to More's narrative that led to its adoption by succeeding chroniclers, without the slightest regard for the truth or consistency of the tale. It was dramatized by Shakespeare, gravely recorded by Lord Bacon, and passed gradually from *mere report* to *asserted fact*. More's tale has for ages been perpetuated as truth by historians who felt more inclined to embellish their writings with the 'tragedyous story' than to involve themselves in the labor of research.

'The experience of every age justifies the great historian of Greece (Thucydides, lib. i. c. 20), in the conclusion to which he was led by his attempts to ascertain the grounds on which so much idle fable had been received as truth by his countrymen: Men will not take the trouble to search after truth, if anything like it is ready to their hands' (Hind's *'Rise and Progress of Christianity'*, vol. ii, p. 58).

No proof is known to exist of Richard being involved in any violence against his nephews. Contemporary accounts afford no basis for accusations irreconcilable with Richard's previous high character and unblemished reputation. His evil reputation is not justified by the contradictory reports by his political enemies or by the prejudiced evidence against him. 'No prince could well have a better character than Richard till he came to be protector and dethroned his nephew. This action, and the views of the Lancastrian faction, gave birth to the calumnies with which he was loaded' (Carte's *Hist. Eng.*, vol. ii, book xiii, p. 818).

Thus, tradition (based on rumors reported by More) has convicted a King of England — a Plantagenet by birth and descent, and the last of a noble and gallant race — of horrible crimes on alleged proofs which are inconclusive and unsupported.

Probable Origin of the Tradition : Has any other English sovereign been convicted on such shallow evidence? Does such odium as attaches to Richard III attach to these monarchs:

King Henry I usurped his brother's rights and caused him fearful suffering.

King John wrested the throne from his nephew and has been suspected of killing him with his own hand.

Edward III, Henry IV, Edward IV, Henry VII, Henry VIII, and Queen Elizabeth are implicated in the cruel execution of dethroned rivals of princely opponents.

Why is it then that Richard III has been cursed as the basest of men and the most ruthless of Kings? Because he was succeeded by the founder of a new dynasty — one who had no right to the throne and had succeeded by treachery. It was therefore to Henry VII's interest to load Richard III with the vilest calumnies and to encourage every report that could blacken his memory (*Carte*, vol. ii. book xiii. p. 818).

Hence later chroniclers, to court the favor of Henry VII and his posterity, adopted as real facts reports based on rumors. They transmitted Richard III to future ages in the most detestable light. From mental depravity they passed to personal deformity 'representing him as crooked and deformed, though all ancient pictures drawn of him show the contrary' (Ibid.). He may have been guilty of the murder of his two nephews but no evidence is on record. No more substantial basis exists for the accusation than the envenomed shaft of political malice.

Mysterious indeed is the fate of the young Princes, and so it is likely to remain. However, it is already admitted that 'the personal monster whom Sir Thomas More and Shakespeare exhibited has vanished'. All advocates of political truth should therefore suspend judgement in a case which has so long darkened the royal annals of England — a case based on rumors and political distortions wholly at variance with the loyalty, ability, wisdom, and character which marked the early life and the reign of King Richard III.

PART 2: SOURCES OTHER THAN HALSTED

Horace Walpole

Walpole says that the picture of Richard III, as drawn by historians, is a character formed by prejudice and invention. Shakespeare's tragedy is not a true representation.

The prime source from which all later historians have taken their materials for the reign of Richard III is Sir Thomas More. Grafton then copied him verbatum as did Holinshed, Shakespeare's source. Grafton tells us in a marginal note that More was only an undersheriff of London when he wrote his History. It covers only a few months in 1483, and he left it unfinished and unpublished. More was born in 1478 and thus, was only *five* when Richard ascended the throne. He wrote his history in 1513, thirty years after the events he narrates (See Chapter IV).

Buck says that More's informant was John Morton, Bishop of Ely, whom Henry VII rewarded by making him Archbishop of Canterbury in 1486, Lord Chancellor in 1487, and Cardinal in 1493. Morton was foremost in the effort to dethrone Richard III and crown Henry Tudor. Could More have drawn from a more corrupt source?

More's account cannot be true. It is full of notorious falsehoods and inconsistencies and there is still no proof that the two Princes were actually murdered.

No inquiry was made into their alleged murders on Henry Tudor's accession. Although such murders would have been the blackest of the crimes charged to Richard, the act of Henry's Parliament attainting Richard does not even mention them.

Two of England's greatest men used their talents to blacken Richard III and to praise a tyrant. More adopted the hearsay and rumors of Henry VII's times. Lord Bacon praised Henry — a King whose nearest approach to wisdom was mean cunning — a sordid usurper. Henry was a mean husband and King. He cheated and oppressed his subjects, bartered England's honor for foreign gold, and eliminated every possible rival for the crown to insure possession of his no-title.

Walpole says that he can neither entirely acquit Richard in the disappearance of the two Princes nor condemn him, because there are no proofs on either side. But a court of justice would absolve Richard because of this lack of evidence.

Gairdner : James Gairdner spent 47 years in the Public Records Office in London. He entered in 1846 and served as assistant Keeper of the Public Records, 1859-1893. He made important contributions to English history. He acknowledged the prejudiced sources, the lack of evidence, and the many inconsistencies of the Lancastrian and Tudor chronicles. Yet, he preferred to rely on tradition and concluded that he had 'no doubt, therefore, that the dreadful deed was done' (*Richard the Third*, pp. 119-127).

He believed, however, that Buckingham had a guilty knowledge (*Letters and Papers*, Book II, Preface).

Markham : Henry VII effectively silenced all comment and destroyed all evidence, such as the Titulus Regius, favorable to Richard III. He employed writers to publish his version of the events leading to his accession to the throne. Shakespeare used their stories — his only source — to write his play. Nothing contrary to the official line was allowed to be printed or said for 160 years. Markham notes Gairdner's weak reasoning and, in the main, follows Walpole (pp. 167-169, 178, 207, 232, 235, 239, 283, 286, 301).

The Complete Peerage (See also Chapter XX). The Editor of the Complete Peerage says that the major reasons for charging *Richard III* with the death of the two Princes are that —

the Princes disappeared while in Richard's custody;

he regarded them as a threat while they were alive; and

the bones found in the Tower in 1674 were presumed to be those of the Princes.

The major reasons for charging *Henry VII* with their death are as follows, *First*, when he became King, Henry Tudor tried to blacken Richard's memory by charging him with every possible crime. The Act which Henry's Parliament passed (Rot. Parl., vol. vi, p. 276) catalogs Richard's alleged crimes. But it does not charge Richard with what would have been the worst crime — the murder of the two Princes. The Act does not even mention them.

Second, the Princes' mother, Elizabeth Woodville, entrusted her five daughters to Richard's care in March 1484, and they attended his court functions. She even advised Dorset, her son by her first marriage, to return to Richard's side, and he tried unsuccessfully to do so. Would the Queen and Dorset have taken these actions if Richard had murdered the Princes?

The freedom enjoyed by the Princes' sisters indicates that Richard did *not* regard them as threats *while their brothers lived*. Yet, if the boys had been murdered, their claims would have passed to their sisters, and they *would* have been a threat to Richard.

Henry VII's Motive : Henry's Parliament repealed the Act (the *Titulus Regius*) which had declared the two Princes to be bastards. Parliament's action legitimised the boys and made the elder King of England, *if he were alive*. In this case, their eldest sister Elizabeth could not head the House of York. Thus, *Henry* had a powerful motive to kill the two Princes, so that Elizabeth could represent the House of York and Henry could succeed in his purpose to unite the Houses of York and Lancaster by marrying her.

The Bones : The essential points are as follows:

The bones found in the Tower in July 1674 were not interred in the marble urn in Westminster Abbey until 1678, *four years later*.

When the urn was opened on July 6, 1933, the bones of *birds* and *animals* were discovered, as well as human bones.

It is uncertain whether the bones interred in *1678* were the bones found in *1674*.

It is medically *not* possible to identify with certainty the human bones found in the urn as being those of the two Princes, (and carbon-dating is not precise enough).

Conclusion : The Editor joins the authorities cited on the last pages of this chapter in dismissing More's story as not worthy of serious consideration. He concludes that the case against Richard III is 'not proven'. (See '*The Princes in the Tower*', *The Complete Peerage*, vol. XII, Part II, ed. Geoffrey H. White, Appendix J, pp. 32, 39, Pitman Periodicals Ltd., successors to St. Catherine Press Ltd., London, 1959.)

Kendall : Kendall observes that, despite hundreds of years of debate, we have no proof that Richard III murdered his two nephews. The only 'evidence' we have is unsupported and conflicting statements from highly prejudiced or uninformed sources. No court of law would convict Richard on the available evidence.

Kendall believes the boys were killed by one of three men — Richard III, Henry VII, or the Duke of Buckingham. The only evidence supplied by *contemporary* sources (Mancini, Guillaume de Rochefort — Chancellor of France, and the Second Continuation of the Croyland Chronicle) is that there were suspicions shortly after Richard was crowned. Also, Buckingham's lieutenants spread rumors of their deaths. The three *intermediate* sources, Fabyan's New Chronicles, the Great Chronicle, and John Rous *Historia Regum Angliae*, add nothing but rumor and suspicion.

The principal testimony from *Tudor* sources comes from More and Vergil. Both are unreliable. More's tale, especially, is not credible. Kendall repeats the same points Halsted made about Sir James Tyrell's alleged confession and about Sir Robert Brackenbury.

As contrasted with the above, there are several major indications that Richard did not murder the two Princes. *First*, relying on Richard's public oath of March 1, 1484, to treat the Queen Dowager and her daughters well if they would come out of sanctuary, the Queen entrusted her five daughters to Richard's care. No complaints were ever made of Richard's treatment of them. The girls appeared at Richard's court, and Richard gave his former enemy, the Queen, a larger annuity and more freedom than her son-in-law, Henry VII, gave her later.

Second, Kendall mentions the Queen's action appealing to her son by her first marriage, the Marquis of Dorset, to leave Henry Tudor and return to England and Richard's court. He tried to do so.

Third, Henry Tudor's actions also indicate that Richard did not murder the Queen's two sons. To paint Richard as a villain and to make himself more secure on the throne, it was important to Henry to prove that Richard had murdered the boys. But the Bill of Attainder enacted by Henry's first Parliament fails to charge Richard with this crime — the worst that could be charged against Richard. Nor did Henry ever press any investigation of the alleged murders.

Fourth, Henry did his best to suppress all evidence of the pre-contract and Parliament's confirmation of Richard's title to the throne by having his first Parliament order the destruction of all copies of the *Titulus Regius* — the Parliamentary Roll revealing that Edward IV's children were bastards and settling the crown upon Richard.

Fifth, Henry waited from 1485 to 1502 — 17 years — when he 'gave out', after Sir James Tyrrel's execution in 1502, that Tyrrel had confessed to the crime. But Henry VII's own historian, Polydore Vergil, writing about 1517-18, and his own biographer, André, writing in 1503, evidently did not believe the alleged confession. They never even mentioned it.

Sixth, the Tudor historians either do not mention the precontract or give false accounts.

Who did kill the Princes, if Richard III and Henry VII didn't? Gairdner refers to Buckingham's 'guilty knowledge'. Kendall goes further, believing that *Buckingham* could have been the culprit. He stayed on a few days in London after Richard started on his progress north. Buckingham had the power as Constable of England, and stronger motives than Richard to kill the boys.

Buckingham's guilt would explain several apparent mysteries. *First*, it would explain the otherwise puzzling actions of the Princes' mother in giving up her daughters to Richard in March 1484 and repeatedly urging her son, the Marquis of Dorset, to leave Henry Tudor and join Richard III. *Second*, it would also explain why Brackenbury steadfastly supported Richard and died for him at Bosworth. *Third*, it would likewise explain why Henry, in February 1487, deprived Elizabeth Woodville of her possessions, put her in a nunnery, and placed her son Dorset in custody until after the battle of Stoke because apparently the Queen Dowager aided Simnel's cause. Her action seems as incomprehensible as her release of her daughters to Richard, since Simnel's success would dethrone her daughter — unless she knew that Buckingham had murdered her sons. *Fourth*, it would explain why Henry did not accuse Richard of the murders in either his letters to his supporters before his landing at Milford Haven or in the Bill of Attainder against Richard (pp. 219, 286-288, and Appendix 1).

Jacob : E.F. Jacob, professor of history at Oxford University in his scholarly *The Fifteenth Century* (Oxford, 1961), gives us important perspective on Richard III. He cautions us not to dwell only on the two Princes. Whilst it is a fascinating mystery, it is only part of Richard's story. He adds that history's past condemnation of King Richard III should not prejudice and color our view of the earlier events of his life leading to his ascending the throne.

History and Shakespeare's play were based essentially on Sir Thomas More's story about Sir James Tyrrel's alleged confession to murdering the two Princes at Richard's direction. Here, Professor Jacob's view is most important. He joins Bacon, Walpole, Kendall and others in concluding that *More's story is discredited*, (pp. 609, 610, 624).

With the collapse of More's testimony, the principal 'evidence' against King Richard III crumbles. But colorful stories have long lives even if untrue, and if they also damage reputations they are practically imperishable.

Chapter XV

RICHARD QUELLS BUCKINGHAM'S REBELLION

Duke of Buckingham rebels

The entire reign of King Richard III is composed of such startling events that it more resembles a highly-colored romance than events of real life. Perhaps no event in Richard's remarkable career is more strange than the insurrection of the Duke of Buckingham.

No one appears to have been more thoroughly ignorant of Buckingham's deep game than the King himself. Richard did not merit Buckingham's enmity. Many documents attest Richard's generosity and the honorable fulfillment of his promises to that nobleman. Rous, the contemporary of both Richard and Buckingham, states the King conferred vast treasures on the Duke. It seems that vanity and inordinate ambition were the true causes of the Duke of Buckingham's perfidious conduct to his royal kinsman. Buckingham is reputed to have taken offense at King Richard's refusing him the Hereford lands (More, p. 136). Documents effectually disprove this allegation. Nothing can be more forcibly worded than were the letters patent (Harl. MSS, 433. fol. 107) 'for restoring to Henry Stafford Duke of Buckingham, the purpartie of the estate of Humfrey Bohun late Earl of Hereford . . .'. This was followed by 'a cedule, or particular of this purpartie, amounting to a great sum yearly' (Ibid.).

Buckingham had been the active instrument in raising Richard to the throne. As a joint descendant from King Edward III he could ill brook to bear the train of a Prince for whom he had secured a crown. Buckingham felt humbled when the Duke of Norfolk carried the crown, the Earl of Surrey the sword of state, and Lord Stanley the much coveted mace of constableship. True, Buckingham was appointed to high office immediately after the coronation, in addition to receiving the de Bohun lands. 'On the 13th of July, in the first year of Richard III, Henry Stafford, Duke of Buckingham, had livery of all those lands whereunto he pretended a right by descent as cousin and heir of blood to Humfrey de Bohun, Earl of Hereford and constable of England; and within two days after was advanced to the high and great office of constable of England . . . '. (Edmondson's *Constables of England*, p. 30.)

Gairdner : Richard's sign manual promised Buckingham a full restitution in the next Parliament and gave him the profits of the Bohun lands from the preceding Easter 'unto the time he be thereto restored by authority of Parliament'. The matter was therefore incomplete, and Buckingham doubted Richard's good faith and despaired of his promises (p. 107. Also see Legge, vol. 2, p. 8).

Kendall : Richard was entirely reasonable in making his grant provisional. Henry VI's share of the Bohun estate was forfeited to the Yorkist crown by parliamentary confiscation, when Parliament attainted Henry in 1461. Therefore, only Parliament could reverse Henry's attainder, as it applied to the Bohun lands (p. 250).

Conspiracy to place Henry Tudor on throne

There is no doubt that the Duke of Buckingham and John Morton entered into a compact in favor of Henry Tudor, and that the southern counties were on the eve of open rebellion to release the young Princes from the Tower (Chron. Croy., p. 567). The two conspirators at Breacknock Castle felt assured that, as soon as a report circulated that the Princes were dead, the insurgents would readily fall into the plot to crown Henry. Morton was violently opposed to King Richard. He hailed with delight any proposal that would shake the stability of the new King and give ultimate hope of uniting the lineage of York and Lancaster (Grafton, p. 160). A trusty messenger, Reginald Bray, was sent to Lord Stanley's wife, the Countess of Richmond, informing her of the high destiny contemplated for her son, Henry Tudor, and requiring her cooperation in the plot. Lady Margaret willingly undertook to break the matter to the widowed Queen and Elizabeth, the young Princess, both still in sanctuary at Westminster (Grafton, p. 162). Dr. Lewis, a physician of great repute, attached to the household of the Countess, was instructed to condole with the Queen on the reported deaths of her sons, and to propose a restoration of the crown to her surviving offspring by the marriage of the Princess Royal, Elizabeth, with Henry Tudor (Ibid.). The Queen entered into the scheme with alacrity, provided always that Henry would solemnly swear 'to espouse and take to wife the Lady Elizabeth, or else the Lady Cecily,

189

if her eldest sister should not be living' (Grafton, p. 166). The Countess returned to the dwelling place of her husband, Lord Stanley, in London. Daily communication passed between the Countess and the Queen in sanctuary through Dr. Lewis. A powerful ally of Buckingham, Hugh Conway, Esquire, with Christopher Urswick, Lady Margaret's confessor, were speedily sent to Brittany 'with a great sum of money' (Grafton, p. 166) to tell Henry Tudor about the fair prospect that had dawned for him.

In the west country, Buckingham and Bishop Morton exerted themselves with equal zeal and determination. But the wily prelate took advantage of the trust reposed in him by Buckingham. Stealthily departing from Breacknock Castle, he proceeded secretly to his see of Ely where he secured both money and partisans. He escaped to France and joining Henry Tudor, devoted himself to Henry's cause during the remainder of Richard's reign (Ibid. p. 163).

Buckingham was greatly mortified by Morton's treachery, but he was now too deeply involved in his scheme. He soon collected sufficient forces to enable him to cooperate with Henry of Richmond. These secret schemes were carried out during King Richard's progress from Warwick to York. On September 24, 1483, a few days after Richard's return to Pontefract, Buckingham directed Henry to land in England on October 18 (Rot. Parl., vi, p. 245), on which day the conspirators had arranged to rise.

Croyland Chronicle: '. . . a rumour was spread that the sons of King Edward before-named had died a violent death, but it was uncertain how. Accordingly, all those who had set on foot this insurrection, seeing that if they could find no one to take the lead in their designs, the ruin of all would speedily ensue, turned their thoughts to Henry, Earl of Richmond . . . '. (p. 491)

Henry Tudor, Earl of Richmond

Henry had no real claim to the throne. He was the illegitimate descendant of John of Gaunt. *(See Appendix III for chart.)*

John of Gaunt had three wives. His first wife was Blanche, heiress of Lancaster, by whom he acquired the title, Duke of Lancaster. By Blanche he had two daughters and one son (afterward King Henry IV, the founder of the Lancastrian dynasty). By his second wife, Constance of Castile, he had one daughter. His third wife, Katherine Swynford, was previously his mistress. She bore him three sons and one daughter, Joan, all born out of wedlock. They were surnamed De Beaufort, from the place of their birth.

The eldest son was John, afterward Earl of Somerset. His son John, Duke of Somerset, was the father of Margaret Beaufort, Countess of Richmond. Joan married Ralph Neville, Earl of Westmoreland, and was the mother of Cecily, Duchess of York, the mother of Edward IV and Richard III. (The other two sons were Henry, the renowned Cardinal Beaufort, Bishop of Winchester, and Thomas, Duke of Exeter and Chancellor of England.)

These four children were eventually legitimated by an Act of Richard II's Parliament. Henry IV, however, added a special reservation, excluding them from succession to the crown: 'We do, in the fulness of our royal power, and by the assent of parliament, by the tenor of these presents empower you to be raised, promoted, elected, assume, and be admitted to all honours, dignities (*except to the royal dignity*) . . . '. (Rot. Parl. vol. iii, p. 343.)

Thus, Henry Tudor could not claim the throne through his *mother, Margaret Beaufort*, because the Beauforts were barred from the crown by the above Act of Parliament.

Henry's descent through his *father* was equally corrupt. Henry V's widow, Katherine of Valois, only daughter of Charles VI of France, had a secret liaison with *Owen Tudor*, a clerk in the wardrobe of her household. He afterward claimed he had married her, but never produced any proof. (In any event, the marriage would have been illegal, since he had never applied for citizenship.) This ill-advised union produced three sons and one daughter. *Edmund Tudor*, the eldest son, married Margaret Beaufort when she was only fourteen. Their son was Henry Tudor, afterward King Henry VII.

Thus Henry Tudor could not claim the throne through his *father, Edmund Tudor*, because Edmund's father, *Owen Tudor*, could produce no proof of a lawful wedding with Queen Katherine.

Jasper Tudor, the second son of Owen Tudor and Queen Katherine, was a chief agent in preserving Henry Tudor's life and subsequently elevating him to the throne.

At the brief restoration of King Henry VI, Henry Tudor was fourteen. He was completing his education at Eton when the Battle of Tewkesbury reestablished the race of York on the throne and ruined the Lancastrian cause. He was secretly taken from England by his uncle, Jasper Tudor. A furious storm cast the fugitives upon the shores of Brittany. Here, the reigning Duke detained Henry as a state prisoner up to the period when his mother sought Buckingham's intercession to effect his release and obtain a pardon from Richard III.

Because of the special reservation of the royal dignity in the patent of legitimation, the Yorkist dynasty appears to have needlessly feared danger from the captured Henry Tudor. But a deadly feud had existed between Richard, Duke of York, father of Edward IV, and John, Duke of Somerset, grandfather of Henry, Earl of Richmond, and the exile was a subject of suspicion and hated by the House of York. Henry VI's affection for Henry Tudor, and young Henry's distinguished position as the nephew of the reigning monarch, Henry VI, linked him closely with the Lancastrian dynasty. Yorkist apprehensions were strengthened after the Battle of Tewkesbury had extinguished the royal line of Lancaster.

Edward IV made many efforts to obtain possession of the attainted Henry, sending costly presents and offering great sums to Francis, Duke of Brittany (Philip de Comines, p. 516). These overtures failing, King Edward, after a few years, adopted a different course. Voicing sympathy for Henry and a desire to bury past differences, Edward sent ambassadors to sue for Henry's release and offered him the hand of his eldest daughter, Princess Elizabeth (Cott. MSS., Dom. A. xviii).

This subtle device almost cost Henry his life, for the Duke of Brittany consented to release his captive. Happily, however, for Henry the plot was made known to him. Escaping into sanctuary, he eluded his enemies (Lobineau, *l'Histoire de Britagne*, vol, i, p. 751). Custody of Henry was a constant source of wealth to Francis of Brittany because of Edward IV's bribes. And Henry was a hostage for unbroken and friendly alliance with England. Therefore, Francis again tendered his protection to Henry of Richmond. He left sanctuary on receiving a pledge that, although he must still be considered a state prisoner, he would no longer be rigorously confined. At Edward IV's death, the attainted Earl had been a captive for thirteen years.

Henry's hopes of liberation were crushed by Richard III's decisive measures immediately after his accession to the throne. One of Richard's first acts was to send costly presents to Francis and his court, renewing the existing treaty and stipulating for Henry's continued imprisonment. Such was Henry's position when 'The Duke of Buckingham, by the advice of the Bishop of Ely, his prisoner at Breaknock, sent to him to hasten to England as soon as he could, to have to wife Elizabeth, elder daughter of the deceased king, and together with her, possession of all the realm' (Cont. Croy., p. 568).

The presence of John Morton, Bishop of Ely, inspired Henry with confidence, and he sought the assistance of Francis, Duke of Brittany. While the recent compact between Francis and Richard III prevented Francis from sanctioning the enterprise, the Duke promised not to oppose it. The vast sums of money sent Henry by his mother enabled him to enlist in his cause many exiled followers of Henry VI, with high military reputation, who had lingered in poverty for years. Henry then pledged to arrive in England by the day fixed for the uprising, October 18, 1483.

Markham : The title, Earl of Richmond, was given to Richard after Henry Tudor's father, Edmund, was attainted, and the title merged in the crown. Therefore, Henry is rightfully referred to as *calling* himself Earl of Richmond (p. 133).

Kendall : Henry Tudor's grandfather, Owen Tudor, came from lowly sources, his father being the Bishop of Bangor's butler. When Henry VI's council discovered the liaison between Owen and Henry V's widow, Queen Katherine, when she died in 1437, they clapped Owen in prison (pp. 156, 157).

Richard III takes precautionary measures

'The conspiracy', says the Croyland Chronicler (p. 508), 'by means of spies was well known to Richard, who . . . with great alacrity and with the greatest vigilance' moved to impede Henry's progress. It is noteworthy that Buckingham, the reputed avenger of the Princes' alleged murder, did not advocate the Earl of Warwick or the Princess Elizabeth. Instead, he selected as successor to the throne an illegitimate scion of the extinct House of Lancaster. Why he did so is a mystery.

Richard felt Buckingham's treachery keenly, as recorded in a postscript in his own handwriting to a letter addressed to the Lord Chancellor, John Russell, Bishop of Lincoln, October 12, 1483: '. . . Here, loved be God, is all well, and truly determined, and for to resist the malice of him that had best cause to be true, the Duke of Buckingham, — the most untrue creature living: whom with God's grace we shall not be long 'till that we will be in that parts, and subdue his malice. We assure you there was never falser traitor . . . '. A few days previously, Richard is stated to have invited Buckingham's personal attendance, to learn the truth of a report he could not bring himself to believe. Buckingham avowed his perfidy by refusing to attend the royal summons.

Richard sent a letter to the York authorities requiring their aid, and proclaimed Buckingham a traitor. When Richard arrived at Leicester on October 21, the greater part of the kingdom was in rebellion, led by the Marquis of Dorset, the Bishop of Exeter and his brother Sir Edward Courtney, and Sir Richard Guildford. Henry sailed from Brittany on October 12, with 500 Bretons and forty ships, hoping to land at Plymouth on October 18, as instructed.

Richard moved promptly. He issued a proclamation at Leicester, offering £1,000, or £100 a year for life, on the capture of Buckingham. The marches of Wales were guarded by trusty bands of soldiers, and vessels of war were stationed to keep a careful watch in the channel.

Buckingham's rebellion collapses

A series of misadventures brought to a speedy close the turbulent career of the capricious Buckingham. On October 18, Buckingham assumed command of the Welsh rebels. Proceeding from Breacknock Castle, he rapidly reached the city of Gloucester where he intended to cross the Severn. He then planned to march southward and join the army raised in the west by the Courtneys. But during the Duke's progress through Wales violent storms and a continual rain of ten days had caused the Severn to overflow its banks. Bridges collapsed, fords became impassable, and cattle drowned. The ensuing scarcity of provisions increased his followers' privations, and he was unable to join his confederates or communicate with them.

Buckingham was reluctantly obliged to yield to the clamors of his soldiers, who murmured at being 'without money, victual or wages', (Grafton, p. 173), and return to Weobly (Chron. Croy., p. 568). Dispirited at the failure of the enterprise, the Welshmen departed to their homes. For all the Duke's fair promises, threatenings, and enforcements, they would 'in no wise neither go farther nor abide'. Richard's proclamation, offering so large a reward for Buckingham's capture and threatening severe penalties for his concealment, completed the measure of his misfortune. He found himself so closely watched that he could 'on no side make his egress with safety' (Chron. Croy., p. 568).

Finding his situation so desperate, Buckingham suddenly left his associates and departed from Weobly in disguise. First, however, he provided for the concealment of his infant heir, Lord Stafford. He sought shelter in the dwelling of Humphrey Banastre, at Lacon near

Shrewsbury. Here he hoped to find a sure but temporary asylum with a follower 'whom he above all men loved, favoured, and trusted' (Grafton, p. 173). 'One thousand pounds, or one hundred a year for life' was a stimulus that urged numbers to find Buckingham. 'Whereof hearing', states Fabyan, 'the foresaid Banastre, were it for need of the same reward, or fear of losing of his life and goods, discovered him to be taken, and so brought into Salisbury, where the king then laid.' (p. 517).

How far Banastre merits the obloquy on his memory is hard to say. Certainly, the Croyland Chronicler's account renders it doubtful whether, at least in the first instance, he was accessory to Buckingham's capture (p. 568). There can be little doubt, however, after a careful review of the whole matter, that Buckingham sought Banastre's protection too late for any human being to shelter him. Banastre, to save himself and his family from destruction, was compelled eventually to sanction the capture of one whose retreat, according to the Croyland Chronicler, was already tracked.

Buckingham's capture and execution

Buckingham was speedily captured by Thomas Mytton, the sheriff of Shropshire (Fabyan, p. 517; Hall, p. 395; Grafton, p. 175) and delivered into Richard's hands (Stafford MSS. in Blakeway, p. 241) by Sir James Tyler, at Salisbury, November 2, 1483. From the large share of Buckingham's wealth then given Sir James Tyrrel, he probably was the individual who delivered the captive to Richard. The early writers were careless, misspelling the names both of Banaster and the sheriff, and they probably caused Tyrrel's name to be misspelled Tyler.

The last act contemplated by Buckingham should sufficiently expose his deadly malice toward the King. The captive reached Salisbury on Sunday, November 2, notwithstanding which Richard, in conformity with the usage of those times, commanded his immediate execution. The Duke earnestly besought, as his dying request, a personal interview with Richard (Fabyan, p. 517) which he denied. Richard's apparent severity was amply justified in after years by the Duke's own son. He admitted that his father had secreted a knife on his person intending to spring upon the King when in the act of prostrating himself to sue for pardon (Herbert's Henry VIII, p. 110). Within a few hours of his arrival at Salisbury, Buckingham was beheaded without trial. His remains, deprived of the head and right arm, the customary sentence of rebellion at that period, are said to have been recently (about 1844) discovered on the site of a very ancient inn which tradition says was built on the spot where the execution took place (Sir R.C. Hoare's *Hist. of Wiltshire*, p. 207).

The fearful storms which led to Buckingham's defeat proved equally disastrous to Henry Tudor. His fleet was scattered and threatened with destruction. After narrowly escaping capture, he was compelled to seek refuge in France with the appalling news of his total defeat and Buckingham's death (Chron. Croy., p. 570). The conspiracy was now ended, its leaders being either in sanctuary, concealment, or escaped in vessels bound for the continent. The few that were captured received no mercy. Richard felt that the stability of his throne depended upon the firmness with which he handled the rebels. In executing the chief conspirators, Richard acted only in accordance with the practice of those times. The very small number who were executed contrasts markedly with the action of Edward IV and Margaret of Anjou on similar occasions.

King Richard returns in triumph

King Richard reached Winchester on November 26, 1483, as evidenced by a remarkable document which shows his principles of justice even to the humblest of his subjects. He signed a warrant to discharge from the office of Privy Seal a chief clerk who had secured his position by bribery, to the discouragement of the under clerks who saw a stranger 'never brought up in the said office put them by of their promotion'. The King then awarded the vacancy to the oldest and most diligent of the under clerks 'for his experience and long continuance in the same' (Harl. MSS. 433. fol. 123). These original memorials provide proof of King Richard's genuine sentiments and actions. They are invaluable considering how little contemporary evidence there is to refute the mass of fable surrounding him.

The odium in which Richard III is reputed to have been held is not supported by the few well-attested facts we have. Wherever he went he was welcome. He received marked respect and affection from the authorities at York, Exeter, Gloucester, and London. Either the dark deeds imputed to him in after years were not charged to him during his lifetime or, if charged, were not believed by the respectable elements of his subjects. Richard entered London, December 1, 1483, amid such cordial acclamations as dismissed all apprehension of danger to himself or the crown.

Richard granted the manor and lordship of Ealding in Kent to Ralph Banastre, Esq., 'in consideration of the true and faithful service which the said Ralph hath lately done for and about the taking and bringing the said rebel unto the king's hands' (Harl. MSS., 433. fol. 133). This grant proves the Lancastrian origin of many charges by the early chroniclers against King Richard, who is accused of having refused the promised reward to Banastre (Hall, p. 395; Grafton, p. 176). Little dependence can be placed on chroniclers who misrepresented King Richard's acts to convert them into evidences of his injustice, tyranny, and avarice.

Richard's generosity and justice

On December 1, 1483, scarcely six weeks after the Duke of Buckingham had sought to dethrone and kill him, Richard awarded Buckingham's widow an annuity of 200 marcs (Harl. MSS., 433. fol. 77). She was the sister of both the dowager Queen and of Lionel, the outlawed Bishop of Salisbury — the leaders in the rebellion. Nevertheless, Richard permitted her, her children, and her servants to come from Wales to London where her royal sister was in sanctuary (Harl. MSS., 433. fol. 135).

To Florence Cheyney, whose husband and brother had 'compassed and imagined the king's death at Salisbury', he showed tenderness and chivalrous compassion. His actions contrast so strongly with the 'spiteful, cruel, and malicious feelings' long imputed to him that a literal copy of the record is included in justice to King Richard's memory. 'Safeguard for Florence, wife of Alexander Cheyney, whom, for her good and virtuous disposition, the king hath taken into his protection, and granted to her the custody of her husband's lands, &c.; though being of late confounded with certain rebels and traitors, he had intended and compassed th' utter destruction of his person, and the subversion of this realm' (Harl. MSS., 433. fol. 135).

King Richard paid Buckingham's debts (Ibid. fol. 136, 200), gave considerable sums to the distressed families of many individuals who were outlawed, and settled annuities even on the relics of others who had died openly opposing him (Ibid.; see various items from fol. 37 to 174). He confirmed charitable grants that had been made by his father (Ibid. fol. 130), renewed others that had been conferred by his brother (Ibid. fol. 205), and rewarded with princely munificence those nobles who had remained faithful to him. He appointed Lord

Stanley Constable of England for life. Apparently Stanley had been kept in ignorance of the coalition between his wife and the conspirators — or satisfied Richard that such had been the case. Richard gave Sir James Tyrrel the stewardship of Wales and the adjoining marches, and appointed Sir Robert Brackenbury, who had loyally guarded the Tower, receiver-general of all demesnes in the King's hands because of attainder or forfeiture and not given by the King (Ibid. fol. 52, 74).

Markham and Kendall : Buckingham had little support from the commons, and only one nobleman deserted to him. Richard executed only ten men for treason. With incredible generosity, he even remitted the attainder of a principal conspirator, Henry Tudor's mother, Margaret Beaufort, Countess of Richmond (Markham, p. 132; Kendall, pp. 275, 276).

The year 1483 closes

King Richard's edicts, grants, warrants, and rewards, as recorded in the Harleian Manuscript, are too numerous to mention. Sufficient has been adduced, however, to indicate his energy, justice, and compassion. Thus, although half the kingdom had been lately openly arrayed in rebellion against him, he celebrated Christmas with extraordinary pomp and ceremony. Philip de Comines states 'he was reigning in greater splendour and authority than any king of England for the last hundred years' (vol. i, p. 514).

So terminated the eventful year 1483, which saw Richard, Duke of Gloucester, progress from Lord Protector to King. Its brief cycle chronicles three Kings of England, two Princes of Wales, and two Queens-Consort. It also saw the execution of the lordly Hastings, the gifted Rivers, and the 'deep, revolving, witty' Buckingham. A year with such stirring scenes and events of wondrous import can scarcely be paralleled in the life of any individual, or in the regal annals of this or any other land.

Chapter XVI

PARLIAMENT CONFIRMS RICHARD'S TITLE: HIS WISE LAWS: SON DIES

King Richard III opens his first parliament

Parliament Confirms Richard's Title : King Richard III personally opened his first Parliament on January 22, 1484 (Rot. Parl., vol. vi. p. 237). It passed an Act — the *Titulus Regius* — settling the crown upon Richard and his heirs. The Act recites that before his coronation a roll containing certain articles was presented to him on behalf of the three estates of the realm by many lords spiritual and temporal, and other nobles and commons in great multitude, and he 'for the public weal and tranquility of the land benignly assented' (Ibid. p. 240). As the three estates were not assembled in the form of a Parliament, 'doubts, questions, and ambiguities had arisen in the minds of many persons. It was therefore enacted that the tenor of the said roll should be recorded, and should be of the same virtue and force, as if the said things had been so said, affirmed, specified, desired, and remembered in a full parliament'. The commons gave their assent to this bill which also designated King Richard's son, Prince Edward, as 'heir apparent to succeed to him in the above said crown and royal dignity . . . '. (Ibid. pp. 240-242.)

Parliament attaints Henry Tudor : Parliament also attainted the leaders of Buckingham's rebellion, including Henry Tudor, Earl of Richmond, and his uncle, Jasper Tudor, Earl of Pembroke (Ibid. p. 244). But Richard showed unwise leniency toward one of the ringleaders, 'Margaret Countess of Richmond (mother of the king's great rebel and traitor, Henry Earl of Richmond'). He merely placed her in the custody of her husband, Lord Stanley and gave him a life interest in her estates, with the reversion to the King (Ibid. p. 250).

Henry pledges to marry Elizabeth of York

The King's enemies reassembled from all points of the French coast, and proceeded with Henry Tudor to the Cathedral of Rennes (Grafton, p. 180). Here, before the high altar on Christmas Day 1483, Henry solemnly renewed his pledge to marry Elizabeth of York, and the assembled warriors vowed to secure his accession to the English crown. (Ibid. p. 181.)

King Richard took strong defensive measures against invasion. Among other things, he ordered the Cinque Ports to send out ships to watch the movements of the Bretagne vessels, took vigorous measures for guarding the coast, and engaged John Bramburgh to make for him 'certain great stuff of gunpowder'.

Clergy eulogizes King Richard

A convocation of the clergy, following Parliament's meeting, petitioned King Richard: 'Seeing your most noble and blessed dispostion in all other things, we beseech you . . . that . . . the liberties of the church may be confirmed . . . '. (Wilk. Council, vol. iii, p. 614.) Among those who thus praised the King were John Russell, Bishop of Lincoln, Lord Chancellor of England, 'a wise man and a good'; Waynfleet, Bishop of Winchester, honored by the personal regard of King Henry VI and distinguished for 'piety, learning, and prudence' (*Archaeologia*, vol. xxv. p. 2); and Fisher, the friend of Erasmus, elected to the bishopric of Rochester by Henry VII 'for his great and singular virtue', but afterwards beheaded by Henry VIII for his uncompromising integrity, virtue, and incorruptible morality (Fuller's *Church History*, p. 205). Macauley says 'One of the most adulatory addresses ever voted by a Convocation, was to Richard III' (*History of England*, iii, 444 — cited by Gairdner, p. 161).

Would these, and the many other churchmen equally eminent, have appealed to the 'blessed and noble disposition' of one whose hands were bloodied by the murder of his nearest kindred? Coupled with the remarkable language of the petition is the absence of all inquiry regarding the young Princes.

King Richard acceded to the clergy's petition. He confirmed them in their former privileges (Harl. MSS., 433, p. 44) and redressed many of their grievances. He released the clergy in the north from heavy impositions levied by Edward IV (Ibid., p. 42) and founded at York a college for one hundred priests (Ibid. p. 72; Rous, p. 215).

Polydore Vergil says that these acts arose from remorse, but there is nothing to justify this allegation by Henry VII's personal historian. Sharon Turner says this eulogy by representatives of the whole body of the English clergy becomes 'a kind of sacred testimony to his character . . . it must either have been a phrase of consummate hypocrisy, or it must be allowed to counterbalance in no small degree the defamation that has pursued him' (Turner's *Middle Ages*, vol. iv. p. 79).

Richard's wise laws alienate nobility

King Richard framed a remarkable series of laws to safeguard individual liberties, to correct economic abuses, and to promote trade (Bacon's *Henry VII*, p. 2; Harl. MSS. pp. 64, 71, 76, 85, 99, 101, 104; Buck, lib. v. p. 138). He founded the valuable and important Heralds' College (Feodera, xii, p. 215), an act that must immortalize his name because of the benefit it has conferred on posterity. The names of such members as Camden, Dugdale, Sandford, and Ashmole, indicate the invaluable assistance the College has afforded historians and antiquaries in providing authentic memorials of past transactions.

In these and many other laws, Richard III gave practical evidence of the statesmanlike qualities which proved him 'jealous of the honour of the English nation'. But, in proportion as he made laws 'for the ease and solace of the common people' (Bacon's *Henry VII*, p. 2), Richard alienated the nobility. They resented the slightest innovation on the unqualified despotism in which they had been nurtured and which they hoped Richard would extend.

The calamities which thickened around Richard III after he was elevated to the throne may, in great measure, be summed up in the words of Henry VII's personal historian, Polydore Vergil, 'the disaffection of his nobles' (p. 565). They had elected as their ruler a monarch whose principles were too liberal for an aristocracy whose privileges had been upheld with almost sovereign power.

[Note : Halsted discusses Richard III's laws in both Chapter XVI and XVIII. The following material from Chapter XVIII is included here for unity and coherence.] Richard III's wise and equitable laws have been widely recognized (Bacon, pp. 2, 3; Sharon Turner, vol. iii, p. 72). He framed laws of such wisdom that to this day many of his statutes remain in full force. 'In no king's reign', states Sir Richard Baker, 'were better laws made than in the reign of this man' (*Chron. of Kings of England*, p. 234).

Even Lord Bacon, the biographer of Richard III's rival, Henry VII, bears testimony to Richard's 'wise and wholesome laws', an admission from the highest legal authority and from one of the most learned Lord Chancellors of England. Bacon adds 'He was a good law-maker for the ease and solace of the common people'. But Bacon reveals his prejudice by commenting that these laws were 'but the brocage of a usurper, thereby, to woo and to win the hearts of the people' (Bacon's *Henry VII*, p. 3).

Richard III unceasingly devoted himself to one point — emancipating the people from the many oppressions under which they had so long suffered. He tried to diffuse a nobler spirit among all ranks by the soundness of his edicts and the high principles of justice, religion, and morality on which they were based.

During a brief visit to Kent, he proclaimed: 'The king's highness is fully determined to see administration of justice to be had throughout his realm, and to reform and punish all extortion and oppression'. He invited the humblest who had been unlawfully wronged to petition 'his highness; and he shall be heard, and without delay have such convenient remedy as shall accord with the laws' . . . 'his grace is utterly purposed that all his true subjects shall live in rest and quiet, and peaceably enjoy their lands and goods according to the laws' (*Harl. MSS.*, 433. fol. 128).

Richard III struck at an evil that had brought the noble institution of trial by jury into contempt. In the future, no juror was to be chosen who was not 'of good name and fame', and only persons who possessed freehold property of at least forty shillings a year were to be eligible to serve on a jury (Statutes of the Realm, vol. ii, p. 479).

He also empowered every justice of the peace to bail persons arrested for felony on suspicion alone (Ibid. p. 478).

But the law that gave the greatest relief to most people prohibited the seizure of property belonging to persons who, *before* conviction, had been imprisoned on a charge of felony (Ibid. p. 479). Thus, the powerful could no longer oppress their weaker opponents and the poor by false indictments.

Other laws framed by King Richard provided for better regulation of the temporary courts held during fairs. These courts were called 'pie-poudre', a corruption of pied-poudre, dusty foot. In the middle ages, these periodical marts were important. They were the only means of bartering with merchants of other lands and diffusing goods to the distant provinces.

Richard also prohibited the practice of fraudulently transferring property before sale.

Gairdner : Gairdner notes that the public Acts of Richard's Parliament were wise and beneficial. The most remarkable enactment abolished benevolences — forced contributions to the crown (pp. 160, 161).

Kendall : Kendall says that King Richard's legislative program was remarkable. His laws, designed to protect individual liberties and eliminate economic injustices, reflected the principles by which he governed. Within the brief period he was King, he developed an orderly legislative program to benefit his subjects — a record unequalled before or since his reign (pp. 281-185, 319).

Elizabeth Wydville and daughters leave sanctuary

For many months the Dowager Queen and her five daughters had been closely watched in their sanctuary in Westminster Abbey because of the compact made by their mother to unite the eldest daughter, Elizabeth, to Henry Tudor. But all present danger from this source seemed to end with the defeat of the rebels and Parliament's vigorous efforts to preserve domestic peace.

On March 1, 1484, just ten months after they entered sanctuary, the King solemnly bound himself, in the presence of the 'lords spiritual and temporal and the mayor and aldermen of the city of London', on the word of a King and the security of written agreement, that if the daughters of Dame Elizabeth Grey, late calling herself Queen of England, would quit their place of refuge and submit to his direction —

> their lives and honor would be secure;
>
> they would not be imprisoned but be supported in a manner suitable to his kinswomen;
>
> he would marry them to gentlemen of birth, giving to each an estate of the yearly value of 200 marks;
>
> he would strictly charge their husbands to treat them as his relations upon pain of his displeasure;
>
> he would allow their mother 700 marks a year (£466 13s. 4d. in 1844); and
>
> he would discountenance any reports circulated to their prejudice (Harl. MSS. 433. fol. 308).

Elizabeth Wydville relied upon Richard's word and sent her five daughters from sanctuary. Richard honorably and conscientiously fulfilled his pledge. 'He caused all his brother's daughters to be conveyed into his palace with solemn receiving, and by familiar and loving entertainment' strove to efface from their minds their recent adverse position (Grafton, p. 200). King Richard and Queen Anne treated the daughters and their mother generously and lavished marked distinction upon the young and beautiful Elizabeth.

Gairdner : Gairdner notes that Richard completely won over the Queen Dowager; she even urged her son, the Marquis of Dorset, to return to England (p. 202).

Kendall : The Queen Dowager wrote to her son, the Marquis, on her own initiative, urging him to return to Richard and he tried unsuccessfully to do so. Elizabeth and Dorset's actions in siding with Richard rather than Henry indicate that Richard was not guilty of killing the two Princes (pp. 408, 409).

Richard and Anne's generosity to Cambridge

By a note dated March 5, 1484, King Richard was warned of threats of invasion. Accordingly, he left London March 6 to visit the threatened districts. He entered Cambridge March 9. A unanimous assembly of the regents and non-regents on March 10, immediately after his departure, acknowledged his liberality to the University and decreed an annual mass during the life of that 'most renowned prince and pious king, Richard, after the Conquest, the third'. He was especially generous to King's College. He founded and erected buildings there and made several grants for churches at King's College (*Harl. MSS.*, 433. fol. 190, 209, 210).

Letters patent, dated March 25, 1483, 'in favour of Margaret College, Cambridge, founded by Anne the Queen consort', prove Anne to have been equally generous (*Rymer's Add. MSS.*, 4616. Art. 63). A solemn service was ordered to be celebrated annually on May 2, 'by the whole congregation of regents and non-regents of the aforesaid university, for the happy state of the said most renowned prince and his dearest consort Anne' (*Cooper's Ann. Cam.*, p. 228).

Richard's visit to Cambridge was preceded by a circular letter he sent to all the prelates of the realm. He called upon them to repress vice, however highly placed the offender might be. 'We therefore . . . require . . . ye . . . punish . . . all such persons . . . not sparing for any love or favour the offender, be he temporal or spiritual' (*Harl. MSS.*, 433. fol. 281).

Scotland threatens again

Open warfare had commenced on the borders of England and Scotland. King James III could neither trust his nobles nor they their King. His brother, the Duke of Albany, ever ready to fan the flames of discord, had fled to England to escape his brother's vengeance. The most friendly feeling had always existed between the Duke and Richard. The perpetual skirmishes on the frontiers and the numerous aggressions at sea threatened serious results unless quelled by pacific negotiations. It was this situation which also prompted King Richard's sudden departure from London and his progress north. Little, however, did Richard anticipate the bitter domestic trial that was about to overwhelm him and in one fatal moment blight his hopes.

Sudden death of Richard's son

'How vain is the thought of man, willing to establish his affairs without God!', said the Chronicler of Croyland, 'for about the feast of St. Edward in the month of April, 1484, this only son, in whom all hope of royal succession was reposed by so many oaths, died after a short illness at Middleham Castle. . . . Then might you have seen the father and mother, having heard the news at Nottingham, where they then dwelt, almost mad with sudden grief' (p. 571).

'His (Richard's) parental feelings were pure and kind' (Turner, vol. iv. p. 15). The young Prince was constitutionally weak. His household accounts include expenses of 'my lord prince's chariot from York to Pontefract' (*Harl. MSS.*, 433. fol. 118). This mode of conveyance was then in use only for state prisoners, females and invalids (Bacon's *Henry VII*, p. 8). By a singular coincidence, Edward, the sole heir of Richard III, died on April 9, 1484, exactly one year after the death of King Edward IV (Memoir prefixed to the *Privy Purse Expenses of Elizabeth of York*, by Sir H. Nicolas, p. 42). No memorial is known to exist about young Edward's funeral.

Richard takes defensive action

The Chronicler of Croyland says that, grievous as was the King's affliction, he 'nevertheless attended to the defense of his realm' (p. 571). It was reported that Henry Tudor, Earl of Richmond, would shortly land in England. He was supported by the exiles, who had sworn fealty to him as their King, in the hope that he would marry Elizabeth of York, King Edward IV's eldest daughter. Also, John Morton, Bishop of Ely, had never rested in his activities to depose Richard and place Henry on the throne.

Richard adopted the admirable plan to guard against sudden invasion introduced by Edward IV during the preceding Scottish war. Under this plan, swift couriers were placed at every twentieth mile. Thus, by their passing letters from hand to hand, he could obtain the news of two hundred miles within two days. Richard also had spies abroad from whom he learned almost all of Henry's intentions (*Chron. Croy.*, p. 571).

Heir apparent — Earl of Warwick — then Earl of Lincoln

As it became necessary to appoint an heir to the crown, Richard nominated as his successor his nephew, Edward, the young Earl of Warwick, son of the ill-fated Duke of Clarence. This selection exonerates Richard from the charge that he ill-treated young Warwick. Edward IV had bestowed Warwick's wardship and marriage on the Marquis of Dorset, the Queen's son by her former husband (*Cal. Rot.*, p. 325). Thus, if the generally accepted opinion is true that Warwick's mind was weakened by cruelty and neglect in childhood, the accusation rests on his early guardian, Dorset. He was Governor of the Tower. Here, he had closely kept the infant Warwick from the period of Clarence's execution until Richard's elevation to the throne opened his prison gate.

George, Duke of Clarence, was executed in the Tower on February 18, 1478. Edward, his son and heir, was then three (Dugdale, vol. ii. p. 102). 'He was a child of most unhappy fortunes, having from his cradle been nursed up in prison' (Sandford, book v. p. 114) '. . . he scarcely knew a hen from a goose, nor one beast from another' (Baker's Chron., p. 225). Nearly all Tudor Chroniclers agree with Hall (p. 55) in his description of Edward's weak intellect which was apparent when in after-years he was brought to the royal palace at Shene to establish Lambert Simnel's imposture. Apparently, the mental powers of the unfortunate Warwick never advanced beyond that of the earliest childhood.

By mid-summer, 1484, Richard apparently had realized the need for a change. He withdrew the name of the young Earl of Warwick and substituted that of Edward's cousin the gallant and chivalrous Earl of Lincoln. Lincoln was the eldest son of King Richard's eldest surviving sister, the Duchess of Suffolk (Rous. p. 217). His abilities were well known to Richard, for they had been tried and proved on many important occasions.

Richard has been unjustly charged with having harshly treated and cruelly imprisoned his unfortunate nephew, Warwick. It is true he sent him to Sheriff Hutton Castle, but not as a prisoner. 'The prince was kept here during the whole of Richard's reign, but he was not treated harshly' (Castel. Hutton., p. 17). The Castle had been the home of young Warwick's ancestors, and was at this identical period occupied by his immediate kindred the Nevilles. King Richard had visited the Castle to examine into its fitness for his nephew's abode (Ibid. pp. 4, 9). 'I saw no house in the North so like a princely lodging', says Leland (*Itin.*, vol. i. p. 73).

Richard plans Henry's capture

Francis, Duke of Brittany, was now so old that the function of governing had fallen almost entirely to his confidential minister Peter Landois (Grafton, p. 189). Landois valued the support of the powerful King Richard III more than the friendship of the exiled and attainted Henry Tudor, Earl of Richmond. Richard sent munificent presents ostensibly to Francis, but judiciously made over to Landois. Francis promised, through his official adviser Landois, to capture and imprison Henry.

But the vigilance of Richard's deadly enemy, John Morton, again preserved Henry and defeated Richard's well-laid plans. Morton had discovered the plan and warned Henry. Concealing his secret knowledge, Henry, with only five followers, went ostensibly to visit one of his adherents in an adjoining village. Having eluded suspicion by his seeming openness, Henry entered a thick wood. Here, assuming the garb of a simple page (Grafton, p. 192), he fled from Brittany to France (Polydore Vergil, p. 555). Henry's escape was not discovered until the fourth day of his departure. Couriers and horsemen were hastily sent to the coast and frontier towns. So fast did they fly that the fugitive 'was not entered into the realm of France scarce one hour' when his pursuers reached the border (Grafton, p. 193). Henry was well received by Charles VIII, because of his enmity toward both England and Brittany.

Francis, Duke of Brittany, wearied of the difficulties of his association with Henry, renounced all further connection with him and concluded a friendly alliance with Richard (Foedera, xii. p. 226).

Richard secures peace with Scotland

King Richard was anxious to negotiate peace with Scotland so he might be free to quit the North and be nearer to the new point of danger — Charles VIII's France. Richard entered Nottingham on July 30, 1484. Here, he received the anticipated letter from James III of Scotland, desiring safe conduct for his ambassadors (Harl. MSS., 433, fol. 263). On August 6, Richard signed the treaty of peace with Scotland, and was now free to direct his attention exclusively to the threat from France.

Richard hangs Collingbourne

Richard knew that he must check the hopes of his own rebellious subjects as well as counteract Henry's plans. He therefore imprisoned many persons of wealth and family who had been corresponding with the exiles. He made an example by executing on Tower Hill one of the most seditious of the ringleaders, William Collingbourne.

Collingbourne had been arrested some weeks earlier on proof of treasonable practices. Nevertheless, he had renewed his communications with Henry Tudor. Although Collingbourne had received from Richard places and emoluments of importance, during his imprisonment he had offered substantial sums to anyone who would join Henry and Dorset and invade the English coast. He assured them that he and others would cause the people to rise in arms for Richmond (see Collingbourne's indictment, in Holinshed, p. 746).

The traditional belief is that Collingbourne was executed merely for a political sarcasm on the King and his three chief advisers, Lord Lovell, Sir Richard Ratcliffe, and Sir William Catesby.

'The Ratte, the Cat, and Lovell our dogge,
Rule all England under the Hogge'.

But Collingbourne's indictment makes it clear that he was not charged alone for striving to bring the King and his government into contempt through rhymes stuck on the doors of St. Paul's Church. The indictment for open and avowed treason charges him also with infusing groundless suspicion into the French King's mind to induce him to aid Henry Tudor in expelling Richard from the throne (*Holinshed Chron.*, p. 746).

Collingbourne merited the death of a traitor. If, in the execution of his sentence unnecessary cruelty was exercised, the odium rested with the civil authorities who carried the sentence into effect. The King, though he sanctioned the execution, was at the time in a distant part of the kingdom.

Richard's letters — a key to his character

Collingbourne was arraigned on July 18, 1484. His previous suspension from office is apparent from a letter King Richard III wrote his mother on June 3, 1484 (Harl. MSS. 433, fol. 2). Collingbourne had apparently held a responsible position connected with Lady Cecily's holdings.

'Madam, — I recommend me to you as heartily as is to me possible. Beseeching you in my most humble and affectuous wise of your daily blessing to my singular comfort and defence in my need. And, Madam, I heartily beseech you that I may often hear from you to my comfort. And such news as be here my servant Thomas Bryan, this bearer, shall show you to whom, please it you, to give credence unto. And, Madam, I beseech you to be good and gracious, Lady, to my Lord my chamberlain, to be your officer in Wiltshire in such as Collingbourne had. I trust he shall therein do you good service. And that it please you that by this bearer I may understand your pleasure in this behalf. And I pray God to send you the accomplishment of your noble desires. Written at Pomfret the 3d day of June 1484, with the hand of

Your most humble son
Ricardus Rex'.

This letter is evidence, from the King's expressed wish 'that I may often hear from you', that he and his mother were on amicable terms and were in frequent correspondence. It is also evidence of the King's true nature. There are no materials for biography so satisfactory as letters — none that so effectively portray the nature and character of the writer. Richard wrote other letters which afford evidence of his character — evidence which contradicts the long held traditional view of Richard as a cruel tyrant. One of the most revealing is a letter about the proposed remarriage of Jane Shore. She had so captivated Thomas Lynom, the King's solicitor, that he wanted to marry her.

Richard was apparently grieved and astonished at this proposed union. Jane Shore was the paramour of Edward IV for many years. She did penance for her irregular life after his death. And she was a prisoner in Ludgate for treasonable practices at the identical period when the solicitor-general sought her in marriage. She was reported to have been Lord Hastings' mistress after Edward IV's death and Dorset's mistress after Hastings' death.

Richard's conduct in this emergency was hardly that of a tyrant or persecutor. He addressed the following remarkable letter to the 'learned and the good' Dr. Russell, Bishop of Lincoln, then Lord Chancellor. It is the letter of a kind and indulgent master, anxious to dissuade a faithful servant from committing an act injurious to his interests but willing to yield to his wishes if persuasion failed to open his eyes. No date is given to this letter which is preserved in Lord Hardwicke's state papers in the Harleian Library, No. 2378, but it was probably written about this period.

'BY THE KING.

'Right Reverend Father in God, &c., signifying unto you that it is showed unto us, that our servant and solicitor, Thos. Lynom, marvellously blinded and abused with the late wife of William Shore, now being in Ludgate by our commandment, hath made contract of matrimony with her, as it is said, and intendeth, to our full great marvel, to proceed to effect the same. We, for many causes, would be sorry that he so should be disposed, pray you therefore to send for him, and in that ye godly may exhort and stir him to the contrary. And if ye find him utterly set for to marry her, and none otherwise would be advertised, then, if it may stand with the law of the church, we be content (the time of marriage being deferred to our coming next to London), that upon sufficient surety found of her good abearing [behaviour] ye do send for her keeper and discharge him of

210

our commandment by warrant of these, committing her to the rule and guiding of her father or any other, by your discretion, in the mean season.

'Given, &c.
'To the Right Rev. Father in God the
Bishop of Lincoln our Chancellor'.

King Richard's letter empowered the Chancellor to release the fascinating Jane from prison, to deliver her into the charge of the person most fitting to succour her — her own father, and even to sanction the marriage provided it held good 'with the law of the Church'. There is no compulsion in this letter, no stretch of regal power, and no threat. Does this conduct indicate a cruel tyrant — the arbitrary, imperious, selfish destroyer of his people's comforts and happiness? And it must be remembered that in Richard's day letters were neither designed for, or liable to, publication. They were the secret deposits of the true sentiments of the writer. What a far cry Richard's letter presents from Shakespeare's Richard III (Act 1, scene 3):

'Look when he fawns he bites; and when he bites,
His venom teeth will rankle to the death'.

Other letters also illustrate King Richard's leniency, forbearance, and kindness. Although letters are rare at this early period of English history, Richard's letters are abundant. The mass of facts connected with his remarkable career precludes including all of his correspondence or numerous extracts from that invaluable register of his reign, the Harleian collection. 'I made the attempt', says Sharon Turner, 'but I found the entries too numerous for insertion: it contains from 2,000 to 2,500 official documents, most of which are the king's beneficial grants' (Turner's *Middle Ages*, vol. iv. p. 58).

Chapter XVII

HENRY TUDOR THREATENS AGAIN: QUEEN ANNE DIES

Unrest in London

King Richard returned to London about August 6, 1484, after six stormy months, subdued in spirit and desolate in heart. Within one year of his father's accession to the throne, young Edward of Gloucester, Prince of Wales, slept in his tranquil grave. Disaffection, too, was spreading over the land.

Richard knew about the seditious spirit in London and the waning of his popularity. The revival of internal feuds between the nobles, the total cessation of commercial intercourse with France and Scotland, and the heavy cost of keeping up armaments by sea and land fostered a spirit of disorder in the citizens of London. The court had been stationary at York for six months, and Richard had shown partiality for his northern subjects. The Londoners feared that the King might move his abode to York. But King Richard was too wise a ruler to be ignorant of the fatal consequences of such a move.

Richard reinters Henry VI at Windsor

In August 1484, King Richard removed the body of Henry VI from Chertsey Abbey to the collegiate church at Windsor, so he might be placed with his royal predecessors. But this act of respect to the memory of the rival of the House of York has been twisted to Richard's disadvantage. 'He envied', said the Tudor partisans, 'the sanctity of King Henry', and removed him from Chertsey 'to arrest the number of pilgrimages to his tomb' *(Wilk. Council.,* iii. p. 635). But this same authority admits that Chertsey was unfitting for the resting-place of a king. And Chertsey was so remote that it could not have caused the revival of compassionate feeling which resulted from Henry VI's public disinterment and removal of his body to the regal mausoleum of his ancestors.

Consider that Henry's mortal remains had reposed at Chertsey for thirteen years. His exhumation was neither caused by public outcry nor required as an act of justice. Yet Richard voluntarily, openly, and without fear of any popular feeling for Henry, transferred his remains to a place of such distinction that visits to his tomb would increase substantially.

Rous was a contemporary Lancastrian writer and a warm partisan of Henry VI. He wrote: 'And in the month of August following the body of King Henry was dug up, and translated to the new collegiate church of Windsor, where it was honourably received and again buried with the greatest solemnity on the south side of the high alter' (p. 217).

Richard's public works

Richard founded a college of priests in Tower Street, near the church called 'Our Lady of Barking' (Rous, p. 215). He commanded the erection of a high stone tower at Westminster, 'a work', says Sir George Buck, 'of good use, even at this day' (lib. v. p. 138). He erected new buildings at the Tower of London and renovated the older portions, 'in memory whereof there be yet his arms, impaled with those of the queen, his wife, standing upon the arch adjoining the sluice gate' (Ibid. p. 139). He also commanded improvements at Windsor Castle, Westminster Palace, and Baynard's Castle.

Peace overtures from Scotland and France

James III of Scotland sent a letter to Richard stating his intention to send commissioners to England to treat not only 'of truce and abstinence from war, but likewise of marriage, between those of the blood of both kings' (*Harl. MSS.*, 433, fol. 263). On the day of Richard's return to London from Nottingham, August 1, 1484, he granted letters of safe conduct to ambassadors from Scotland.

Messengers arrived from the French King also requesting letters of protection for ambassadors appointed to treat for peace (*Feodera*, xii. p. 235). Richard issued the required letters on September 1. An opening was thus afforded for a renewal of commercial intercourse with both kingdoms.

Richard concludes truce with Scotland and Brittany

Richard left London and, on September 16, 1484, at Nottingham, gave audience to the deputies from Scotland. Richard was seated under a royal canopy, surrounded by his court and the chief officers of state. James III's secretary and orator, Archibald Quhitlaw, delivered an eloquent oration in Latin, extolling Richard's high renown, noble qualities, great wisdom, virtue, and prudence, and concluding that 'Nature never united to a small frame a greater soul, or a more powerful mind'. Sharon Turner says 'If Richard had not been short the prelate who came ambassador to him from Scotland would not, in his complimentary address delivered to him on his throne, have quoted these lines; nor would he have made such an allusion, if it had not been well known that Richard cared not about it' (*Middle Ages*, vol. iii, p. 476).

On September 20, 1484, Richard concluded a truce with Scotland. On the same day, the Scottish Commissioners and officials of the English government signed a contract of marriage between the heir to the Scottish throne, King James' eldest son, the Duke of Rothesay, and Lady Anne de la Pole, daughter of the Duke of Suffolk and sister of the Earl of Lincoln, when Richard III had nominated his successor to the throne. The Duke of Rothesay had previously been engaged to the Princess Cecily. His faithless performance was the origin of the war in which King Richard, before his accession to the throne, acquired such high military reputation.

This second contract of marriage was also destined to end in a similar manner and mortify another of Richard's nieces. 'Upon the breach thereof', says Buck, 'the young affianced, resolving to accept no other motion, embraced a conventual life, and ended her days a nun in the monastery of Sion' (lib. i. p. 33). James IV of Scotland was united to Princess Margaret, the eldest daughter of King Henry VII and his Queen, Elizabeth of York, on August 8, 1503 (*Let. Cott.*, iv. fol. 205).

During Richard's stay in Nottingham, Francis, Duke of Brittany, sought ratification of peace negotiations with England. An English mission sailed to Brittany on October 13, 1484, and established a friendly alliance between the two countries.

Richard receives cordial reception in London

Having at last restored peace within the realm and cemented friendly relations with Scotland, France and Brittany, Richard returned to London for the winter of 1484-1485. Here he was welcomed by the citizens with demonstrations of popularity and joy fully as great, if not greater, than those when he made his triumphal entry into London one year before. And here Richard celebrated the festival of Christmas, 1484, with great splendor.

Thus restored to public favor, Richard encouraged such sports and pastimes as were consistent with the customs of the age. Falconry and hawking especially engaged his attention. But the recreation to which Richard himself seemed most devoted was music. He made many grants to minstrels from the royal funds. He kept a band of trumpeters at a yearly payment and promoted a very large choral ensemble. In an act illustrating the despotism of the period and the little personal freedom enjoyed by the people of England, he empowered 'John Melynek, one of the gentlemen of the chapel royal, to take and seize for the king all such singing men and children, being expert in the science of music, as he can find, and think able to do the king's service . . . '. (*Harl. MSS.*, 433, fol. 46, 78, 96, 104, 189, 190, 210).

Henry Tudor threatens: Richard takes defensive measures

But Richard's peaceful days were few in number and of short duration. The treaties with France, Brittany, and Scotland had temporarily allayed suspicion of danger. As early after his return to London as December 6, 1484, he received intelligence which led him to doubt the good faith of the French. Accordingly, Richard issued a strong edict stating that 'our ancient enemies of France' conspire to subvert the realm and calling for the punishment of those sending seditious writings or spreading rumors to promote discord (*Harl. MSS.*, 787. fol. 2).

Richard learned that the rebels planned to land at Harwich, and promptly took strong defensive measures. These measures were so effective that the threatened danger was dispelled and King Richard was able to celebrate Christmas, 1484, in tranquility. The festivities ended on the day of the Epiphany when Richard presided at an entertainment of extraordinary magnificence in Westminster Hall, 'the king himself wearing his crown and holding a splendid feast in the great hall similar to that at his coronation' (Chron. Croy., p. 571).

Little did Richard imagine that this would be the last feast at which he would preside — the last time he would display his crown in peace before his assembled peers. For events following these festivities were to be far different from the tranquility following the coronation. 'On the same day tidings were brought to him by his seafaring intelligencers that, in spite of all the power and splendour of his royal estate, his enemies would, beyond all doubt, enter or attempt to enter, the kingdom during the approaching summer' (Ibid.).

Upon receiving this new intelligence, Richard commanded the knights, squires, and gentlemen of the county of Chester, 'to obey the Lord Stanley, the Lord Strange, and Sir William Stanley, who had the rule and leading of all persons appointed to do the king service, when they shall be warned against the king's rebels' (Harl. MSS., 433. fol. 201). He issued a similar commission to the knights of other counties 'to do the king's grace service, against his rebels, in whatsoever place within the realm they fortune to arrive' (Ibid., fol. 203, 205).

Richard is forced to adopt benevolences

Edward IV had suffered tumult and insurrection when he invoked benevolences to extort money from his subjects. King Richard III had not only condemned this mode of taxation at his accession, but had afterwards abolished it by an Act of Parliament (Statutes of the Realm, vol. ii. p. 478). But now, forced to adopt this obnoxious measure, he incurred the displeasure of the church and the citizens. For the edict specified the sums the clergy as well as laymen were required to give (*Harl. MSS.*, 433. fol. 275).

The Croyland Chronicler says that Richard, because of Henry Tudor's impending invasion, sent chosen men 'who, by prayers and threats, extorted from the chests of almost all ranks very large sums of money' (p. 571). Fabyan corroborates this account and depicts Richard's distress at having to rely on benevolences. 'And in the month of February, King Richard, then leading his life in great agony and doubt, trusting few of such as were about him, spared not to spend the great treasure which before King Edward gathered in, giving of great and large gifts. By means whereof he alone wasted, not the treasure, but also he was in such danger that he borrowed many notable sums of money of the rich men of this realm, and especially of the citizens of London, whereof the least sum was forty pounds, for surety whereof he delivered to them good and sufficient pledges' (Fabyan, p. 518).

Richard's use of benevolences was different in at least three respects from Edward IV's use of this unpopular measure. *First*, Richard was confronted with an emergency. He needed money 'for such great and excessive costs and charges as we must hastily bear and sustain, as well for the keeping of the sea as otherwise for the defence of the realm' (*Harl. MSS.*, 433. fol. 276). *Second*, it is well known that Richard pledged even his plate and jewels to raise money in this emergency. His want of money appears from the warrants in the Harl. MSS., 'for pledging and sales of his plate' (Turner's *Middle Ages*, vol. iv. p. 29). *Third*, Richard adopted this strong measure with the consent and approval of his Privy Council. The letter delivered to those from whom a loan was requested was prefaced with the words 'to be delivered to those from whom the *commons* requested loans in the king's name'. And the letter stated 'for that intent his grace and all his lords thinking that every true Englishman will help him in that behalf'. This language is proof that Richard had the approval of his Privy Council. It indicates that Richard did not act tyrannically but followed the advice of leading members of both Houses of Parliament.

Queen Anne dies

Queen Anne Becomes Ill : From the time of the death of her son Edward, Prince of Wales, on April 9, 1484, there were reports of Queen Anne's precarious state of health (Buck, lib. ii. p. 44). The Croyland Chronicler says the King's grief at the loss of his son almost approached insanity (p. 570). And it appears that Queen Anne never recovered from the shock of her son's death.

There seems little doubt that consumption was the true cause of the 'gradual decay' which is stated to have overcome the two daughters of the Earl of Warwick, Queen Anne and her elder sister Isabel. 'Isabel Duchess of Clarence, only sister of Anne queen-consort of Richard III, died of a deep decline, the 12th of December, 1476 in the twenty-fourth year of her age, having been born September 5th, 1451' (Sandford, book v. p. 412).

Accusations Against Richard : Richard has been accused of poisoning his wife in order to marry his niece Elizabeth of York. There is, in fact, not the slightest basis for imputing to Richard such an unnatural crime. His accusers have advanced no stronger proof than the fact that the youthful Princess Elizabeth appeared in robes of a similar form and texture as those worn by Queen Anne, after the reconciliation of her mother, Elizabeth Wydville, and her uncle, King Richard.

The ecclesiastical reporter who has perpetuated the report did not even hint at it until Richard had incurred the Church's anger by his renewal of benevolences (Chron. Croy., p. 572). It is reasonable to suppose that Queen Anne would soften the painful position of her young relative, now appearing in court as the daughter of Dame Elizabeth Grey, instead of, as heretofore, the Princess Royal of the line of York. Thus, Queen Anne would want to attire her as became the niece of the King, whom the Queen loved 'as a sister'. Moreover, the peculiar favor quickly lavished upon Elizabeth gave rise to the surmise that she was to be the bride of the young Prince of Wales (Lingard, p. 262). But the death of the young Prince left Elizabeth still the betrothed of Henry Tudor and, as such, a cause of anxiety to her uncle, King Richard.

The accusation that Richard poisoned his wife rested on conjecture alone. But the question of whether he did want to marry his niece is also important to an evaluation of Richard's character. The Croyland Chronicler asserts that Richard contemplated a union with the Princess Elizabeth, but this accusation was gratuitous and based on a rumor. Fabyan, another contemporary writer, is silent on the subject. So is Rous the only remaining contemporary historian, although he includes the alleged poisoning of Anne in summing up Richard's imputed crimes (p. 215). His summary of alleged crimes is compiled with an obvious prejudice against the House of York and favor toward the House of Lancaster and includes every possible accusation against King Richard with no support for any allegation. Thus, Rous' account possesses not a shadow of historical authority. Grafton, Hall, and Holinshed, and other chroniclers who reported the accusations, penned their works during the Tudor dynasty. Their works were commenced very many years after King Richard's death, and rest on rumor.

Nothing approaching evidence that King Richard wished to marry his niece has ever been adduced except for a letter cited by Buck. '. . . she desires him (the Duke of Norfolk) to be a mediator to the king in behalf of the marriage propounded between them, who, as she wrote, was her only joy and maker in this world; and that she was his in heart and thought: withal insinuating that the better part of February was passed, and that she feared the queen would never die'. 'All these be her own words, written with her own hand; and this is the sum of her letter which remains in the autograph or original draft, under her own hand, in the magnificent cabinet of Thomas Earl of Arundel and Surrey' (Lib. iv. p. 128).

The valuable collection of manuscripts by Thomas Earl of Arundel, now termed 'The Arundelian Library' has been most carefully examined, but no trace appears of this extraordinary letter. Sir George Buck, throughout his history of Richard III, inserts at full length copies of almost every other instrument to which he refers, or gives marginal references to the sources on which his statements are made (see pp. 23, 31, 48, 119, 121, 137, 139). Although every search has been made for the alleged autograph, no trace of it has ever been discovered.

Princess Elizabeth was distinguished by her moral and religious principles throughout a life of peculiar trial and vicissitude. 'From her youth, her veneration for the Supreme Being and devotion to Him were admirable. Her love to her brothers and sisters was unbounded. Her affection and respect to the poor and to religious ministers were singularly great' (Bern. Andreas, Cotton MS., Dom. xviii). It is difficult to reconcile the fact of Elizabeth's piety and moral principles with Buck's allegation.

Richard and Anne had lived on affectionate terms since infancy. No record exists, either positive or implied, in the preceding, present, and succeeding reigns, to intimate that the cousins, after their marriage, were unhappy or indifferent to each other. She was Richard's companion in his regal progress and in his sojourn in more troubled times in the North. They lived in harmony and affection.

A Scholar's Conclusions : Sir Harris Nicolas, the learned biographer of Elizabeth of York, made a keen and searching examination of the accusations against Richard. Here are extracts from his Memoir of 'Elizabeth of York':

'Richard's detractors have insisted that after he discovered the intentions of the friends of Elizabeth and of the Earl of Richmond to blend their respective pretensions to the crown by their marriage, he was impressed with the policy of strengthening his own title by making her his queen; that this became apparent in the similarity of her costume to the dress of her majesty, as early as Christmas 1484, and that to promote his wishes he actually poisoned his wife'.

It was not in King Richard's 'interest to marry the Princess

Elizabeth, and consequently the strongest testimony is necessary to prove that he intended to do so. . . . His title to the crown would not have been strengthened by marrying a woman whom the law had declared a bastard; and to have repealed that declaration would be to call into existence his right to the crown, and to proclaim himself an usurper. A measure so inconsistent with his safety, so contradictory to the whole tenor of his policy, seems incredible; and can it for a moment be believed that he endeavoured to effect it by the murder of a wife who was fast hastening to the tomb with disease, and by a marriage which even the authority of the Pope could not, it is said, reconcile to the feelings and manners of his subjects? . . . The worst enemies of the usurper have represented him as an atrocious villain, but not one of them has described him as a fool'.

Sir Harris Nicolas concludes 'that the whole tale was invented with the view of blackening his (Richard's) character to gratify the monarch (Henry VII) in whose reign all the contemporary writers who relate it flourished'. He adds that it is a charge which deserves attention for no other reason than as it affords a remarkable example of the manner in which ignorance and prejudice sometimes render what is called history little better than a romance (See Sir Harris Nicolas' Memoir prefixed to his *Privy Purse Expenses of Elizabeth of York*, fol. 42-46).

Death of Queen Anne : Queen Anne lingered until March 1485 'about the middle of which month, on the day of the great eclipse of the sun [March 16, 1485] she died, and was buried at Westminster, with all honour befitting a queen' (*Chron. Croy.*, p. 571). The solemnity of Anne's funeral was characterized by the tears King Richard III shed when he personally attended her remains. She was buried near the high altar of Westminster.

So ended the life of Queen Anne, the only surviving daughter of the Earl of Warwick. She had been King Richard III's partner for twelve years. Anne sank to rest in the thirty-first year of her age, after wearing the crown as Queen for only twenty months. Her contemporary, John Rous, portrays Richard, Anne, and their son, Edward, on a roll of velum, nearly eight yards long, of the Earls of Warwick. The original illuminated MS is still preserved in the College of Arms. Queen Anne is represented as standing between the rival crowns of Lancaster and York, extending her hand to King Richard. Beneath her feet rests, muzzled, the bear — the badge of the Earls of Warwick. King Richard and the Prince of Wales are in armor with surcoats of the royal arms. Richard wears his crown and holds his sceptre in his right hand, while Edward's brow is encircled with the coronet of heir apparent. Father and son each stand on the boar, the usual cognizance of King Richard III.

Kendall : Kendall concludes that the rumors about Richard poisoning his wife were part of Henry Tudor's plan to discredit the King by slander (p. 326).

Chapter XVIII

TREACHERY AT BOSWORTH: RICHARD KILLED

Richard denies plans to marry Elizabeth

The King was aware of the rumors spread by his enemies that he intended to marry his niece, Elizabeth of York. Amid all the rumors and speculation, three facts are clear. *First*, Richard never sought to divorce his wife, Queen Anne. *Second*, he never professed his intention to marry Elizabeth. *Third*, he promptly took steps to deny such intention.

It is clear that Richard left no means untried to stop the rumors and to testify, by his actions how badly he had been defamed. Immediately after the deceased Queen had been buried, Richard summoned a council of state to repel the rumors of his proposed marriage with his niece. Richard did not stop with this explicit denial before his great officers of state. He resolved to make his denial still more public and decisive. Accordingly, a 'little before Easter', in the great hall of St. John's Priory, Clerkenwall, Richard, 'in the presence of the mayor and citizens of London, with a clear and loud voice, repeated the aforesaid disavowal' (Chron. Croy., p. 572). He denied ever 'acting otherwise than is according to honour, truth, and the peace and rightfulness of this our land' (Francis Drake, *Eboracum, or the History and Antiquities of the City of York*, London, 1736, p. 119).

Sir Harris Nicolas notes that the legality or illegality of a marriage of relations must depend upon the rules of the church to which the parties belong. It was undoubtedly forbidden by the canon law. The Pope, however, was considered to possess a dispensing power. He not only might, but often did, authorize the marriage of uncles and nieces (*Memoir of Elizabeth of York*, p. 42).

Sir Harris Nicolas adds that 'if a statement which stands on very dubious authority cannot be believed without assigning to him to whom it relates conduct directly at variance with that which the public records show he pursued, and if credence on that statement can only be given by imputing to the person an inconsistency so great, and a change of opinion so flagrant, that his political existence must have been endangered, there is just cause for rejecting every thing short of positive proof' (Ibid., p. 46).

In an act that provides the strongest proof of the untruth of the rumors, Richard removed the Princess Elizabeth to a place far distant from himself or his court. He sent her to share the nominal captivity of the young Earl of Warwick at Sheriff Hutton, 'a goodly and a pleasant house of his own in Yorkshire, where he had liberty, large diet, all pleasure, and safety' (Buck, lib. v. p. 135). Richard neither imprisoned Elizabeth nor concealed her place of abode from her friends or the world. Every latitude and indulgence was permitted consistent with the vigilant watch that was necessary over Edward of Warwick and Elizabeth of York. Henry's supporters would gladly have seized them as the persons best suited to insure the downfall of Richard.

Kendall : Kendall says it was Thomas Rotherham, Archbishop of York who started the rumors that Richard intended to marry his niece, Elizabeth of York. It was also Rotherham who kept John Morton informed of Richard's parleys with Brittany to secure Henry Tudor.

Kendall makes an impressive case for Richard's chivalry and integrity. The chief basis for Henry Tudor's strength was his promise to marry one of Edward IV's daughters. Thus, the emergence of the daughters from sanctuary gave Richard a golden opportunity. He could destroy Henry, his sole threat, by giving them in marriage. Yet, Richard never did this (pp. 326, 333).

Blount and Oxford defect to Henry

Sir James Blount, the governor of Hammes, was a veteran soldier in whom Richard had the greatest confidence. He not only abandoned his trust and deserted to Henry Tudor but released from captivity the Earl of Oxford, a skilled general and a determined enemy of the House of York. The castle and town of Hammes was promptly recaptured, but immediately thereafter Sir John Fortescue and some of the garrison at Calais deserted to Henry. John Morton, Bishop of Ely, is considered to have plotted these moves. Henry timed his reappearance to coincide with these desertions.

Richard III moves to counter Henry

King Richard must have realized that some powerful agent was tampering with his officers and troops. Accordingly, 'a little before Pentecost' he once more left London and 'proceeded to the north' (*Chron. Croy.*, p. 572). Although it was rumored that the rebels were hastening their approach to England, Richard could get no decisive information on where they intended to land (Ibid.). As he moved from town to town, he saw little indication of internal revolt. Finally, in June 1485, he fixed his temporary abode at Nottingham, whose fortress was strong and centrally located.

Richard left Francis Lord Lovell, his faithful chamberlain and friend of his youth, at Southampton in command of the fleet which was stationed there to resist any invasion of the southern coasts (Ibid.). On arriving at Nottingham, Richard sent a letter, dated June 22, 1485, to the commissioners of array in every county throughout England commanding them to . . .

> 'review the soldiers . . . and see that they be able persons well horsed and harnessed . . . ';
>
> 'give straitly in commandment to all knights, esquires, and gentlemen to prepare and array themselves in their proper persons to do the king's service upon an hour's warning . . . ';
>
> proclaim that 'all men be ready to do the king's service within an hour's warning . . . ' and
>
> 'all manner quarrels, grudges, rancours, and unkindness lay apart . . . ' (*Harl. MSS.*, 433. fol. 220).

Richard followed up these letters the same day by sending copies with a strong letter to the sheriffs of every county, requiring their 'continual abode within the shiretown of their office . . . where they might be found' in the event of danger (Ibid. fol. 221).

Richard proclaims Henry a traitor

King Richard summed up his various manifests of June 22, 1485, by a lengthy proclamation the same day denouncing 'Henry Tydder, son of Edmund Tydder, son of Owen Tydder' as a traitor. '. . . he hath no manner, interest, right, or colour, as every man well knoweth, for he is descended of bastard blood, both of father's side and of mother's side; for the said Owen, the grandfather, was bastard born, and his mother was daughter unto John Duke of Somerset, son unto John Earl of Somerset, son unto Dame Katherine Swynford, and of their indouble avoutry (double, or perhaps indubitable adultery) gotten . . .'.

The proclamation charged that Henry had 'covenanted and bargained with . . . France to give up and release in perpetuity all the right, title, and claim that the King of England have had, and ought to have to the crown and realm of France, together with the duchies of Normandy, Anjou, and Maine, Gascoign and Guyne Cascell (Castle) and towns of Calais, Guynes, Hammes, with the marches appertaining to the same . . .'.

Richard called upon all 'good and true Englishmen' for 'the defence of them, their wives, children and goods' against the 'rebels and traitors' (*Paston Letters*, vol. ii. p. 319; *Harl. MSS.*, 433. fol. 221).

Henry defies Richard

Henry Tudor met Richard's proclamation with a powerful reply. He avowed his intention to contest the throne and branded King Richard as 'homocide unnaturall tyrant which now unjustly bears dominion over you' (*Harl. MSS., 787.* fol. 2).

Charles VIII, yielding to Henry Tudor's pleas, advanced him a large sum and furnished him with 3,000 men. Henry thereupon left the French court for Harfleur, the rendezvous of his troops. He left as hostages for repayment of the assistance given him Sir John Bourchier and the Marquis of Dorset who had tried unsuccessfully to escape King Richard and had been overtaken at Compeigne (Buck, lib. ii. p. 57; Grafton, p. 207).

Henry rested at Rouen to allow time for mustering his forces and provisioning his shipping. Here, learning of the rumors that Richard intended to marry Princess Elizabeth, he acted to effect a Welsh alliance by sending messengers to Sir Walter Herbert with proposals to marry his sister and to the Earl of Northumberland, hoping to enlist his aid. Here, also, to his surprise and joy, he received 2,000 Bretons sent unsolicited by Francis Duke of Brittany (Grafton, p. 208; Buck, lib. ii. p. 58).

No obstacle remained to prevent Henry from proceeding with his long threatened invasion of England.

Philip de Commynes says that few forces could have been more contemptible than the soldiers furnished by France — an evil lot

(p. 356). But their inefficiency in military skill was offset by the reckless hardihood of these desperate soldiers of fortune (*Memoires*, ed. J. Colmette and J. Durville, Paris, 1924-25).

Kendall: Kendall says that Henry's 2,000 men from France were the scum from jails in Normandy, released only to fight England (pp. 339, 340).

Lord Stanley acts suspiciously

The great secret of Richard's downfall was the defection of his so-called friends. Neither Henry Tudor nor the combined forces of France and Brittany could have vanquished King Richard had he been more suspicious of his counsellors, more avaricious and mercenary, and less chivalrous and generous in the treatment of his nobles. Richard III, one of the ablest generals and wisest legislators of his age, was the victim of systematic treachery.

There was one illustrious member of his household, high in his confidence and with powerful influence in the west, whose ambiguous and suspicious conduct caused the King deep and unceasing anxiety. It was Lord Stanley, husband of the Countess of Richmond, Henry Tudor's mother (Grafton, p. 202).

Richard, as Lord Protector, had been decidedly opposed to Stanley. Yet he acted most generously to this nobleman. He had released Stanley from prison and pardoned him for his reputed connection with Lord Hastings' conspiracy. He had advanced Stanley to the highest offices in the government and to the most trustworthy places about his royal person. On discovering that Lady Stanley had helped to foment the Duke of Buckingham's rebellion, he had abstained from involving Stanley in his wife's treason. Richard had even greatly softened the sentence so justly due her, in consequence of her husband's integrity. It is only fair to add that, up to the present crisis, Lord Stanley had continued faithful in the trust reposed in him.

This much is very certain, however, King Richard for some time had entertained just reason to doubt the stability of this nobleman, the Lord Steward of his household and the High Constable of the realm. Lord Stanley chose this time to ask for leave to quit the presence of his King and to return to 'his country to visit his family and to recreate his spirits' (Chron. Croy., p. 573). This request convinced Richard that Stanley was moving to be in perfect readiness to receive Henry Tudor (Grafton, p. 203).

Richard was too wise to accelerate Stanley's disaffection by premature and possibly uncalled-for suspicion. However, he would not let Stanley depart until he had consented to send as a hostage Lord Strange, his 'first begotten son and heir' (*Chron. Croy.*, p. 573).

Succeeding events prove the wisdom of Richard discretion. They also remove all doubt that the Attorney-General, Morgan Kydwelly, and Lord Stanley were leagued together. Kydwelly was the means for communicating with the rebels in France, while Stanley was the organ for effecting the plan that was to end in the junction of the exiles with their English supporters.

For about the same time that Lord Stanley left the court, Henry Tudor was advised by the crafty Kydwelly 'to make quick expedition, and shape his course directly for Wales'. Sir William Stanley, Lord Stanley's brother, held the responsible position of Chamberlain in the north part of Wales. By virtue of his office, therefore, he could leave any portion of the coast unguarded. He could even prevent all hostile opposition to the invaders from the royal forces stationed there by King Richard. The King had, in the preceding winter, placed these forces under the sole command of the two Stanleys for the protection of the West Country (*Harl. MSS.*, 433, fol. 200).

Kendall: Kendall mentions Lord Stanley's political agility. He swore allegiance to Henry VI and Edward IV and betrayed both oaths. Yet, he managed to end up with positions of great power and accumulated vast possessions (pp. 334-337).

Henry lands at Milford Haven

Henry followed Kydwelly's instructions. He embarked on July 26, 1485 (Blakeway's *Shrewsbury*, vol. i. p. 242) and had actually sailed from Harfleur before King Richard learned this news. Richard established relays of cavalry on all the high roads to get news to him of Henry's movements. At Richard's request, the great seal was surrendered to him by the Bishop of Lincoln in the old Temple, London, on July 29 (*Feodera*, xii. p. 271).

But Richard's vigilance was in vain. So prosperous was the wind, so favorable the weather, that Henry reached the Welsh coast on the seventh day after leaving France. Here he learned that an opposing garrison which had been waiting for him at Milford

Haven throughout the winter had been removed. Henry made direct for that port and disembarked without opposition on the evening of August 1 (Grafton, p. 209; *Chron. Croy.*, p. 573).

Henry commenced his march forthwith, and before sunrise he had reached the town of Haverfordwest. The astonished populace welcomed him with joy. Henry's descent from their native princes seemed to realize a long-held superstition. The people believed that the sceptre which had been usurped from the ancient British kings by the Saxons, the Danes, and the Normans, would be restored to them by a native of Wales, a descendant of the renowned King Arthur (Baker's *Chron.*, p. 252). Taking advantage of this superstitition, Henry caused a banner, displaying the insignia of Cadwallader, the last of their kings, to be carried in front of his troops.

Henry had landed at a point where there was no regular communication with the court. Choosing the wildest mountain passes, he headed for the northern part of Wales, hoping to increase his strength by winning over many of the Welsh chieftains and to join Sir William Stanley. Thus, Henry was in the heart of the kingdom before Richard knew of his having sailed from Harfleur.

Richard moves to repel Henry

Richard commanded the Duke of Norfolk, who had been guarding the eastern counties, to join him with his full strength at Nottingham. The King also summoned the Earl of Northumberland from the north and Lord Lovell and Lord Stanley from the south and west. He sent a mandate to the Tower of London enjoining the attendance of the faithful Brackenbury and placed under his command 'divers other knights and esquires, in whom the king placed less confidence' (Grafton, p. 204). Letters were despatched to every county 'forbidding all who were born to any inheritance in the realm to withdraw from the ensuing conflict on pain of forfeiture of life, and goods, and possessions' (*Chron. Croy.*, p. 573).

Stanley's son confesses treason

The Lords of Norfolk, Northumberland, and Lovell obeyed promptly. But Lord Stanley excused himself on the plea of sickness. This pretence was so shallow that Richard was confirmed in his conviction that, like the excuses of the faithless Buckingham, Lord

Stanley's illness was merely a feint to conceal his traitorous designs.

This connection was soon confirmed. Lord Stanley's son, Lord Strange, whom Richard was holding as a hostage for his father's appearance, attempted to escape. He was arrested and when in danger of his life confessed his guilt. He acknowledged that his uncle, Sir William Stanley, Sir John Savage, and other members of his family were leagued with Henry Tudor and intended to join him with their forces. He absolved his father, however, from all participation in this plot and promised that, if his life were spared, Lord Stanley would prove his loyalty by speedily joining the King. Accordingly, he sent letters to his father explaining the peril he was in and begging him to hasten to his relief. (Ibid.) But Lord Stanley never again returned to Richard's court to prove his loyalty.

As usual, King Richard acted with great moderation. Although Sir William Stanley and Sir John Savage were immediately denounced as traitors, neither Lord Stanley nor Lord Strange were included in the denunciation.

The Tudor chronicler, Grafton, admits that vast multitudes thronged to Richard's standard (p. 215). The realm was not opposed to his government. His enemies, however, preferred to impute his downfall to that source rather than admit the systematic treason and perjury by which it was effected.

Richard was loyally supported and had taken every means to repel the invaders. Thus, when he learned of Henry's landing, he expressed satisfaction that 'the day had at length arrived, when having easily triumphed over the exiled faction, his subjects would from thenceforth enjoy undoubted peace' (*Chron. Croy.*, p. 573). He was justified in this feeling because no part of England or Wales betrayed symptoms of riot or insurrection.

Henry stealthily and cautiously pursued his course, keeping near the sea coast within reach of his shipping. Marching in a wild and half-populated country, he was obliged to contest the mountain passes and to assault many places opposed to his progress (Blakeway's *Shrewsbury*, vol. i. p. 244; Grafton, p. 211).

Henry Tudor had ample cause to tremble for the result. His slender band of 3,000 French and 2,000 Bretons was only increased by a few native chieftains. Sir Walter Herbert, on whose aid he had counted, remained true to King Richard (Grafton, p. 211). The Earl of Northumberland, too, was with the King.

Happily for Henry, the Shrewsbury authorities permitted him to pass through on his pledge to do so peaceably. Here, Henry was met by Sir Rice Ap- Thomas, one of the most powerful of the

Welsh chieftains, whom Richard had appointed to command the royal forces in the south of Wales (Blakeway's *Shrewsbury*, vol. i. p. 245). Despite his solemn oath of allegiance to Richard, this chieftain joined Henry on his promise of being made Governor of Wales if Henry gained the throne (Ibid. p. 244; see note to Turner's *Middle Ages*, vol. iv. p. 33).

At Newport, the rebels were joined by Sir Gilbert Talbot, 'with the whole power of the young Earl of Shrewsbury, then being in ward, which were accounted to the number of 2,000 men' (Grafton, p. 213). This incident affords a striking example of the abuse of wardship at this period. The young Earl of Shrewsbury remained true to King Richard (*Harl. MSS.*, 542, fol. 34) and joined his banner. Yet, as a minor, he had no command over his tenantry all of whom were carried over to Henry's army by his uncle and guardian, Sir Gilbert Talbot (Grafton, p. 213).

Sir William Stanley met Henry at Stafford. Upon his advice, Henry went direct to Litchfield where he was received like a prince (Grafton, p. 213). His father-in-law, Lord Stanley, had paved the way for Henry's favorable reception. Stanley left Litchfield on learning of Henry's approach to avoid sacrificing the life of his son who had been left with King Richard as a hostage for his fidelity.

King Richard moves to Leicester

King Richard, having learned that Henry Tudor's object was to proceed direct to London, resolved to intercept his progress. Despite the King's precautionary measures, he found that Henry was moving by 'day and night right in his face' (Chron. Croy., p. 573). Richard therefore had to move promptly from Nottingham, although many of his trusty commanders had not yet reached the castle. He learned with great indignation of the defection of the Talbots, the perfidy of Ap-Thomas, and the welcome given to Henry at Litchfield. His spies informed him of a private interview between Sir William Stanley and Henry at Stafford (Grafton, p. 213) and of Lord Stanley's departure for Atherstone the day before the rebels entered Litchfield. Accordingly, Richard decided to move to Leicester to prevent a junction between Henry and his step-father and to give battle before Henry's forces were further augmented.

Richard marshalled his troops in the market place at Nottingham. He separated the foot soldiers into two divisions, five abreast, and divided his cavalry so as to form two wide-spreading wings. He placed his ammunition and artillery in the center and took up his own position in a space immediately behind it. Gorgeously attired in splendid armor, with his helmet surmounted by the crown, and surrounded by a gallant band of archers and picked men-at-arms, King Richard III rode upon a superbly caparisoned milk-white charger, attended by his body guards. They displayed the banner of England and innumerable pennons glittering with the silver boar and other insignia. Thus Richard wended his way on the morning of August 6, 1485, down the steep hill and left the castle of Nottingham forever. He was about to fight his last battle but he knew it not (Huttons *Bosworth*, p. 46; Grafton, p. 215). See W. Hutton, *The Battle of Bosworth Field*, 2nd edition, ed. J. Nichols, London, 1813. King Richard's army covered the road for three miles and was 'more than an hour in marching out of Nottingham, and as long in entering Leicester', which he reached at sunset. His army was so large that the Croyland Chronicler states it was 'a greater number of men than was ever before seen in England fighting on one side (p. 574; Hutton, p. 46). John of Gaunt's castle of Leicester was too ruinous for occupation, so Richard took up his abode in the town's chief hostelry, known in later ages as the Blue Boar.

On August 17, Richard marched to Hinckley and fixed his camp at the village of Elmsthorpe. Learning that Henry had not left Litchfield, Richard took up his station on August 18 on rising ground at Stableton where no enemy could approach unseen. Here he was probably joined by the Duke of Norfolk, the Earl of Surrey, and Sir Robert Brackenbury (Hutton, p. 50).

At Stony Stratford, Sir Walter Hungerford and Sir Thomas Bourchier, both 'esquires of the body' (Harl. MSS. 433. pp. 16, 27, 142) left Brackenbury under cover of the night and joined the enemy's ranks. And Sir John Savage, Sir Simon Digby, and many other individuals, whom gratitude alone ought to have bound to their King, proclaimed themselves supporters of the rebels.

Richard's suspicions were again excited when he learned that Henry had moved from Litchfield and arrived at Tamworth late on the evening of August 18 (Hutton, p. 195). Here, the troops commanded by Lord Stanley and his brother William separated the royal forces from Henry's army. Thus, secret interviews between Henry Tudor and his kindred were facilitated. August 19 and 20 apparently were spent by both sides in watching their opponents' movements and placing their camps as advantageously as possible. The hostile armies were now so close that an engagement had become inevitable.

Gairdner: 'The chronology of Richard's movements given by Hutton in his "Battle of Bosworth Field", pp. 49, 50 is quite impossible. Mr Hutton thinks, apparently, that Richard arrived at Leicester on the evening of the 16th, and that he marched out of it on the 17th . . . But the Croyland writer distinctly says that Richard moved out of Leicester . . . on the 21st August, the day before the battle took place; and this is confirmed by the Rolls of Parliament (vi. 276) . . .'. (p. 232.)

'. . . the theory started by Hutton that Richard encamped at Stapleton, about three miles south of Market Bosworth, is not very probable . . . If Richard had encamped on the 21st so far south as Stapleton he would naturally have attacked his enemy on the south side of Ambien Hill; whereas it would appear that Henry's forces marched northwards along a marsh that lay west of Ambien Hill before the battle began' (p. 254).

The armies meet near Redmore Plain

Henry again followed the footsteps of his step-father. He quit Tamworth and arrived at Atherstone shortly after Lord Stanley's departure. Stanley had marched to within three quarters of a mile of the royal troops the better to deceive the King. The Duke of Norfolk and the Earl of Northumberland, each with his own powerful body of men, were also encamped on advantageous positions. All parties felt that the time had now arrived for the long threatened and much desired combat.

A broad extent of uninclosed country separated the rival forces. The scene of action eventually fixed upon was Redmore Plain, since better known as Bosworth Field, because of its proximity to the town of Market Bosworth. 'Redmore, or Red-moor, is so named from the colour of the soil, as the meadows in the west are called white-moors for the same reason' (Hutton, p. 68). It was somewhat of an oval form, about two miles long and one mile wide, intersected by a thick wood. It was bounded on the south side by a small river running through a low swampy country and on the north side partly by rising ground and partly by a boggy flat, Amyon Lays. Amyon Hill rose gently northward. The rival commanders speedily occupied high ground knowing that the battle would inevitably occur on the plain below.

Richard's camp consisted of two lines, covering about eighteen acres. It was fortified by breastworks 300 yards long and about 50 broad. Hutton, in his *Battle of Bosworth Field*, states that on his first visit to Bosworth Field vestiges of the camps were yet visible (p. 62). Although Henry Tudor's forces covered only seven acres, the experience of the Earl of Oxford, Sir James Blount, and other renowned warriors fully compensated for his smaller numbers (Hutton, p. 50).

Lord Stanley and his brother, Sir William Stanley, had craftily placed themselves on two eminences. One was to the extreme left a little in advance of the royal camp. The other was to the extreme right, but somewhat to the rear of that camp. Although seemingly attched to King Richard because of their closeness to his forces, they were in the best position for accelerating his downfall at the proper time.

During the night of August 20, 1485, the celebrated interview between Henry Tudor and the two Stanleys is said to have taken place. The brothers informed Henry of their intentions and also apparently intimated to him the probable defection of the Earl of Northumberland (Hutton, p. 57; Grafton, p. 218).

At daybreak on August 21, Henry broke up his camp at Atherstone, crossed the Tweed, and encamped on Bosworth Field. The same day, King Richard, learning of Henry's movements, advanced to meet him. Although he had encamped his forces so as to preclude Henry's further advance toward London, Richard appears to have made Leicester his headquarters. He rode out of Leicester in the same royal state in which he made his entry into that town. He was accompanied by the Duke of Norfolk, the Earl of Surrey, Lord Lincoln, Lord Lovell, most of his personal friends, and a vast concourse of people. With his royal crown upon his head, King Richard was borne on a noble war-steed of uncommon size, whose costly trappings accorded with the rich suit of polished steel armor he had worn fourteen years before at the battle of Tewkesbury. Thus, Richard, the last English King to go into battle, presented himself before his soldiers as became a defied and insulted monarch on the eve of engaging in deadly battle.

Both armies were within view of each other the greater part of August 21. But it was Sunday, and as if by mutual consent each party remained inactive until towards evening. The King then broke up his encampment and took up his position for the night on the brow of the hill overlooking Bosworth plain.

Sir William Stanley had already been proclaimed a traitor. However, he had not arrayed himself publicly under Henry's banner, thus creating doubts as to his ultimate intention. But Lord

Stanley had been wary in his conduct. Although Richard must have resented his contemputous disregard of his summons, yet he could not justly charge him with treason. Stanley had avoided a junction with Henry, although still pleading severe illness as his excuse for not obeying Richard's summons (*Harl. MSS.*, 542, fol. 34).

And now, on the eve of the battle, Lord Stanley had encamped near Richard and at a considerable distance from Henry. Sir William observed the same policy. Although ranged on the side of the field occupied by Richard, he had intentionally allowed the whole royal army to separate his band from that of his brother. Under such circumstances to have concluded perfidy and to have denounced the Stanleys would perhaps accelerate the very evil Richard wished to prevent.

King Richard awoke on the morning of August 22 determined to ascertain beyond doubt the sentiments of Lord Stanley. He sent the trusty Brackenbury with a message forthwith requiring Lord Stanley's personal attendance at his camp. Richard was well aware that Lord Stanley had espoused Henry Tudor's mother. Sir William had been admitted to be faithless by his own nephew, Lord Strange. And the King's suspicions had been further stirred by the following message affixed during the night to Norfolk's tent (Grafton, p. 230):

> 'Jocke of Norfolk, be not too bold,
> For Dickon thy master is bought and sold'.

Suspicion had opened Richard's mind to a danger greater than Henry's trivial band of 7,000 men arrayed against the royal forces of more than double that number.

Battle of Bosworth Field

Fable and misrepresentation have added greatly to the horrors of Bosworth Field. It is known, however, that on Lord Stanley's refusal to obey the royal summons, the King commanded the immediate execution of Stanley's son, Lord Strange, who had been a hostage for his father's fidelity. But the day had long dawned and both armies were on the alert. Richard was again prevailed upon to spare his captive or at least to suspend his execution until the battle ended (*Chron. Croy.*, p. 574; Grafton, pp. 283, 284).

Recovering his usual self-possession, King Richard arranged his forces with the military skill and precision for which he was noted. He spread his force of about 16,000 men to the greatest advantage,

234

covering the eminence which rose from the center of the plain from its base to its summit. Henry's troops were ranged in the valley beneath. His troops were protected by the wood, and the marshy swamps which intervened between that and the rivulet. The two Stanleys had placed their forces so that the four bands formed an irregular square closer to Richard than to Henry (Hutton, pp. 87, 88).

Both armies were drawn up in similar order of battle, each in two lines. The archers were in the front, the bill-men in the rear, and the horse forming the wings. King Richard entrusted his front line to his faithful friend the Duke of Norfolk, assisted by the Earl of Surrey. The second line appears to have been commanded by Lord Ferrers, with the Earl of Northumberland. The King, in person, commanded the center. It comprised a dense square of 'seven score of serjeants, that were chained and locked in a row, and as many bombards and thousands of morrispikes, harquebusses, &c. &c.' Henry's front was commanded by the Earl of Oxford, supported on his right by Sir Gilbert Talbot and on the left by Sir John Savage. Henry's second line, ostensibly commanded by himself, was in effect commanded by his uncle, the Earl of Pembroke, a veteran warrior of great skill (Hutton, p. 81; Grafton, p. 220; *Harl. MSS.*, 542, fol. 34).

According to later writers — Grafton and Hall — both leaders are said to have made powerful orations to their troops. But none of the contemporary historians — the Chronicler of Croyland, the historian Rous, or the city annalist, Fabyan, mention such orations. Nor are they mentioned in the manuscript which appears to have been written by some person present at the conflict (*Harl. MSS.*, 542, fol. 34).

As Henry's army slowly advanced, the royal archers bent their bows. From the moment the trumpets sounded and actual strife commenced, King Richard exhibited the utmost heroism. He encouraged his troops by the example of his own invincible courage. Had he been adequately supported, Henry and not Richard III would probably have fallen on Bosworth Field.

But in the heat of the battle, Lord Stanley passed over to Henry Tudor, thus neutralizing the advantage which the devoted Norfolk had obtained over the Earl of Oxford (Grafton, p. 227). Henry's strengthened forces then made a desperate attack upon the yet unbroken front of the royal forces. But the Earl of Northumberland, commanding the second line, instead of supporting his sovereign — with feelings more despicable than open revolt — stood aloof. Richard was thus deprived of aid from the quarter on which he had

235

most relied for support (Grafton, p. 251; Hall, p. 419).

Richard was stung to the quick by such base perfidy and furious at witnessing the death of the valiant Norfolk, the capture of the Earl of Surrey, and the slaughter of several other trusty commanders who had hastened to their rescue. He determined to seek out Henry Tudor and, by challenging him to single combat, end the battle at once. Quitting his protected central position, he rushed down the hill towards the enemy's ranks, followed by Lovell, Brackenbury, Ratcliffe, Catesby, and many other devoted friends (Grafton, p. 218; Hutton, p. 108).

As they passed a spring between the opposing lines, tradition states that the King slaked his thirst. It still retains the name of 'King Richard's Well'. Refreshed, he reclosed his helmet, and again rushed towards the spot where Henry stood indifferently guarded. He dashed into the midst of the enemy's ranks with a vigor that nothing could withstand, followed by his chosen band. In spite of opposition, Richard made his way almost to Henry before his intention had become apparent to Henry or his supporters (Grafton, p. 228).

King Richard maintained his perilous position by almost superhuman strength. He killed with his own hand Sir William Brandon, Henry Tudor's standard-bearer and unhorsed Sir John Cheney, one of the most powerful men of his time. Carrying terror and destruction into the very heart of his enemies' ranks, the King now called upon Henry to meet him in single combat. But Henry's friends knew that he was no match for Richard III, the best warrior of his time. Henry's flight or destruction seemed inevitable and King Richard's success certain (Ibid. p. 229).

Treachery of the Stanleys and Northumberland

Sir William Stanley had been neutral up to this crisis. Seeing Henry's peril, Sir William speedily joined Henry with 3,000 fresh soldiers. Surrounding Richard III, he at once cut him off from his own army or flight, and thus decided the fortune of the day (Ibid; Hutton, p. 112).

'Then to King Richard there came a knight and said "I hold it time for ye to fly; yonder Stanley his dynts be so sore, gainst them may no man stand. Here is thy horse, another day ye may worship again." "Not one foot will I fly" ' was his answer, ' "so long as breath bides within my breast; for by Him that shaped both sea and land, this day shall end my battles or my life; I will die King of England" ' (*Harl. MSS.*, 542. Fol. 34).

Betrayed, vanquished by treachery alone, Richard continued to fight with the desperation induced by his perilous situation. All his followers, one by one, were numbered with the dead. His standard-bearer alone remained and waved the royal banner on high until life was quite extinct. Still Richard remained undaunted, slaying all who approached within his sword's length.

Death of King Richard III

At last, overpowered by numbers and weakened by loss of blood, his strength was exhausted, although his courage was unabated. The Croyland Chronicler says 'in battle and not in flight the said king, stricken with many mortal wounds, fell on the field like a courageous and most daring prince' (p. 574).

Thus perished King Richard! Thus ended the Yorkist dynasty! He died like its founder, his gallant sire at Wakefield Green, the victim of base treachery.

Richard's death was not caused by open insurrection, by popular feeling over the reputed murder of his nephews, by efforts to restore the crown to its lawful owner, or to kill a tyrant whose savage deeds had driven his subjects to desperation. These were the insinuations of Henry's chroniclers in after-years. On the contrary, the last of the Plantagenet kings had been accompanied to the field, as had been his predecessors, by the flower of English chivalry. The list of these gallant knights who on the eve of the battle swore that Richard should wear the crown shows that neither the nation nor her nobles as a body had rejected their King.

Richard believed that Henry could oppose but 7,000 men to his own force of 16,000. But Richard was basely deserted by Lord Stanley's 5,000 men and one third of his army who were withdrawn by the Earl of Northumberland (Vergil, p. 563; Grafton, p. 234; Hall, p. 419).

Even Rous, who was no friend of Richard acknowledged: 'If I may speak the truth to his honour, although small of body and weak in strength, he most valiantly defended himself as a noble knight to his last breath, often exclaiming that he was betrayed, and saying — Treason! treason! treason!' With these words on his lips, King Richard III expired on August 22, 1485, after a brief reign of two years and two months — the victim of faithless conspirators. His death established the truth of the warning — the King of England was indeed 'both bought and sold!'

Polydore Vergil : Henry Tudor's official historian admits: 'King Richard, alone, was killed fighting manfully in the thickest press of his enemies'.

Kendall : Kendall notes that contrary to Henry's expectations, the Welshmen did not flock to his banner.

Henry Percy, Earl of Northumberland, remembered that his great-grandfather had died at Shrewsbury resisting Henry IV, and that his father had been killed at Towton battling Edward IV. Now, he stood aloof from contests for the throne, content to guard only the future of the House of Percy.

Henry had about 5,000 men and the Stanleys about 6,000 men, or about 11,000 in all. Richard had only about 6,000 men, excluding Northumberland's 3,000, who remained idle during the conflict. Thus, with the defection of the Stanleys and Northumberland's idleness, Henry's forces outnumbered Richard's almost two to one.

The main forces which betrayed Richard III, the troops of Lord Stanley, Sir William Stanley, the Earl of Northumberland, and Ap Thomas, were reflecting the interests of their leaders — not the interests of the nation (pp. 341, 350, 353, 361).

Turner : 'If Northumberland had charged with the forces he kept aloof, when Sir William Stanley surrounded the king, he would have preserved his life, and prevented his defeat. We can hardly conceive how a nobleman who had . . . taken or kept so many honors and bounties from him, could stand, with cool faithlessness, and see his sovereign exert the most heroic valor against such ungenerous odds, and be almost, if not quite, in the hearing of his death-cries of treason — yet not move one step, or send one man to his assistance. To let the king he had sworn to defend be thus beaten down and slain in his immediate presence, treacherously withholding relief, was one of the most stubborn efforts of human insensibility that history has recorded'.

'No talents could save Richard, amid associates like these. With such a nobility, he was environed in a fatal labyrinth, from which death only could release him' (*Middle Ages*, Book IV, pp. 526-528).

'Thus fell Richard, the victim of treachery unparalleled; for there seems to have been no national movement in favor of Richmond. It was a perfidious combination of five noblemen, which destroyed Richard. Exclusively of the force of the two Stanleys, Henry came to the battle with only 5,000; of these he had brought 2,000 with him, and 2,000 were the earl of Shrewsbury's under Talbot; so that, excepting these, all the rest who had joined him from his landing at Milford to Bosworth field, including the mighty Rice ap Thomas, amounted but to 1,000 men. Hence, it was four English noblemen; the two Stanleys, Shrewsbury, and Northumberland; and . . . Sir Rice, who dethroned Richard, by betraying and deserting him. The nation had no share in the conflict, notwithstanding all that is said of the king's unpopularity. It was an ambush of a few perfidious and disaffected noblemen, against the crown, which succeeded by their hypocrisy; and Richard perished by one of those factions in his aristocracy, from which, by taking the crown, it seemed likely that he had rescued himself. He had suppressed violently what he thought dangerous, and he was overwhelmed by the explosion of a new mine, which he had not suspected to be forming beneath him, because it was prepared and fired by those whom gratitude, honor and conscience ought to have made faithful and attached. Whatever had been his conduct towards his nephew, he had done nothing to them, to deserve that they should have destroyed him . . . '. (pp. 530-531.)

Chapter XIX

HENRY CROWNED KING; OVERPOWERS BARONS

Henry Tudor is crowned King

The battle of Bosworth Field ended with King Richard's life. It had lasted only two hours. Terror-stricken, the royal troops fled in all directions. But Henry's forces pursued them ferociously, killing about 4,000 men (*Harl. MSS.*, 542 fol. 34; Hutton, pp. 128, 129; Hume, Chap. xxiii p. 273).

Henry, accompanied by Lord Stanley, the Earl of Pembroke, the Earl of Oxford and others paused on the summit of a steep hill. Here he received from his step-father, Lord Stanley, the crown which had cost King Richard his life. During the heat of the battle, and shortly before Richard's death, his crown had been cleft from his helmet. Falling to the ground, it was picked up by a soldier and concealed in a hawthorn bush. There, Sir Reginald Bray found it and presented it to Lord Stanley, who placed it on his step-son's head and hailed him as Henry VII, monarch of England (*Harl. MSS.*, 542. fol. 34; Hutton, p. 132; Grafton, p. 233).

Norman and Tudor invasions contrasted

King Richard III was the only sovereign of England, except Henry V at Agincourt, who went into battle wearing his crown. Richard also was the only English monarch slain in battle since the Norman conquest. The conduct of Henry Tudor's invaders of the fifteenth century affords a painful contrast to the generous feeling which marked the Norman conqueror four centuries before.

The Normans warred with the living and not with the dead. They fought as became men — not as ruthless savages. Henry's forces acted far differently even though the Lancastrian and Tudor historians openly admired Richard's bravery and heroism. 'Richard died by the hands of a multitude, who cut his body in the most shocking and barbarous manner, while he was breathing his last' (Nicholls' *Leicestershire*, vol. ii, p. 298).

With Harold's death, all personal rancor ceased. William, honoring Harold's valor, delivered his body to his mother to be honorably buried (Baker's *Chron.*, p. 29). Henry Tudor's conduct towards Richard was far different. With a barbarity discreditable to the victors, they stripped Richard of his gorgeous apparel. In outrage of decency and common humanity, they placed Richard's body naked across his war steed, 'like a hog or a calf, the head and arms hanging on the one side of the horse, and the legs on the other side'. Thus all besprinkled 'with mire and blood', Richard III was carried back to Leicester as a trophy of the morning's victory, to be presented in the most degrading manner (Grafton, p. 234; Hutton, p. 141; Fabyan, p. 518).

This shameful action reflects the vindictive feelings of Richard's foes. These feelings manifested themselves later in the fearful rumors and accusations designed to blacken Richard's memory forever and to exalt Henry Tudor.

Disposition of Richard's body

King Richard had left his tent standing, so that the spoils were immense (Hutton, p. 79; Bacon's Henry VII, pp. 133, 135). King Henry VII entered Leicester the same night with great pomp. Richard's body was there 'laid openly that every man might see and look upon him', and be satisfied that he was indeed deceased.

King Richard's closest friends were slain including the Duke of Norfolk, Sir Richard Ratcliffe, Sir Robert Brackenbury — Constable of the Tower of London, John Kendall — secretary, and Sir Robert Percy — comptroller of the household. The most zealous of Richard's personal friends, regarding 'more his oath, his honour, and promise made to King Richard, like a gentleman and a faithful subject to his prince . . . manfully died with him, to his great fame and laud' (Grafton, p. 230). Sir William Catesby was beheaded two days after the battle.

During the two days Henry stayed at Leicester, 'Many other nobles and gentlemen got into foreign countries and sanctuaries, obscuring themselves till the storm and smart of that day's memory was past' (Buck, lib. ii. p. 64). During these two days, King Richard's mutilated remains were exposed to the rude gaze of the populace.

After two days, Henry VII and his army left for Coventry on his progress to London. Upon his departure, Richard's body was denied even the humble sepulchre which had been awarded to the lowest of his soldiers. 'King Richard III being slain at Bosworth', remarks the county historian, 'his body was begged by the nuns at Leicester, and buried in their chapel there'. He adds that at the suppression of the monasteries by King Henry VIII, Richard's tomb was utterly defaced, 'since when, his grave, overgrown with nettles and weeds, is not to be found'. His body is traditionally reported to have been thrown over Bow Bridge (Nicholl's *Leicestershire*, vol. ii, p. 298).

But positive proof may be said to exist, and on the high authority of Christoper Wren, that King Richard's remains were suffered to rest finally in consecrated ground. 'At the dissolution of the monastery where he was interred, the place of his burial happened to fall into the bounds of a citizen's garden; which being purchased by Mr Robert Heyrick, some time mayor of Leicester, was by him covered with a handsome stone pillar three feet high, with this inscription, "Here lies the body of Richard III sometime King of England". This he shewed me walking in the garden, 1612' (Wren's *Parentalia*, p. 114).

No remains, however, of this or of any other monument now mark the place where King Richard was interred.

Gairdner : Gairdner notes that Richard's body, covered with dust and blood, naked, and with a rope around his neck, was trussed across the back of a horse and carried into Leicester (pp. 244, 245).

Kendall : Kendall states that Richard's body later was cast into the Soar (p. 493).

Richard's illegitimate children

Richard III left two illegitimate children — a son and a daughter. Both were apparently older than the young Prince of Wales, with whom they were probably brought up at Middleham (Harl. MSS., 433. fol. 269). They seem to have been educated with great care and were recognized by the King as his offspring. Richard knighted the elder child, John, and on March 11, 1485, appointed him Captain of Calais for life and governor of the fortresses of Rysbank, Guisnes, Hammes, and all the marches of Picardy belonging to the English crown. Nothing is known, however, of his subsequent fate.

Richard's other child, Katherine, seems to have ranked high in her father's favor. She was early married to William Herbert, Earl of Huntingdon, secretary to the young Prince of Wales (*Harl. MSS.*, 433, fol. 34).

Tradition numbers a third child, bearing his father's name (See Peck's *Desiderata Curiosa*, Seymour's *Top.*; and *Hist. Survey of Kent*, Leland's *Kent*; and Gent's Mag. vol. xxxvii. p. 408; vol. lxii, p. 1,106). It is said that he did not learn of his parentage until the eve of the battle of Bosworth. Richard then apparently sent for him and said he intended to acknowledge him as his offspring if he survived the battle and defeated Henry Tudor. When the battle ended, the stripling fled and, after great privation, worked as a stone mason at Eastwell in Kent, where he lived obscurely and in penury to the age of between 70 and 80. Shortly before his death, he made his history known to an ancestor of the present Earl of Winchelsea, who allowed him to erect a cottage in his grounds.

Singular as this romantic tale may appear, there are facts which throw over it an air of credibility. The registry of Richard's death and burial at Eastwell, in 1560, is yet extant, and the author has a certified copy which reads —

'Anno Domini, 1560
Rychard Plantagenet was buried the xxii daye of Decembre,
   Anno di supra'.

The Gentleman's Magazine of August 10, 1767, has a very interesting letter entitled *The Story of Richard Plantagenet authenticated*. The rector of the parish of Eastwell, in the same year, stated 'It is also remarkable that in the same register, whenever any of noble family was buried, this   mark is prefixed to the name; and the same mark is put to that of Richard Plantagenet' (T. Parsons, Rector of Eastwell, July, 1767).

Appearance of Bosworth Field

Owing to the learned Dr. Samuel Parr, the site of the well from which King Richard drank will be preserved for posterity. Dr. Parr learned that the well was in danger of being destroyed by cattle and from the draining of the land. Accordingly, he journeyed to Bosworth Field in the year 1813. Having discovered, by means of local information, the identical spot, he took measures to have it preserved by means of an inscription in Latin — in English thus:

243

With water drawn from this well,
Richard the Third, King of England,
When fighting most strenuously and intensely
With Henry Earl of Richmond,
Quenched his thirst;
Before night about to be deprived
Alike of his life and sceptre,
11th of the Calends of September, A.D. 1485.

This inscription deeply cut on white stone, is placed immediately over the spring. Within, a small building of unhewn stone of a pyramidal form has been rudely constructed.

Power shifts from barons to King

The battle of Bosworth, fiercely as it raged, lasted but two hours (Grafton, p. 231). Yet, those two hours were fraught with the most important results to England. The downfall of King Richard proved the downfall also of that overwhelming baronial ascendancy which had led to his destruction. It had been the aim of the House of York to curb the inordinate power of the arrogant nobles and to check the undue influence of the priesthood.

The Yorkist rule was characterised by one vast and desperate struggle between the sovereign and the aristocracy. Every King of England must be in danger so long as the real control of affairs rested virtually in her turbulent barons. King Richard III had undertaken to suppress the hosts of private military retainers and had enacted prohibitions against the ancient custom of giving badges, liveries, and family devices to multitudes of armed followers. By these measures, Richard struck at the root of the evil which arose from each chieftain having a standing and well-disciplined army to command, to over-awe the crown and perpetually disturb the peace of the realm (*Harl. MSS.*, 433, fol. 111, 138, 188, 230). But these daring measures to limit the power of the nobles led, by the treason and treachery of a very few, to King Richard's ruin.

It was left to the calculating Henry VII to consummate the policy which the Yorkist Kings, with their shining abilities, had failed to effect. None but a prince so cautious, so mistrustful, so secret in his habits and reserved in his manners as the founder of the Tudor dynasty could have perfected the policy initiated by the Yorkist Kings. 'A dark prince, and infinitely supicious' (Bacon, p. 242).

Henry's execution of Sir William Stanley within ten years after Bosworth shows that he saw the need of watching his personal attendants 'Through the agency of secret spies, which he did employ both at home and abroad, by them to discover what practices and conspiracies were against him' (Ibid. p. 240). 'He kept a strict hand on his nobility, and chose rather to advance clergymen and lawyers which were more obsequious to him, but had less interest in the people, which made for his absoluteness, but not for his safety' (Ibid. p. 242).

Richard's evil reputation not merited

The legend of Richard's deformities were not derived from contemporary writers but arose in Tudor times and was perpetuated and elaborated upon by Tudor chroniclers. The physical power which Richard displayed when seeking out Henry of Richmond on Redmore Plain must prove to every impartial mind how great a mixture of fable has been intermingled with historal fact. A withered arm could not have slain Sir William Brandon, or unhorsed Sir John Cheyney, the most powerful man of his time. If Richard's arm had been withered from his birth, Richard could not have performed corresponding acts of heroism at Barnet.

There is scarcely an action connected with Richard III's memorable career that has not been reported with political bias. And Shakespeare's genius perpetuates Richard's evil reputation. But the great bard had no access to sources contemporary with Richard. He relied upon the sources available to him, Hall and Holinshed, both of whom had adopted Sir Thomas More's portrait of Richard.

Shakespeare's most destructive scene, as regards King Richard's reputation is found in act v, scene 3. Here, the ghosts of Edward of Lancaster, Henry VI, George Duke of Clarence, Rivers, Grey, Vaughan, Hastings, the two young Princes, Queen Anne, and the Duke of Buckingham visit the doomed Richard. They flit before him with reproaches for every crime which posthumous calumny and legendary lore has fastened upon him. What wonder is it that by this terrific scene the mind of succeeding generations of spectators were convinced of Richard III's guilt?

Even the catalog of Richard's virtue could not offset Shakespeare's brilliant imagination and the prejudice of his Tudor source:

Richard's steadfast loyalty and service to his brother, Edward IV amidst every reverse and temptation;

Richard's stern resistance to the French King's bribes;
his neutrality in the intrigues of the English court;
his wise legislative program; and
his generosity and clemency.

Instead, Henry VII's writers have produced a monster of depravity whose very name has come to symbolize bodily and mental deformity. This impression has prevailed for ages, and to a certain degree, still prevails regarding an English King whose actions and character deserve a more just and faithful review.

The nation was indebted to King Richard for wise statutes of lasting good. He was a firm protector of the Church and a strict administrator of justice. Richard was a generous enemy. That his clemency and forbearance did not arise from personal fear is evidenced by the bravery and courage which even his enemies have perpetuated.

A close examination of the records will prove that, among all the fearful charges brought against Richard III, few, if any, originate with his contemporaries. The dark deeds which have made his name so odious were first promulgated as rumor, and admitted as such by Fabyan, Polydore Vergil, and Sir Thomas More in the reign of his deadly enemy and successor, Henry VII. They were multiplied in number and more surely attributed to him by Grafton, Hall, and Holinshed, during the ensuing reign. And toward the close of the Tudor dynasty, Lord Bacon, Sir Richard Baker, and many others cast every reservation aside and recorded the rumored dark deeds as historical truths. These charges were made yet more appalling by the moral and personal deformity with which King Richard was invested by the genius and imagination of Shakespeare, relying on Hall and Holinshed.

The Croyland Chronicler terminated his valuable work with the death of King Richard. He intimated very plainly the little probability there was of truth prevailing in subsequent narratives about Richard. 'Forasmuch as the custom of those who write histories is to be silent on the actions of the living, lest the description of their faults should produce odium, while the recital of their virtues might be attributed to the fault of adulation, the afore-named writer has determined to put an end to his labour at the death of Richard III' (Gale, p. 577). This he did on April 30, 1486, about eight months after King Henry's accession. This period was sufficiently long for him to perceive that silence was desirable regarding Henry's actions and that odium would be incurred by admitting his faults.

If Richard resolutely pursued a domestic policy which would ameliorate the condition of his people and contribute to the country's prosperity, then surely it is time that justice was done to him. Time, and the publication of many contemporary documents, have furnished proof of his eminent virtue and noble exemplary deeds. They already suffice to rescue King Richard's memory from at least some of the crimes which have made his name odious and have inspired great doubts as to the truth of other accusations.

Lord Bacon panegyrised 'his wholesome laws' and pronounced him 'jealous for the honour of the English nation' (p. 2). Grafton admitted 'that if he had continued lord protector the realm would have prospered, and he would have been praised and beloved' (p. 235). Polydore Vergil, writing for Henry VII, commended his 'piety and benevolence' and lauded 'the good works which his sudden death alone rendered incomplete' (p. 565). Contemporary writers testify to his noble conduct in the field, and the treachery which destroyed him (*Chron. Croy.*, p. 574; Rous, p. 217). Fabyan said that before his accession he was so 'loved and praised' that many would have 'jeaparded life and goods with him' (p. 517). The Universities of Oxford and Cambridge perpetuate his love of letters, his patronage of the arts, and his munificence to these Universities (Gutch's *Hist. Oxford*, p. 639; Cooper's Annals of Cambridge, p. 228). The register of his public acts abounds in examples of Richard's liberality to the church and his equity, charity, beneficence, and piety (*Harl. MSS.*, fol. 433).

Gairdner : Gairdner notes that the Tudor Age began in dark mystery and so continued to the end. State matters were not to be the concern of citizens. Any opposition was punished. It was a secret, tyrannical, and, frequently, a cruel government (pp. 258, 259).

Conclusion

Mystery will probably surround portions of Richard's career because of the destruction of original documents and the great distance of time. Yet so great an advance has already been made as the admission by D'Israeli that the 'personal monster whom More and Shakespeare exhibited had vanished' (*Amenities of Literature*, vol. ii p. 105). It is to be hoped that more attention will be given to the origins of Richard III's evil reputation and the conclusions to be drawn from the many facts we know, as distinguished from the unsupported charges originating with Richard's enemies, tradition, and Shakespeare's brilliant play.

Chapter XX

THE BONES FOUND IN THE TOWER (Editor's Notes)

Halsted

Bayley, the historian of the Tower, says 'It is a very general opinion that the building called 'The Bloody Tower' received its appellation from the circumstances of the royal children having been stifled in it, and it is commonly and confidently asserted that the bones were found under a staircase there; yet both of these stories seem wholly without foundation' (Bayley, vol. ii. p. 64; Halsted, p. 221).

'The whole story of the two royal brothers having been destroyed in the Tower, comes to us in so questionable a shape, that it can never be entertained without some serious doubts' (Ibid.).

'Between the reign of Henry VIII, when this building was called the Garden Tower, and the year 1597, when it was known as the Bloody Tower, the Tower was crowded by delinquents of all descriptions; and as the structure in question was no doubt then frequently used as a prison, it more probably derived its present name from some of the horrid deeds which distinguished that era' (Bayley, vol. i. p. 264; Halsted, p. 223).

Bayley adds we do not need stronger proof 'that the name of the building did not originate in the circumstance in question' because that designation was not used 'till upwards of a century after the supposed act' (Bayley, vol. i. p. 264; Halsted, p. 222).

'The identity of the bones', observes Mr Laing, 'is uncertain; the Tower was both a palace and a state prison, the receptacle of Lollards, heretics, and criminals, within which those who died by disease or violence were always buried; the discovery, therefore, of bones, is neither surprising nor perhaps uncommon; but we must guard against the extreme credulity perceptible in the officers, who, persuaded that the princes were secretly interred in the Tower, appropriated every skeleton to them . . . '. (Laing in *Henry*, vol. xii. p. 419; Halsted, pp. 228, 229).

Thus, it appears that More's legend of the Bloody Tower vanishes by testing its validity. *First*, the name Bloody Tower was not assumed until 1597, the year of Queen Elizabeth's survey of the fortress, over 100 years after the alleged murder. *Second*, the bones that were supposed to confirm the tradition were found in a part of the fortress far removed from the burial place reported by More.

On a discovery thus vague and inconclusive has King Richard's guilt been considered firmly proved. And this despite the untenable legend of the 'Bloody Tower' and the absence of all proof of Tyrrel and Warbeck's reputed confessions. 'King Henry's great and culpable omission in this instance', (the alleged confession of Warbeck) 'as in the case of the examination of Tyrrel and Dighton, was, in not openly publishing a statement, signed and verified by competent authorities, which would have been far more satisfactory than "the court fumes", which, adds Bacon, "commonly print better (i.e., more strongly impress themselves on the public mind) than printed proclamations" ' (Documents relating to Perkin Warbeck, *Archaeologia*, vol. xxvii. p. 153; Halsted, pp. 222, 223, 227).

The Complete Peerage (See also Chapter XIV)

The Complete Peerage contains a succinct review of the controversy surrounding the discovery of the bones found in the Tower of London. The Editor, Geoffrey H. White, in a summary entitled 'The Princes in the Tower', says that Sandford, writing in 1677, bases his story on the account of John Knight, King Charles II's principal surgeon.

Sandford (in *Genealogical History of the Kings of England*, p. 402) says 'that on a Friday in July 1674 workmen at the Tower of London, digging under the stairs which led from the King's lodgings to the Chapel, about 10 feet in the ground, found the bones of two "striplings" '. . . . The workmen threw away the bones and rubbish, but were later made to sift the rubbish and recover some bones, which were 'presumed to be the bones of the two Princes'. Knight could not 'have been present when the bones were first dug up, as he would have prevented the discarding of the bones, but he may have witnessed the sifting. Although the bones were found in 1674, they were not enclosed in a marble urn until 1678 — *four years later*'.

'The urn was opened for examination on July 6, 1933, in the presence of the Dean of Westminster and others, including Lawrence E. Tanner, Archivist and Librarian of Westminster Abbey. The bones were submitted to Professor William Wright for anatomical examination, resulting in a surprising discovery. The urn contained not only human bones but a large variety of other bones, such as fish, duck, chicken, rabbit, sheep, pig, and ox'.

In their final report, Tanner and Wright concluded that the bones were indeed those of the two Princes — between 12 and 13 for the elder and about 10 for the younger. They attributed a red stain on the skull of the elder to the possibility of congestion caused by suffocation, and admitted the impossibility of determining sex from the bones (See 'Recent Investigations regarding the fate of the Princes in the Tower', *Archaeologia*, vol. 84, 1935, pp. 1-25, by Lawrence E. Tanner and Professor William Wright).

Twenty years later, Kendall's experts (1) confirmed the impossibility of ascertaining sex, (2) rejected the theory that suffocation caused the reddish stain on the larger skull, and (3) differed among themselves and with Professor Wright on the possible ages of the children (pp. 497-498).

The Editor of the Complete Peerage notes it is incredible that all the authorities who examined the bones in 1674, including the Royal Surgeon, were 'so ignorant of anatomy that they supposed all these bones of animals and birds to be human bones. . . . The only possible solution seems to be that a number of the original bones . . . were given away or sold as relics; and that when the bones were called for, four years later, to be interred in the Abbey, the persons in whose charge they were hurriedly collected any bones on which they could lay hand in an emergency in order to make the quantity pass muster with the undertakers'.

In brief —

the bones found in 1674 were not actually enclosed in a marble urn until four years later, 1678;

we do not know who had custody of the bones and where they were kept from 1674 to 1678; and

there is evidence that some of the bones were given away during these four years.

The Editor concludes —

It seems impossible to determine with any certainty whether these bones were or were not those of Edward V and his brother Richard';

'*prima facie* the bones of 1678 were not those of 1674'; and

'So here again (as with the death of the two Princes) it seems necessary to record a verdict of "not proven" ' (*The Princes in the*

Tower, The Complete Peerage, vol. XII, Part II, ed. Geoffrey H. White, Appendix J, pp. 32-39, London, 1959).

Dr. R.H.G. Lyne-Pirkis, Godalming, England, with assistance of Dr. Kenneth Oakley and Dr. Barker of the British Museum, Professor Charles Dent of University College, Professor Richard Harrison of the London Hospital, and Sir Bentley Purchase, the Paddington Coroner (Condensation of lecture to Richard III Society, London, February 1963).

Dr. Lyne-Pirkis states that his review of the evidence tends to completely invalidate the conclusions in the 1933 Tanner-Wright report. He points out that the scientific evidence to support the sweeping conclusions in that report are very meager. There has been considerable progress in scientific methods since 1933, principally the research of Professor Wingate Todd in America.

Before Professor Todd, students merely accepted what was taught them at medical school about how bones and teeth look at different ages. But no one had really examined the matter. Something is told or taught you when you are young, you accept it, and this may go on for generations. Then, someone asks — but what is the *evidence*? And often there is no evidence.

So, in 1926, Professor Todd began his great pioneer work on how bones develop and grow old and on how to accurately date the age of a child from a skeleton. He died in 1938, but his successors continued his research and are still doing so.

Professor Wright dated the bones, in part, on the basis of the status of ossification — cartilege turning into bone. Professor Todd's research demonstrated, however, that this yardstick is unreliable. After many years of research, Professor Todd found that, even in a homogeneous group of children, there was a big difference in the maturity of bones.

Now we need to distinguish between *chronological* age and *skeletal* age or maturity. Chronological age is the actual age of the child; skeletal age or maturity is the apparent age the bones show. Thus, a child's bones will appear to be older or younger than its actual age, depending on whether the child is fast or slow in developing. Professor Todd's research revealed that there is a big difference in normal children as to the actual maturity or the apparent age of the child. *This discovery at once disposes of any attempt to state the precise age of a skeleton from the appearance of the bones, as Professor Wright attempted to do.*

Professor Wright could not say whether the bones were those of boys or girls. Even today we would not be able to do so. Until children reach puberty, bones are very similar in both sexes.

But, you may say, Professor Wright relied mainly on the *teeth*. In his day, it was assumed that the time when teeth erupted was fairly uniform. Well, Professor Todd examined the teeth as well as bones of the skeleton. He found it was quite impossible to arrive at the *exact* age of a child from the time the teeth erupted because here, also, there are enormous variations even in normal children.

Dr Lyne-Pirkis, reviewing the feasibility of *radio-carbon dating*, said this technique is accurate only to within plus or minus about 100 years. So, if we used radio-carbon dating, we would only get an answer of from 1370 to 1570 — not very helpful. And the process would destroy most of the bones.

Are we ever likely to find a more precise method of dating bones of this approximate age? In London, Professor Miles has been working at the Royal Dental College on dating babies' bones by measuring the thickness of the enamel on the baby teeth before they come through. This method seems to provide extremely precise dating. Unfortunately, baby teeth stop growing at the age of about four hundred days — about 1¼ years, so this method would be of no help here.

It is just possible that one day someone may endeavor to cut sections across a bone and examine it under the microscope to see whether it shows growth rings like trees do. This possibility may seem odd, since human beings are not trees. But, in fact, this phenomenon does occur in other animals, such as earplugs in whales and the tusks in walruses and hippopotamuses.

Sir Thomas More says that the two Princes were suffocated. In fact, there is no authentic evidence to support his story. The only persons who gave any purported details were More and Polydore Vergil. Vergil was Henry VII's personal historian and was anxious to blacken the reputation of Henry's dead rival, Richard III. Both were supporters of the Tudor dynasty and were therefore quite naturally biased in their views. Kings were absolute monarchs in those days, and it was not wise to suggest any unpleasant things about them if you wanted to live long.

In summary, Professor Todd's research invalidates the scientific bases for Professor Wright's conclusions. Wright said by no possibility could either Prince have been alive on August 22, 1485, when Henry Tudor ascended the throne as Henry VII. In other words, Henry could not have killed them. The inference was that Richard, or someone acting for him, had murdered them. We are certain now, however, that we can not be nearly as accurate as Professor Wright thought he was in 1933. We cannot date bones nearer than plus or minus two years. Thus, if these were indeed the bones of the two young Princes, *it would still have been possible for them to be alive when Richard III died on Bosworth Field.*

But we do not know whether these were actually the bones of the Princes. All we can say is that bones of children were found in the Tower, but we can not state their precise chronological age. *No one today would accept Professor Wright's estimate of age, because it was based on wrong premises.*

Kendall : Kendall says that the bones found in the urn at Westminster Abbey cannot be identified with certainty as those of the two Princes (p. 498).

Chapter XXI

EDITOR'S COMMENTARY
— SUMMARY

> When to the sessions of sweet silent thought
> I summon up remembrance of things past . . .

Shakespeare, Sonnet XXX

We asked in the Foreword — was Richard III the deformed monster pictured by Shakespeare and 500 years of tradition, or is his story, as it has come down to us, a hoax? What picture of Richard emerges when we review the evidence?

The stubborn fact is that Edward IV's two sons disappeared from public view after they came into Richard III's custody. On the other hand, there is no proof that would sustain a verdict of Richard's guilt in a court of law.

As we have seen, the tradition is based on prejudiced sources. It is worth noting that the evil things we read about Richard originated in rumors, speculation, and unproven allegations. But the good things we read about Richard — his just rule, wise legislation, valiant conduct in battle, and concern for his subjects' welfare — are undisputed even by apologists for Henry VII.

We shall probably never know with certainty what happened to the two young Princes. But we can perhaps arrive at a more satisfactory personal judgment of Richard III's character by —

reviewing again the actions of those who knew Richard best;
examining Henry Tudor's actions after the battle of Bosworth;
comparing the reigns of Richard III and Henry VII very briefly;
briefly summarizing the views of several scholars;
showing with a specific example how false legends grow; and
noting another tradition about Richard III, also 500 years old.

Actions of Edward IV and the dowager Queen

The judgments and actions of those who knew Richard best are revealing. Probably, no person knew Richard better than his brother, Edward IV. Richard had been at Edward's side through every adversity, in contrast to the fickle George, Duke of Clarence. It was to Richard alone that Edward IV, in his will, entrusted the care of his son and the rule of England during Edward V's minority (Andre, p. 23; Vergil, p. 530).

The actions of Edward IV's widow Elizabeth Woodville, also tell us something. The mother of the two young Princes accepted Richard's promise to treat her and her daughters well. She sent them out of sanctuary and entrusted them to Richard's care. They danced at his court, and no complaint was ever made of his treatment of them. Richard treated the dowager Queen better than her future son-in-law, Henry VII, would later treat her. She even wrote to her son, the Marquis of Dorset, urging him to flee Henry Tudor and return to Richard who would treat him well. Dorset, evidently preferring Richard to Henry, tried to escape, but Henry's agents captured him.

Henry Tudor's actions after Bosworth

If Richard III had, in fact, murdered his two nephews, Henry VII's actions after the battle of Bosworth cannot be logically explained.

Henry based his title on conquest, since he had no real claim to the throne. Thus, it was of paramount importance to him to strengthen his title. So, his first action was to order that all copies of the *Titulus Regius* be destroyed on pain of severe punishment. The *Titulus Regius*, as we have seen, was the enactment of Parliament on January 23, 1484, rehearsing and confirming the bill drawn up by the Parliament of June 25, 1483. That bill declared Edward IV's marriage to Elizabeth Woodville bigamous, because of his precontract with Lady Eleanor Butler, and conferred the crown upon Richard and his issue.

To further strengthen his hold on the crown, Henry VII had his Parliament attaint Richard and his followers. Since Richard III was a legally crowned King of England on the date of the battle of Bosworth, Henry used the dishonest device of dating his reign from the day *before* the battle, August 21, 1485.

The strongest actions Henry VII could have taken to strengthen his title and to discredit Richard III would have been the following:

Charge Richard, in the bill of attainder, with the murder of the two Princes.

Exhume and produce their bodies, if they had, in fact, been murdered.

Conduct an open investigation into their disappearance and publish his proofs of Richard's villainy.

Prove that Edward IV had no legal precontract of marriage with Lady Eleanor Butler.

The remarkable fact is that Henry VII did not take a single such action. Thus, he undermined the case against Richard III. If Henry had had any proof, he certainly would have produced it.

Richard III and Henry VII compared

Kendall believes that Henry VII's government cannot compare with Richard III's reign in terms of domestic tranquility, prosperity, stable government, effective diplomacy, and measures to protect the lower classes from abuses by the nobility. Richard was accessible to his subjects and concerned for their welfare. He developed an outstanding legislative program which reflected this concern. As a result, his government was popular.

In sharp contrast, Henry's reign was marked by aloofness, disorder, misery, oppression, spying, hangings, and miserly extortion of money from his unhappy subjects (pp. 307, 318, 319, 378-382).

Views of several scholars

E.F. Jacob : (Professor of History, Oxford University). Professor Jacob, in his monumental work, *The Fifteenth Century*, (Oxford, 1961), states that More's tale of Richard's alleged villainy, his *Richard III* — the ultimate source of Shakespeare's famous play — is now discredited (p. 624). Professor Kendall agrees (pp. 398-406; 421-423).

George Bosworth Churchill : In *Richard the Third up to Shakespeare*, Palaestra X, Mayer & Muller, Berlin, 1900.

Kendall (p. 498) cites Churchill as a principal source for the development of the Tudor tradition. In his preface, Churchill states his book grew from a desire to examine the nature of Shakespeare's raw material when he began to write his *Richard III*.

Churchill notes we have long known that Shakespeare's Richard was not the Richard of history. Richard's reputation was molded by Tudor sources — those who wrote in the reign of Henry VII and Henry VIII. Two of them — Polydore Vergil and Bernard Andre — wrote at the express request of Henry VII. All had the strongest incentive to blacken Richard's character and to praise Henry VII.

Sir Thomas More's *History of King Richard* is of paramount importance in forming the traditional picture of Richard III. It was copied, with only slight changes, by all the succeeding chroniclers, including Hall and Holinshed, who were Shakespeare's sources. Thus, More's Richard III became essentially Shakespeare's Richard III.

Buck, Walpole, Gairdner, Jacob, and Kendall are among those who join Churchill in discrediting More's history because —

it has many inaccuracies;

it has apparently willful misstatements of fact;

over one-third of the history is taken up with long speeches — all imaginary; and

It is filled with a feeling of actual hatred of Richard.

More's extreme bias may be traced to the fact that, as a boy, he was placed in the household of John Morton, Richard's deadly enemy and the person principally responsible for Henry Tudor's seizure of the crown (preface, introduction, and pp. 118-127).

Kendall : Kendall states (p. 421) that, because of More's hatred that is evident throughout his history, many have alleged that Morton himself wrote the Latin version of More's *Richard III*, which apparently formed the basis for the English version. In any event, it is clear that More got most of his information about Richard from Morton.

Francis Drake : Drake's *Eboracum*, 1736, reflects the great love the people of the North had for Richard III. Their sadness on learning of Richard's defeat and death at Bosworth is reflected in the following quotation from the York City Council records:

'Wer assembled in the counsail chambre, wher and when it was shewed . . . by *John Spon* sent unto the *feld of Redemore* to bring

tydings from the same to the citie that king *Richard* late *lawfully*
reigning over us was through grete treason . . . *piteously slane and
murdred* to the grete hevyness of this citie . . . ' (emphasis as shown —
Order of York City Council, August 23, 1485).

Drake summarizes the people's contrasting views of Richard III
and Henry VII as follows:

> 'It is plain that Richard, represented as a monster of mankind by most,
> was not so esteemed in his life time in these northern parts. And had the
> Earl of Northumberland staid and raised forces here, he might have
> struck Henry's new acquired diadem into the hazard. Wanting that
> nobleman's personal appearance among them, our city had nothing to
> do, but with the rest of the kingdom, to submit to the conqueror. His
> policy taught him to shew great acts of clemency at his entrance into
> government, though he must know, that neither his title, nor his
> family, were recognized or respected, in these northern parts of the
> kingdom' (*Eboracum: or the History and Antiquities of the City of
> York*, William Bowyer, London, 1736, pp. 120, 124).

Sharon Turner : In *History of England During the Middle Ages*,
4 vols., the Longman Group, successors to Longman, Rees, Orme,
Brown, and Green, London, 1830.

[Kendall states (p. 428) that Turner is the first professional
historian to free himself of the Tudor myth and examine the evidence
in an objective way.]

Turner says 'Our ablest lawyers have acknowledged that his
(Richard III's) statutes were wise and useful. . . . He was too liberal to
be personally rapacious' and refused money offered him by the
corporations of London, Gloucester, and Worcester. 'There was
nothing mean or sordid about him . . . he emptied his exchequer by
his bounties to men, who were enabled by his own generosity more
effectually to betray him . . . '.

Richard III moved against the private armed forces maintained by
the nobility and gentry. 'While such masses of military retainers
obeyed the orders of the great nobility and gentry, it was of small
avail to a king to be popular among the nation, if the aristocracy were
either indifferent or averse to him . . . the common population . . .
were but a mob, that was sure to be broken as soon as attacked . . . '.
So, Richard prohibited the ancient custom of giving distinctive
clothing or badges. 'In these public benefits of Richard, we see the
real cause of his unpopularity with the higher orders. . . . He was
becoming too good a king to suit their interests . . . ' (lib. V, Chapter
I, pp. 18-22).

A.R. Myers : Professor of Medieval History, University of Liverpool, author of *England in the Late Middle Ages*; editor, *English Historical Documents* (vol. 4, 1327-1485). 'The Character of Richard III' in *History Today*, vol. 4, 1954, pp. 511-521.

' "Shakespeare, the only history of England I ever read", the great Duke of Marlborough is said to have remarked; and Shakespeare's enormous influence in shaping subsequent concepts of fifteenth-century England is nowhere better illustrated than in the case of Richard III. His picture is the more effective because it so skilfully simple — the portrait of evil incarnate . . . ' (p. 511).

'. . . [T]here was little to be learnt of Richard III from books when More wrote [1513]. The short but mostly excellent account of the Yorkist period by the *Continuator of the Croyland Chronicle*, who had been a councillor of Edward IV, was composed in 1486; but it was unkown in More's day and remained unprinted until 1684. Moreover, it is questionable whether More regarded himself as writing history; his story is much more like a drama, unfolded in magnificent prose, for which fidelity to historical fact is scarcely relevant. . . . Certainly, the serious errors of fact, and the blanks left in the manuscript for the insertion of various dates and names, seem to indicate that More never revised his *Richard III* and did not intend it to be published as he left it. Yet it exercised enormous influence; it was embodied with only slight alterations in all subsequent chronicles of importance, such as those of Hall, Grafton, Holinshed, and Stow, and formed the basis of much of Shakespeare's picture'.

'The history of Polydore Vergil, which was second only to More's biography in importance for shaping the Elizabethan view of Richard, makes a greater attempt at impartiality. . . . Yet Vergil's work was much influenced by the fact that (as Henry VII's official historian) he had been called upon to produce an apologia for the House of Tudor and . . . it was necessary for an unpopular foreigner to be very circumspect to keep the favour of Henry VIII. . . . And as succeeding chroniclers used Vergil's history, bodily or as a basis, for those parts of the Yorkist reigns not touched upon by More, Vergil's accusations against Richard became very potent'.

'*It is this peculiar characteristic of the sources for Richard's life — that all those which formed the Elizabethan picture of the king were written after his death under influences hostile to him . . . '* — emphasis added (p. 515).

'. . . [D]uring his brief reign he displayed many qualities which, if he had come to the throne in a more acceptable way, might have helped him to a long and successful reign. He showed zeal for trade and English interests abroad; he tried to repress disorder and promote justice; he made it easier for poor suitors to present their petitions to him and his council; he strove to make financial reforms and lessen the burden of royal demands for money; he instigated a land law (on uses) which foreshadowed an important reform of Henry VIII. His public policy in these matters, together with his tenderness to clerical privileges, his building of churches, his advocacy of morality among the people, and his patronage of learning, moved the clergy assembled in convocation to praise him for his "most noble and blessed disposition". He endeavored to win popular approval by his magnificent dress, his princely building, his care for heraldry and pageantry, his generous magnanimity towards the dependents of some of his fallen opponents, his many recorded acts of kindness to petitioners in distress, . . . we find the Bishop of St. David's writing to the Prior of Christ Church, Canterbury: "He contents the people wher he goys best that ever did prince; for many a poor man that hath suffred wrong many days have be relevyd and helpyd by hym . . . God hathe sent hym to us for the wele of us al" . . . what brought him to defeat and death at Bosworth Field was not the feeling of the nation at large but the desertion of a few great nobles and their forces' (p. 520).

'. . . If Edward IV had lived to the age of fifty, instead of dying at forty, Richard might have gone down in history as a very commendable character, with a possible share in the murder of Henry VI as the only conspicuous blemish. He might have been remembered as an able and energetic administrator, a brave and skilful soldier, a faithful brother and affectionate father, a kind and generous man of culture, fond of music and architecture, a patron of learning and a devoted son of the Church . . . as Bishop Stubbs rightly said, he owes "the general condemnation, with which his life and reign have been visited, to the fact that he left none behind whose duty or whose care it was to attempt his vindication" . . . ' (pp. 520, 521).

Richard S. Sylvester : Professor of English, Yale University; editor, volume 2 of *The Complete Works of St. Thomas More* (*The History of King Richard III*), Yale University Press, 1963.

Professor Sylvester stated that More liked to construct imaginary scenes in his polemic writings to create a dramatic situation. He disliked careful analysis, tended to fictionalize, and made heavy use of quotations — all imaginary. These characteristics will not surprise those who know More's earlier writings, such as his *Richard III*

(Lecture, *St. Thomas More: The Polemical Art*, The Folger Shakespeare Library, Washington, D.C., October 10, 1969).

Lehrer C. Wessel, Eschwege, Germany : *Richard III In Shakespeare's Plays compared with Richard III in history* (in *Realschule II, Ordnung und Proggymnasium*, April 6-7, 1876).

Wessel states that very few Englishmen joined Henry Tudor after he landed in England in August 1485. Richard III fell not by a revolt of the people but by the treason of a few nobles whom Richard had treated generously. After his fall, none dared to mention his good qualities, his wise rule, and his beneficial laws.

It is a curious fact that Richard becomes more depraved and his crimes more numerous as the time interval between Bosworth Field and the chronicler increases. '. . . [S]ometimes the atrocities which the latest writer relates as a fact, are mentioned merely as a rumor by the chronicler from whom he got his information, whilst contemporary writers are silent about them. When Shakespeare wrote his plays wicked Richard was firmly established in Holinshed's and Hall's chronicles . . . and if he represented Richard as he found him there, he did not mean to do him any wrong. Yet there is no writer who has wronged Richard more than Shakespeare because for centuries the English have got their knowledge of the history of Richard's time but from Shakespeare's plays . . . '.

'Now, had Richard been the bloody monster he has been represented by Shakespeare and tradition, he certainly would have persecuted all those he knew to be his enemies, or whom he could not trust. But he did nothing of the kind . . . '. He tried to redress all wrongs and required magistrates to administer strict justice. He gave Oxford and Cambridge large sums of money to improve learning and was concerned to give his people good laws. 'Of all this nothing is said in Shakespeare's play'.

Gairdner : The following statements by Gairdner, an apologist for Henry VII, might well serve as Richard's obituary:

'It is admitted on all hands that he was a good general in war, and that he was liberal. . . . He alone, when Duke of Gloucester, refused the gifts of Louis and protested against the ignoble peace with France. As king he seems really to have studied his country's welfare; he passed good laws, endeavored to put an end to extortion, declined the free gifts offered to him by several towns, and declared he would rather have the hearts of his subjects than their money'. (pp. 246, 247).

The public acts of Richard's Parliament, which met on January 23, 1484, and concluded on February 20, 1484, 'have always been noted as wise and beneficial' (p. 160).

Richard's innovative Council of the North lasted for over 150 years. His good rule of the borders 'was remembered long after his day as a very model of efficiency'. At the time of his brother's death, April 9, 1483, 'no man stood in higher honour than Richard through-out the kingdom generally' (p. 42).

Richard's acts of clemency toward his enemies 'were done graciously and in no grudging spirit. Whatever other evil there was in Richard, there was nothing mean or paltry' (p. 251).

'. . . [H]e saw clearly the importance of checking corruption and promoting economy in the service of the state' (p. 149).

A legal scholar's view

H.G. Hanbury, Vinerian Professor of English Law, University of Oxford, presents an interesting appraisal of Richard III in his article *The Legislation of Richard III*, in *The American Journal of Legal History*, Temple University, vol. 6, 1962.

'. . . [T]he traditional view of him as a monster of iniquity is borne out by little contemporary evidence'. During Richard's reign, More 'was a mere child'. Both More and the Monk of Croyland were 'much under the influence of Morton, Bishop of Ely, and afterwards Archbishop of Canterbury, whose hostility to Richard was notorious and persistent . . . ' (p. 95).

'Of the private statutes the most interesting is Titulus Regius itself (the Act of Parliament settling the crown upon the King and his issue, 1484, Rot. Parl. VI, 240). It was repealed by Henry VII who ordered the destruction of all copies, the original, of course, as Gairdner points out, being always preserved in the custody of the Master of the Rolls. The repeal, in restoring the legitimacy of his queen, Elizabeth of York, furnished Henry with one more support, wherewith to bolster up his weak title through conquest, and his title by descent, which was weaker still. It was, however, a support whose usefulness he was very unwilling to acknowledge as is shown by his ungracious delay in allowing the queen's coronation . . . ' (pp. 96, 97).

'. . . Richard's magnanimity (to Margaret Countess of Richmond) is in striking contrast to the unscrupulous chicanery of Henry, as shown in the Act of Attainder passed in the first year of his reign, against Richard's faithful followers. Henry's enactment may be described as conviction and confiscation by fiction, as it dated his accession as having occurred on the day before the Battle of Bosworth . . . this nauseating falsification of history disgusted not only the contemporary Monk of Croyland, but also Henry's zealous apologist Gairdner. The distaste of the English people took very practical shape ten years later, in the form of an Act of 1495, which laid down that in no case could loyalty to one who was at the time king *de facto* be treated as treason to a subsequent king' (pp. 97, 98).

'The second statute is probably the most beneficent of all the legislation of Richard III. It provides, quite simply, that 'the subjects of this realm shall not be charged with any benevolences, etc.' . . . When we recall to mind Richard's unfailing devotion to his brother Edward IV, we must acknowledge that this statute is a very strong demonstration of Richard's even greater devotion to 'the ease and solace of the common people . . . " ' (p. 104).

'But benevolences, to which Richard III, in his direst extremity, scorned to stoop, were unashamedly revived by the insatiable greed of Henry VII. . . . Some of his predecessors might have been justly condemned as spendthrifts, but of all rulers the most odious must be the inveterate miser, who hoards for the sake of hoarding' (p. 106).

In discussing the former Queen, Elizabeth Woodville, Professor Hanbury says that 'Richard III had no intention of really impoverishing her . . . she lived on the friendliest terms with Richard, and brought her daughters to his court, thus providing, incidentally, an almost unanswerable argument against the view that Richard was responsible for the deaths of Edward V and his brother . . . Henry VII . . . early in 1487, enclosed her for the rest of her life at Bermondsey, having first stripped her of all her property. . . . It was expressly given as the reason for her treatment by Henry VII, that, as Bacon puts it, "she had delivered her two daughters out of sanctuary to King Richard, contrary to promise" ' (pp. 112, 113).

'Richard III suffered, throughout Tudor times, from the calumnies of a chorus of detractors. In more modern times his character has been vindicated by zealous apologists. This paper will have served its purpose if it has succeeded in portraying him as a singularly thoughtful and enlightened legislator, who brought to his task a profound knowledge of the nature of contemporary problems, and an enthusiastic determination to solve them in the best possible way, in the interests of every class of his subjects . . . ' (p. 113).

Growth of a Legend

Sharon Turner says that no part of English history has been more disfigured by prejudice, inaccuracy, and injustice than the reign of Richard III. Henry VII, and the chroniclers writing for him, tried in every way to blacken Richard's memory (*History of England During the Middle Ages*, 3rd edition, 1830, III, p. 345).

I have seen no better example of how the Tudor myth about Richard's character developed than the following case cited in *English Historical Documents*, vol. IV, 1327-1485, ed. A.R. Myers, Eyre Methuen Limited, London 1969; New York, Oxford University Press, 1953-1975, No. 188, pp. 314, 315.

Contemporary writers plainly say that Edward, Prince of Wales, son of Henry VI's Queen, Margaret of Anjou, was *slain in the field*, at the battle of Tewkesbury, May 4, 1471. Yet, later writers charged that Richard murdered Edward in cold blood.

Note from the following example how Edward Hall, writing 71 years after the battle, has perfected the myth, citing no new authority for his tale:

188. The growth of a legend: the death of Edward Prince of Wales at Tewkesbury, 1471

(i)
(*The Tewkesbury Abbey Chronicle*, 1471, ed. C.L. Kingsford,
English Historical Literature in the Fifteenth Century
[Clarendon Press, 1913])
(376[Latin])

Also in the same year, on May 3rd, that is, on the feast of the Finding of the Holy Cross, there came to Tewkesbury Prince Edward, son of King Henry VI, with a great army, and on the morrow entered the great field which is called Gastons. When King Edward IV arrived with his army, he slew prince Edward in the field, when also John Somerset, brother of the Duke of Somerset, the Earl of Devon, and Lord Wenlock with many others were killed.

(*Ibid*. 377[English])

These are the names of the noblemen that were slain at Tewkesbury field. Lord Edward, prince of King Henry, in the field of Gastum beside Tewkesbury, slain, and buried in the midst of the convent quire in the monastery there; for whom God worketh.

(Warkworth's *Chronicle*, c. 1473, 18[English])

And Prince Edward . . . held forth his way to the town of Tewkesbury, and there he made a field not far from the River Severn; and
King Edward and his host came upon them, the Saturday the 4th day
of May . . . 1471. . . . And there was slain in the field Prince Edward,
which cried for succour to his brother-in-law the Duke of Clarence.

(*The Second Continuation of the Croyland Chronicle*, 1486
[W. Fulman, *Rerum Anglicarum Scriptores [1684]*, 555]
[Latin, trans. H.T. Riley [Bohn's Antiquarian
Library, 1893], 466])

When both armies had now become so extremely fatigued with the
labour of marching and thirst that they could proceed no further,
they joined battle near the town of Tewkesbury. After the result had
long remained doubtful, King Edward at last gained a glorious
victory. Upon this occasion, there were slain on the queen's side,
either on the field or after the battle, by the avenging hands of certain
persons, Prince Edward, the only son of King Henry, the Duke of
Somerset, the Earl of Devon, and all and every the other lords above-
mentioned.

(*The Great Chronicle of London, 1512*, ed. A.H. Thomas and
I.D. Thornley (1938), 218[English])

The king assembled his people and drew towards his enemies and
finally met with them at a place or village called Tewkesbury, where
after a short fight he subdued his enemies and took Queen Margaret
and her son alive. The which being brought into his presence, after
the king had questioned a few words of the cause of his so landing
within his realm, and he gave unto the king an answer contrary to his
pleasure, the king smote him on the face with the back of his gauntlet.
After which stroke so received by him, the king's servants rid him out
of life forthwith.

Edward Hall, *The Union of the Two Noble and Illustre Famelies
of Lancastre and York* (1542, ed. H. Ellis (1809), 301 [English])

[After the Battle of Tewkesbury] The queen was found in his chariot
almost dead for sorrow, the prince was apprehended and kept close
by Sir Richard Crofts. . . . After the field was ended, King Edward
made a proclamation that whosoever could bring Prince Edward to

him alive or dead should have an annuity of 100 pounds during his life, and the prince's life would be saved. Sir Richard Crofts, a wise and valiant knight, not at all mistrusting the king's former promise, brought forth his prisoner Prince Edward, being a goodly girlish looking and well-featured young gentleman. When King Edward had viewed him well, he asked him how he durst so presumptuously enter into his realm with his banner displayed. The prince, being bold of stomach and of a good courage, answered saying, 'To recover my father's kingdom and heritage, from his father and grandfather to him, and from him, after him, to me lineally descended'. At which words King Edward said nothing, but with his hand thrust him from him (or, as some say, struck him with his gauntlet) whom at once they that stood about, which were George, Duke of Clarence, Richard, Duke of Gloucester, Thomas, Marquis of Dorset, and William, Lord Hastings, suddenly murdered and pitifully slew. The bitterness of which murder some of the actors afterwards in their latter days tasted and assayed by the very rod of justice and punishment of God. His body was interred in homely fashion . . . in the church of the monastery of black monks at Tewkesbury.

Another tradition — remembrance of things past

Jerome Beatty, Jr., tells of another tradition about Richard III that has endured for 500 years. (See article in *The Saturday Review* of April 13, 1968, p. 18, about a meeting in New York City, March 24, 1968, of The Richard III Society, Inc., a branch of The Richard III Society of England.)

'I thought the most appealing presentation was by Jean di Meglio, who was born and raised in a hamlet on the edge of Bosworth Field. She brought folklore and sentiment to bear on the adamant historian [Professor A.L. Rowse, who had just addressed the meeting.]

' "Richard III first came to my notice", she said, "as the King Dick of King Dick's Well, a place pointed out to me by my father when I was a little girl. The affectionate diminutive was used exclusively in speaking of him, so that only when I was nine years old and studying the Wars of the Roses in the village school did I find that he was actually King Richard III. At the same time, I also learned of Henry VII, who until then was known to me only as 'that 'Enry Tudor' who came over the Brockey Fields in August, ruining the ripening wheat, instead of marching his men up Barwell Lane as any decent man would have done. Under their King Dick, the country people had begun to recover from the years of civil strife. They had expected to reap their harvest, and the bitterness of their disappointment when Henry Tudor destroyed the crops has lasted for 500 years" '.

' "My history lessons about the Wars were given by a teacher who encouraged us to take sides. Some of us went so far as to wear roses — mostly white. The red roses were, in the main, worn by children whose older brothers and sisters had told them the winner. But few of us were swayed by this advance information, for we had no question which was the right side. My village of Earl Shilton sent men to Bosworth for Richard, and, although the common grave of those who died is only an unevenness in a green field by the church, it is said that there is where the men of Bosworth lie. The unmarked mounds in the neighboring hamlet, Elmesthorpe, were pointed out to me as a child as the graves of men who went to fight for their King and died in vain" '.

' "Such affection and veneration for his memory would not have been passed down through 500 years of unwritten folk history had King Dick been a tyrant and a villain. Indeed, Richard III must have been well loved in his day to be remembered as he is" '.

APPENDIX I.

(All appendices are by the Editor)

ROTULI PARLIAMENTORUM (ROLLS OF PARLIAMENT): THREE IMPORTANT ACTS

TITULUS REGIUS

AN ACT FOR THE SETTLEMENT OF THE CROWN UPON THE KING AND HIS ISSUE, WITH A RECAPITULATION OF HIS TITLE

(passed by the Parliament of Richard III, 1484)

In May 1483, before any question regarding the legitimacy of Edward IV's children had arisen, the council considered whether Richard's protectorship should be continued. It was agreed that the principal matter for which the Lords and Commons would be summoned was their approval for continuing the protectorship until Edward V became of age.

Accordingly, the Lords and Commons met on Wednesday, June 25, 1483, having been legally convened several weeks before by Edward V (Royal Wills, p. 347, as cited by Halsted, vol. II, p. 103). In the meantime, however, Bishop Stillington's revelation of the bastardy of Edward IV's children meant that the Parliament was not opened in due form, Edward IV being dead and his children illegitimate. In all other respects, however, it was a legal Parliament. The eminent authority, Blackstone, has held that if the throne becomes vacant or empty, whether by abdication or by failure of all heirs, the two Houses of Parliament may dispose of it (cited by Halsted, vol. II, p. 106).

A roll declaring Richard's title to the throne was unanimously approved and presented to the Protector the next day, Thursday, June 26, 1483. The throne being empty, Richard acceded to the petition unanimously tendered by the legally constituted authorities and took the royal oath that day in Westminster as Richard III. He was formally crowned in a coronation ceremony, Sunday, July 6, 1483, attended by virtually the entire peerage of England.

* * *

Where late, heretofore, that is to say, before the Consecracon, coronation, and Inthronizacion of oure Soveraign Lord the King Richard the Thirde, a Rolle of Perchemont, conteignying in writeing certeine Articles of the tenour undre writen, on the behalve and in the name of the thre Estates of this Reame of Englond, that is to wite, of the Lords Spūalls and Temporalls, and of the Comōns, by many and diverse Lords Spūalls and Temporalls, and other nobles and notable persons of the Comōns in grete multitude, was presented and actually delivered unto our said Souveraine Lord the King, to th' entent and effect expressed at large in the same Rolle; to which Rolle, and to the Consideracions and instant Peticion comprized in the same, our said Souveraine Lord, for the public wele and tranquillite of his Land, benignely assented.

Now forasmoche as neither the said three Estats, neither the said personnes, which in thair name presented and delivered, as is abovesaid, the said Rolle unto oure said Souverain Lord the King, were assembled in fourme of Parliament; by occasion whereof, diverse doubts, questions and ambigiutees, been moved and engendred in the myndes of diverse personnes, as it is said: Therefore, to the perpetuall memorie of the trouth and declaration of the same, bee it ordeigned, provided, and stablished in this present Parliament, that the tenour of the said Rolle, with all the contynue of the same, presented, as is abovesaid, and delivered to our before said Souverain Lord the King, in the name and on the behalve of the said three Estates out of Parliament, now by the same three Estates assembled in this present Parliament, and by auctorite of the same, bee ratifyed, enrolled, recorded, approved, and auctorized, into removying the occasion and doubtes and ambiguitees, and to all other lawfull effect that shall mowe thereof ensue; soo that all things said, affirmed, specifyed, desired and remembred in the said Rolle, and in the tenour of the same underwritten, in the name of the said three Estates, to the effect expressed in the same Rolle, bee of like effect, vertue, and force, as if all the same things had ben soo said, affirmed, specifyed, desired and remembred in full Parliament, and by auctorite of the same accepted and approved. The tenoure of the said Rolle of Parchement, whereof above is made mencione, foloweth and is such.

To the High and Myghty Prince Richard Duc of Gloucester.

Please it youre Noble Grace to understande the Consideracon, Election, and Petition underwritten, of us the lords Spuelx and Temporelx, and comons of this Reame of Englond, and thereunto agreably to yeve your assent, to the comon and public wele of this

Lande, to the comforte and gladnesse of all the people of the same.

Furst, we considre how that heretofore in tyme passed, this Lande many years stode in great prosperite, honoure, and tranquillite; which was caused, forsomoch as the Kings than reignyng, used and followed the advice and counsaill of certaine Lords Spuelx and Temporelx, and othre personnes of approved sadnesse, prudence, policie, and experience, dreding God, and havyng tendre zele and affection to indifferent ministration of Justice, and to the comon and politique wele of the Land; than oure Lord God was dred, luffed and honoured; than within the Land was peas and tranquillite, and among Neghbours concorde and charite; than the malice of outward Enemyes was myghtily resisted and repressed, and the Land honorably defended with many grete and glorious victories; than the entrecourse of Merchandizes was largely used and exercised: by which things above remembred, the Land was greatly enriched, soo that as wele the Merchants and Artificers, as other poure people, laboryng for their livyng in diverse occupations, had competent gayne, to the sustentation of thaym and their households, livyng without miserable and intollerable povertie. But afterward, whan that such as had the rule and governaunce of this Land, delityng in adulation and flattery, and lede by sensuality and concupiscence, folowed the counsaill of personnes insolent, vicious, and of inordinate avarice, despisyng the counsaill of good, vertuouse and prudent personnes, such as above be remembred; the prosperite of this Land daily decreased, soo that felicite was turned into miserie, and prosperity into adversite, and the ordre of polecye, and of the Laws of God and Man, confounded; whereby it is likely this Reame to falle into extreme miserie and desolation, which God defende, without due provision of couvenable remedie bee had in this behalfe in all goodly hast.

Over this, amonges other things, more specially wee consider, howe that, the tyme of the Reigne of Kyng Edward the IIIIth, late decessed, after the ungracious pretensed Marriage, as all England hath cause soo to say, made betwixt the said King Edward, and Elizabeth, sometyme Wife to Sir John Grey Knight, late nameing herself and many years hertofore Quene of Englond, the ordre of all poletique Rule was perverted, the Lawes of God and of Gods Church, and also the Lawes of Nature and of Englond, and also the laudable Customes and Liberties of the same, wherein every Englishman is Inheritor, broken, subverted and contempned, against all reason and justice, soo that this Land was ruled by selfewill and pleasure, feare and drede, all manner of Equite and Lawes layd apart

271

and despised, whereof ensued many inconvenients and mischiefs, as Murdres, Extorsions and Oppressions, namely of poore and impotent people, soo that no Man was sure of his Lif, Land ne Lyvelode, ne of his Wif, Doughter ne Servaunt, every good Maiden and Woman standing in drede to be ravished and defouled. And besides this, what Discords, inwarde Battailles, effusion of Christian Mens Blode, and namely, by the destruction of the noble Blode of this Londe, was had and comitted within the same, it is evident and notarie thourough all this Reame, unto the great sorowe and hevynesse of all true Englishmen. And here also we considre, howe that the seid pretensed Mariage bitwixt the above named King Edward and Elizabeth Grey, was made of grete presumption, without the knowyng and assent of the Lords of this Lond, and also by Sorcerie and Wichecrafte, committed by the said Elizabeth, and her Moder Jaquett Duchesse of Bedford, as the comon opinion of the people, and the publique voice and fame is thorough all this Land; and hereafter, if and as the caas shall require, shall bee proved sufficiently in tyme and place convenient. And here also we consider, howe that the said pretensed Mariage was made privaly and secretely, without Edition of Banns, in a private Chamber, a prophane place, and not openly in the face of the Church, aftre the Laws of Godds Churche, bot contrarie thereunto, and the laudable Custome of the Church of Englond. And howe also, that at the tyme of contract of the same pretensed Mariage, and bifore and longe tyme after, the seid King Edward was and stode maryed and trouth plight to oone Dame Elianor Butteler, Doughter of the old Earl of Shrewsbury, with whom the same King Edward had made a precontracte of Matrimonie, longe tyme bifore he made the said pretensed Mariage with the said Elizabeth Grey, in maner and fourme abovesaid. Which premisses being true, as in veray trouth they been true, it appeareth and foloweth evidently, that the said King Edward duryng his lif, and the seid Elizabeth, lived together sinfully and dampnably in adultery, against the Lawe of God and of his Church; and therefore noo marvaile that the Souverain Lord and the head of this Land, being of such ungodly disposicion, and provokyng the ire and indignacion of oure Lord God, such haynous mischieffs and inconvenients, as is above remembred, were used and comitted in the Reame amongs the Subgectts. Also it appeareth evidently and followeth, that all th' Issue and Chilren of the seid King Edward, been Bastards, and unable to inherite or to clayme any thing by Interitance, by the Lawe and Custome of Englond.

Moreover we considre, howe that afterward, by the thre Estates of this Reame assembled in a Parliament holden at Westm', the XVIIth yere of the Regne of the said King Edward the IIIIth, he than being in possession of the Coroune and Roiall Estate, by an Acte made in the same Parliament, George Duc of Clarence, Brother to the said King Edward nowe decessed, was convicted and atteinted of High Treason; as in the same Acte is conteigned more at large. Bicause and by reason wherof, all the Issue of the said George, was and is disabled and barred of all Right and Clayme, that in any wise they might have or chalenge by Enheritance, to the Crown and Dignite Roiall of this Reame, by the auncien Lawe and Custome of this same Reame.

Over this we considre, howe that Ye be the undoubted Son and Heire of Richard late Duke of Yorke, verray enheritour to the seid Crowne and Dignite Roiall, and as in right Kyng of Englond, by wey of Enheritaunce; and that at this tyme, the premisses duely considered, there is noon other persoune lyvyng but Ye only, that by Right may clayme the said Coroune and Dignite Poyall, by way of Enheritaunce, and howe that Ye be born withyn this Lande; by reason whereof, as we deme in oure myndes, Ye be more naturally enclyned to the prosperite and comon wele of the same; and all the thre Estatis of the Lande have, and may have, more certayn knowlage of youre Byrth and Filiation aboveseid. Wee considre also, the greate Wytte, Prudence, Justice, Princely Courage, and the memorable and laudable Acts in diverse Batalls, whiche as we by experience knowe Ye heretofore have done, for the salvacion and defence of this same Reame; and also the greate noblesse and excellence of your Byrth and Blode, as of hym that is descended of the thre moost Royall houses in Cristendom, that is to say, England, Fraunce, and Hispanie.

Wherefore, these premisses by us diligently considred, we desyryng affectously the peas, tranquillite, and wele publique of this Lande, and the reduccion of the same to the auncion honourable estate and prosperite, and havyng in your greate Prudence, Justice, Princely Courage, and excellent Vertue, singuler confidence, have chosen in all that that in us is, and by this our Wrytyng choise You, high and myghty Prynce, into oure Kyng and Soveraigne Lorde &c., to whom we knowe for certayne it apperteygneth of Enheritaunce soo to bee chosen. And herupon we humbly desire, pray, and require youre seid Noble Grace, that, accordyng to this Eleccion of us the Thre Estates of this Lande, as by youre true Enherritaunce, Ye will accepte and take upon You the said Crown and Royall Dignite, with all thyngs therunto annexed and apperteynyng, as to You of Right bilongyng, as wele by Enheritaunce as by lawfull Eleccion: and, in caas Ye so do, we promitte to serve and to assiste your Highnesse, as true and feithfull Subgietts and Liegemen, and to lyve and dye with You in this matter, and every other juste quarrell. For certainly wee be determined, rather to aventure and comitte us to the perill of oure lyfs and jopardye of deth, than to lyve in suche thraldome and bondage as we have lyved long tyme heretofore, oppressed and injured by Extorcions and newe Imposicons, ayenst the Lawes of God and Man, and the Libertee, old Police, and Lawes of this Reame, wheryn every Englishman is enherited. Oure Lorde God, Kyng of all Kyngs, by whos infynyte goodnesse and eternall providence all thyngs been pryncipally gouverned in this world, lighten youre soule, and graunt You grace to do, as well in this matier as in all other, all that that may be accordyng to his wille and pleasure, and to the comen and publique wele of this Lande; so that, after great cloudes, troubles, stormes and tempestes, the Son of Justice and of Grace may shyne uppon us, to the comforte and gladnesse of all true Englishmen.

Albeit that the Right, Title, and Estate, whiche oure Souveraigne Lorde the Kyng Richard the Third, hath to and in the Crown and Roiall Dignite of this Reame of Englond, with all thyngs therunto within the same Reame, and without it, united, annexed and apperteynyng, been juste and lawefull, as grounded upon the Lawes of God and of Nature, and also upon the auncien Lawes and laudable Customes of this said Reame, and so taken and reputed by all such persounes as ben lerned in the abovesaid Lawes and Custumes. Yit neverthelesse, forasmoche as it is considred, that the most parte of the people of this Lande is not suffisantly lerned in the abovesaid Lawes and Custumes, whereby the trueth and right in this behalf of liklyhode may be hyd, and nat clerely knowen to all the people, and thereupon put in doubt and question. And over this howe that the courte of Parliament is of suche auctorite, and the people of this Lande of suche nature and disposicion, as experience teacheth, that manifestacion and declaration of any trueth or right, made by the Thre Estates of this Reame assembled in Parliament, and by auctorite of the same, maketh, before all other thyngs, moost feith and certainte; and, quietyng men's myndes, remoeweth the occasion of all doubts and seditious langage: Therefore, at the request, and by assent of the Thre Estates of this Reame, that is to say, the Lords Spuelx and Temporalx, and Comens of this Lande, assembled in this present Parliament, by auctorite of the same, bee it pronounced, decreed and declared, that our saide Soveraign Lorde the Kinge was and is, veray and undoubted Kyng of this Reame of Englond, with all thyngs thereunto within the same Reame, and without it united, annexed and apperteynyng, as well by right of Consanguinite and Enheritaunce, as by lawfull Elleccion, Consecration, and Coronacion. And over this, that at the request, and by the assent and auctorite abovesaid, bee it ordeigned, enacted and established, that the said Crowne and Roiall Dignite of this Reame, and the Enheritaunce of the same, and other thyngs thereunto within this same Reame, or withoute it, unite, annexed, and nowe apperteigning, rest and abyde in the personne of our said Souveraigne Lorde the Kyng, duryng his Lyfe, and, after his Decesse, in his heires of his Body begotten. And in especiall, at the request and by the assent and auctorite abovesaid, bee it ordeigned, enacted, establed, pronounced, decreed, and declared, that the High and Excellent Prynce Edward, Son of our said Souveraign Lorde the Kyng, be Heire Apparant of the same our Soveraign Lord the Kyng; to succede to hym in the abovesaid Crown and Roiall Dignite, with all thyngs as is aforesaid thereunto unite, annexed, and apperteignyng; to have them after the Decesse of our saide Souveraign Lorde the Kyng, to hym and to his heires of the Body lawfully begotten.

(Rolls of Parliament, Vol. 6, pp. 240-242)

AN ACT ATTAINTING RICHARD III AND HIS FOLLOWERS

(passed by the first Parliament of Henry VII in 1485)

Henry VII's first Parliament attainted Richard III and 28 of his followers of high treason by the dishonest method of dating Henry's reign from August *21*, 1485, the day *before* the Battle of Bosworth. The Croyland Chronicler spoke out against Henry's deceitful act, questioning what security future kings could have if they could thus be attainted of treason. And H.G. Hanbury, Vinerian Professor of English Law at Oxford University, states that the revulsion against Henry's chicanery resulted in an Act of 1495, ten years later, which provided that in no case could loyalty to one who was at the time king *de facto* be treated as treason to a subsequent king.

In enumerating the crimes alleged against Richard III, the most important charge Henry could have made to blacken Richard and strengthen his own weak title to the throne would have been to charge that Richard murdered the two young sons of his brother, Edward IV. This the Act does *not* do.

* * *

FORASMOCHE as every King, Prince, and Liege Lord, the more hie that he be in estate and prehemenence, the more singularly he is bound to the advancement and preferring of the indefferent vertue Justice; and promoteinge and rewarding Vertue, and bi oppressinge and punishinge Vice: Wherefore oure Soveraigne Lord, calleinge unto hys blessed remembraunce thys high and grete charge adjoyned to his Royall Majestie and Estate, not oblivious nor puttinge out of hys godly mind the unnaturall, mischeivous, and grete Perjuries, Treasons, Homicides and Murdres, in shedding of Infants blood, with manie other Wronges, odious Offences, and abominacons ayenst God and Man, and in espall oure said Soveraigne Lord, committed and doone by Richard late Duke of Glouc', callinge and nameinge hymself, by usurpacon, King Richard the III^d, the which, with John late Duke of Norff', Thomas Erle of Surrie, Francis Lovell Knt Visc' Lovell, Walter Devereux Knt, late Lord Ferrers, John Lord Zouche, Robert Harrington, Richard Charleton, Richard Ratcliffe, William Berkley of Welley, Robert Brakenbury, Thomas Pillkington, Robert Midlestoune, James Harrington, Knts, Walter Hopton, Wiilliam Catesby, Roger Wake, William Sapcott, Humfrey Stafford, William Clerke of Wenlocke, Jeffrey St Jermin, Richard Watkins,

Herrauld of Armes, Richard Revell of Derbyshyre, Thomas Poulter of the Countee of Kent the Younger, John Walsh otherwyse called Hastings, John Kendale, late Secretarie to the said Richard late Duke, John Buck, Andrew Ratt, and William Bramton of Burford, the *XXIst daie of August*, the first yere of the Reigne of oure Sovereigne Lord, assembled to theyme atte Leicestre in the Countee of Leicestre a grete Hoste, traiterously intendinge, imagininge and conspireinge the destruccon of the Kinges Royall psoune, oure Soveraigne Leige Lord. And they, with the same Hoste, with Banners spred, mightyly armed and defenced with all manner armes, as Gunnes, Bowes, Arrowes, Speres, Gleves, Axes, and all other manner Articles apt or needfull to gef and cause mightie Battaille agen oure said Soveraigne Lord, kept togedre from the said XXII^d daie of the said Month thanne next followinge, and theyme conduced to a Feld within the said Shyre of Leicestre, there bi grete and continued deliberacone, traiterously levied Warre ayenst oure said Soveraine Lord, and his true Subjects there being in his service and assistance under a Banner of oure said Soveraine Lord, to the subversion of this Realme, and Comon weale of the same. Wherefore, by the advise and assent of the Lordes Spuell and Temporell, and of the Coens, in this present Parliament assembled, and bi auctoritee of the same, be it enacted, stablished and ordeyned, deemed and declared, that the said Richard Duke of Glouc', otherwise called King Richard the III^d, John late Duke of Norff' . . . (repetition of all of the above names) . . . stand and be convicte and atteinte of High Treason, and disabled and forejugged of all manner of Honors, Estate, Dignitee and Prehemenence, and the names of the same, and forfeit to oure said Sovereigne Lord, all Oastelles, Mannors, Lordshipps, Hundreds, Franchisees, Libertees, Prividges, Advousons, Nominacons, Presentacons, Lands, Tents, Rents, Services, Reversions, Portions, Annuities, Pensions, Rights, Hereditaments, Goods, Cattelles and Debts, whereof they or eny other to the use of eny of theym, were seised or possessed the said *XXIst daie of August*, or att any tyme after, within the Reame of England, Ireland Walles or Caleys, or in the Marches thereof, in Fee Simple, Fee Taille, or Terme of Lyfe or Lives. . . . (There is considerably more text regarding the land laws, rights of wives of the persons attainted and their heirs, provisions for the tenants on the lands seized by King Henry, etc. Underscoring added.)

(*Rolls of Parliament*, Vol. 6, pp. 275-278)

AN ACT ORDERING DESTRUCTION OF ALL COPIES
OF TITULUS REGIUS
(passed by the first Parliament of Henry VII in 1485)

One of the first things Henry Tudor did after being crowned as Henry VII was to see that his first Parliament ordered the destruction of all copies of *Titulus Regius* under pain of severe punishment. A copy, however, was found in the 17th century. Apparently, to strengthen his own weak claim to the throne, he tried to conceal the twin facts that Edward IV's children were bastards and therefore ineligible to succeed to the throne, and that Richard III had been a lawfully anointed King of England.

If Bishop Stillington's revelation of the bastardy of Edward IV's children was not true, why did Henry try to destroy all copies of *Titulus Regius*?

* * *

Where afore this tyme, Richard, late Duke of Glouc', and after in dede and not of right King of England, called Richard the III^d, caused a false and seditious Bille of false and malicious ymagincones, ayenst all good and true disposicion, to be put unto hyme, the beginning of which Bill is thus:

Please it youre noble Grace to understand the Consideracons, Elleccon and Peticon under written, &c.

Which Bille, after that, with all the continue of the same, by auctoritee of Parliament, holden the first yeere of the usurped Reigne of the said late King Richard the III^d, was ratified, enrolled, recorded, approved and authorised; as in the same more plainly appereth. The King, atte the speciall instance, desire and prayer of the Lordes Spirituell and Temporell, and Comons, in thys psent Parlement assembled, woll it be ordeined, stablished and enacted by the advys of the said Lordes Spuell and Temporell, and the Comunes, in this present Parlement assembled, and by auctoritee of the same, that the said Bill, Acte and Ratificacion, and all the circumstances and dependants of the same Bill and Acte, for the false and seditious ymaginacons and untrouths thereof, be void, adnulled, repelled, irrite, and of noe force ne effecte. And that it be ordeined by the said auctoritee, that the said Bill be cancelled, destrued, and that the said Acte, Record and enrollinge, shall be taken and avoided out of the Roll and Records of the said Parliament of the said late King, and brente, and utterly destroyed. And over this, be it ordeined by the same auctoritee, that every psoune haveing anie Coppie or Remembraunces of the said Bill or Acte, bring unto the Chaunceller of England for the tyme being, the same Coppies and Remembraunces, or utterlie destrue theym, afore the Fest of Easter next comen, upon Peine of ymprissonment, and makeing fyne and ransome to the Kinge atte his will. So that all thinges said and remembred in the said Bill and Acte thereof maie be for ever out of remembraunce, and allso forgott. And over thys, be it ordeined and enacted by the said auctoritee, that thys Acte, ne any thing conteined in the same, be anie way hurtfull or prejudiciall to the Acte of stablishment of the Croune of England to the Kinge and to the Heyres of hys body begotten.

(*Rolls of Parliament*, Vol. 6, p. 289.)

APPENDIX II.

A TABLE OF
BRITISH REGNAL YEARS

Sovereign	Accession	Length of reign
William I	Oct. 14, 1066	21
William II	Sept. 26, 1087	13
Henry I	Aug. 5, 1100	36
Stephen	Dec. 26, 1135	19
Henry II	Dec. 19, 1154	35
Richard I	Sept. 23, 1189	10
John	May 27, 1199	18
Henry III	Oct. 28, 1216	57
Edward I	Nov. 20, 1272	35
Edward II	July 8, 1307	20
Edward III	Jan. 25, 1326	51
Richard II	June 22, 1377	23
Henry IV	Sept. 30, 1399	14
Henry V	March 21, 1413	10
Henry VI	Sept. 1, 1422	39
Edward IV	March 4, 1461	23
Edward V	April 9, 1483	—
Richard III	June 26, 1483	3
Henry VII	Aug. 22, 1485	24
Henry VIII	April 22, 1509	38
Edward VI	Jan. 28, 1547	7
Mary	July 6, 1553	6
Elizabeth	Nov. 17, 1558	45
James I	March 24, 1603	23
Charles I	March 27, 1625	24
The Commonwealth	Jan. 30, 1649	11
Charles II	May 29, 1660	37
James II	Feb. 6, 1685	4
William and Mary	Feb. 13, 1689	14
Anne	March 8, 1702	13
George I	Aug. 1, 1714	13

(Black's Law Dictionary 4th Ed., p. 1795)

APPENDIX III.

GENEALOGICAL CHARTS
(see text page 190)

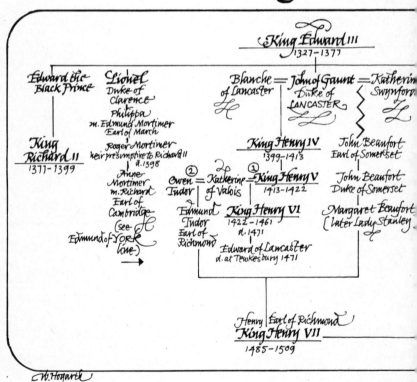

The Descendants of King Edward III

King Edward III
1327–1377

Edward the Black Prince

Lionel Duke of Clarence
+
Philippa m. Edmund Mortimer Earl of March

Blanche of Lancaster = John of Gaunt Duke of LANCASTER = Katherine Swynford

King Richard II
1371–1399

Roger Mortimer heir presumptive to Richard II d.1398

King Henry IV
1399–1413

John Beaufort Earl of Somerset

Anne Mortimer m. Richard Earl of Cambridge (see Edmund of YORK line)

② Owen Tudor = Katherine of Valois = ① King Henry V
1413–1422

John Beaufort Duke of Somerset

Edmund Tudor Earl of Richmond

King Henry VI
1422–1461
d.1471

Margaret Beaufort (later Lady Stanley)

Edward of Lancaster d. at Tewkesbury 1471

Henry Earl of Richmond
King Henry VII
1485–1509

W. Hogarth

282

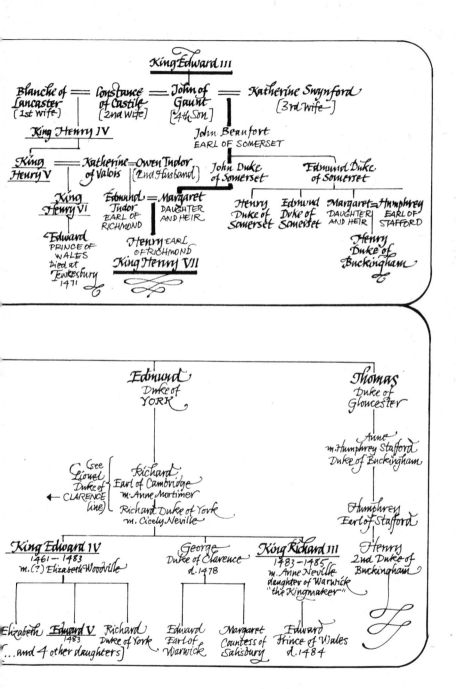

King Edward III

Blanche of Lancaster (1st wife) = Constance of Castile (2nd Wife) = John of Gaunt [4th Son] = Katherine Swynford [3rd wife]

John Beaufort EARL OF SOMERSET

King Henry IV

King Henry V = Katherine of Valois = Owen Tudor [2nd Husband] — John Duke of Somerset — Edmund Duke of Somerset

King Henry VI — Edmund Tudor EARL OF RICHMOND = Margaret DAUGHTER AND HEIR — Henry Duke of Somerset — Edmund Duke of Somerset — Margaret DAUGHTER AND HEIR = Humphrey EARL OF STAFFORD

Edward PRINCE OF WALES Died at Tewkesbury 1471 — Henry EARL OF RICHMOND King Henry VII

Henry Duke of Buckingham

Edmund Duke of YORK — Thomas Duke of Gloucester

Anne m. Humphrey Stafford Duke of Buckingham

(See Lionel Duke of CLARENCE line) { Richard, Earl of Cambridge m. Anne Mortimer
Richard Duke of York m. Cicely Neville }

Humphrey Earl of Stafford

King Edward IV 1461–1483 m. (?) Elizabeth Woodville — George Duke of Clarence d. 1478 — King Richard III 1483–1485 m. Anne Neville daughter of Warwick "the Kingmaker" — Henry 2nd Duke of Buckingham

Elizabeth [...and 4 other daughters] — Edward V 1483 — Richard Duke of York — Edward Earl of Warwick — Margaret Countess of Salisbury — Edward Prince of Wales d. 1484

283

ACKNOWLEDGMENTS

I gratefully acknowledge the courtesies extended to me by the following, including permission, where necessary, to use copyrighted material:

OXFORD UNIVERSITY PRESS AND EYRE METHUEN LTD : *The growth of a legend; the death of Edward Prince of Wales at Tewkesbury, 1471, in English Historical Documents*, Vol. IV, item 188, p. 314; ed. by A.R. Myers.

CAMBRIDGE UNIVERSITY PRESS: *History of the Life and Reign of Richard the Third*, by James Gairdner.

AMERICAN JOURNAL OF LEGAL HISTORY, Temple University School of Law: The article *The Legislation of Richard III*, by H.G. Hanbury, Vol. 6, 1962.

HISTORY TODAY: The article *The Character of Richard III*, by A.R. Myers, Vol. 4, 1954.

LONGMAN GROUP LIMITED:
Richard III as Duke of Gloucester and King of England, by Caroline Amelia Halsted
History of England During the Middle Ages, by Sharon Turner.

PITMAN PERIODICALS LTD : The article *The Princes in the Tower*, by Geoffrey H. White, from *The Complete Peerage*, Vol. XII, Appendix J.

WEST PUBLISHING COMPANY: *A Table of British Regnal Years*, p. 1795 in *Black's Law Dictionary* (4th ed.)

DR. R.H.G. LYNE-PIRKIS, Godalming England, with assistance of Dr. Kenneth Oakley and Dr. Barker of the British Museum; Professor Charles Dent, University College; Professor Richard Harrison, London Hospital; and Sir Bentley Purchase, the Paddington Coroner: Transcript of Dr. Lyne-Pirkis' lecture to the Richard III Society, London, 1963, *The Bones Found In The Tower*.

Jerome Beatty, Jr., and Jean di Meglio gave me permission to quote from the article on a legend about Richard III, in the 'Trade Winds' section of *The Saturday Review*, April 13, 1968. The genealogical chart is included by permission of V.B. Lamb and Isolde Wigram.

I am indebted to William Hogarth for the cover design and genealogical charts, and to Linda B. McLatchie for her assistance and suggestions.

For the use of the unparalleled resources of the Folger Shakespeare Library in Washington, D.C., I thank the Director, Dr. O.B. Hardison, Jr., and his staff.

For their advice and encouragement, I am indebted to Peter Hammond, Caroline Hammond, Geoffrey Wheeler, Jeremy Potter, Patrick Bacon and Isolde Wigram in England, and William Hogarth and Elizabeth D. Haynes in the United States. My wife, Janet, gave me valuable suggestions and support.

BIBLIOGRAPHY

ANDRÉ, Bernard, *Memorials of King Henry VII*, ed. J. Gairdner, London, 1858.

British Museum; *Cotton MSS. Harleian MS.* 433

BUCK, George, *The History of the Life and Reigne of Richard The Third*, W. Wilson, London, 1647.

BUCK, Sir George, *The History of King Richard The Third*, ed. A.N. Kincaid, Alan Sutton, 1979.

Chronicles of London, ed. C.L. Kingsford, Oxford, 1905.

CHURCHILL, George Bosworth, *Richard the Third up to Shakespeare*, Palaestra X, Mayer & Muller, Berlin, 1900.

COMMYNES, Philippe de, *Memoires*, ed. J. Calmette and G. Durville, Paris, 1924-5.

CORNWALLIS, Sir William, *Encomium of Richard III*, ed. A.N. Kincaid, Alan Sutton, Dursley, Gloucestershire.

DAVIES, Robert, *Extracts from the Municipal Records of the City of York, during the reigns of Edward IV, Edward V, and Richard III*, J.B. Nichols and Son, London, 1843.

DRAKE, Francis, *Eboracum; or the History and Antiquities of the city of York, from its origin to the present times*, William Bowyer, London, 1736.

DU BOULAY, F.R.H., *An Age of Ambition*, Viking Press, New York, 1970.

English Historical Documents, 10 vols., gen. ed., David C. Douglas; vol. IV, 1327-1485, ed. A.R. Myers, Eyre Methuen Limited, London, 1969; New York, Oxford University Press, 1953-1975.

FABYAN, Robert, *The New Chronicles of England and France*, ed. H. Ellis, London, 1811.

GAIRDNER, James, *History of the Life and Reign of Richard The Third* (rev. ed.), Cambridge University Press, 1898.

The Great Chronicle of London, ed. A.H. Thomas and I.D. Thornley, London, 1938.

The Great Debate, ed. P.M. Kendall, Folio Society, London, 1965.

HALSTED, Caroline Amelia, *Richard III as Duke of Gloucester And King of England*, the Longman Group Ltd., successors to Longman, Brown, Green and Longmans, London, 1844.

'Historiae Croylandensis Continuatio' in *Rerum Anglicarum Scriptorum Veterum*, ed. W. Fulman (Oxford, 1684); trans. and ed. Henry T. Riley, *Ingulph's Chronicle of the Abbey of Croyland* (Bohn's Antiquarian Library, London, 1854).

HUNT, Percival, *Fifteenth Century England*, University of Pittsburgh Press, Pittsburgh, 1962.

HUTTON, W., *The Battle of Bosworth Field*, 2nd edition, ed. J. Nichols, London, 1813.

JACOB, Ernest Frager, *The Fifteenth Century, 1399-1485*, Oxford, Clarendon Press, 1961.

KENDALL, Paul Murray, *Richard the Third*, Allen & Unwin Ltd., London, 1955. ALL CITATIONS ARE TO THIS EDITION.

LAMB, V.B., *The Betrayal of Richard III*, Coram Ltd., London, 1959.

LANDER, J.R., *The Wars of the Roses*, Secker & Warburg, London, 1965.

LEGGE, Alfred O., *The Unpopular King*, Ward and Downey, London, 1885.

LITTLETON, Taylor, and Rea, Robert R., *To Prove a Villain*, The Macmillan Company, New York, 1964.

MANCINI, Dominic, *The Usurpation of Richard III*, ed. C.A.J. Armstrong, Oxford, 1936.

MARKHAM, Sir Clements R., *Richard III: His Life & Character*, London, Smith, Elder, and Co., London, 1906.

MORE, Sir Thomas, Saint, 1478-1535, ed. Richard S. Sylvester; vol. 3, Yale edition of the Works of St. Thomas More, Yale University Press, 1976.

MYERS, A.R., *England in the Late Middle Ages*, Penguin, 1952.

MYERS, A.R., *The Character of Richard III*, in 'History Today', vol. 4, 1954, pp. 511-521.

Rotuli Parliamentorum; ut et petitiones et placita In Parliamento (Rolls of Parliament), ed. J. Strachey, 6 vols., London, 1767-77, vol. VI.

RYMER, T., *Foedera Conventiones* (etc.), 20 vols., 1704-35.

SCOFIELD, Cora L., *The Life and Reign of Edward the Fourth*, 2 vols., the Longman Group Ltd., successors to Longmans, Green & Co., London, 1923.

STOW, John, *The Annales or Generall Chronicle of England*, London, 1615.

TANNER, L.E. and Wright, W., *Recent investigations regarding the fate of the Princes in the Tower*, 'Archaeologia', vol. LXXXIV (1935), pp. 1-26.

The Trial of Joan of Arc, transl. by W.S. Scott, The Folio Society, London, 1968.

TURNER, Sharon, *History of England during the Middle Ages*, 4 vols., the Longman Group Ltd., successors to Longman, Rees, Orme, Brown, and Green, London, 1830.

VERGIL, Polydore, *Anglicae Historiae*, ed. H. Ellis, Camden Society, 1844.

WALPOLE, Horace, 4th Earl of Orford, *Historic doubts on the life and reign of King Richard the Third*, J. Dodsley, London, 1768.

WESSEL, Lehrer C., *Richard III in Shakespeare's plays compared with Richard III in history*, Eschwege, A. Rossback, 1876, in Realshule und Progymnasium zu Eshwege.

WHITE, Geoffrey H., *The Princes in the Tower*, The Complete Peerage, vol. XII, Appendix J, pp. 32-39, Pitman Periodicals Ltd., successors to St. Catherine Press, Ltd.

WILLIAMS, C.H., *England: The Yorkist Kings*, The Cambridge Medieval History, vol. VIII, Chapter XII, Cambridge, 1936.

The Richard III Society (65, Howard Road, Upminster, Essex) has published in its quarterly publication, *The Ricardian*, the following research articles, edited by P.W. Hammond, and the separate publications mentioned below:

RICARDIAN ARTICLES

March 1977   *As the King Gave Out*, Susan E. Leas, pp. 2-4.

June 1977   *Richard III's 'tytylle & right', A New Discovery*, Anne Sutton, pp. 2-8.

Sept. 1977   *The Valois-Tudor Marriage: A Missing Statute Found*, Mary O'Regan, pp. 21-23.

Dec. 1977   *Richard III's 'tytylle & right'*, P.W. Hammond, pp. 27-28.

Dec. 1977   *The Burial Place of Richard III*, P.W. Hammond, pp. 30-31.

March 1978   *George Buck Senior and George Buck Junior*, A.N. Kincaid, pp. 2-8.

The Encomium of Richard III by Sir William Cornwallis the Younger, ed. by A.N. Kincaid. Book review by Allison Hanham, pp. 23-26.

June 1978   *The Deformity of Richard III*, P.W. Hammond and Marjorie Weeks, pp. 21-24.

SEPARATE PUBLICATIONS

The College of King Richard III, Joyce Melhuish.

1971   *Battle of Tewkesbury*, P.W. Hammond, Howard Shearring, and Geoffrey Wheeler.

1971	*Battle of Tewkesbury, A Roll of Arms*, Geoffrey Wheeler.
1973	*Edward of Middleham*, P.W. Hammond.
1976	*The Bones of the Princes in Westminster Abbey*, P.W. Hammond.

FICTION

Carleton, Patrick,	*Under the Hog*, E.P. Dutton & Co., Inc., New York, 1938.
Jarman, Rosemary,	*We Speak No Treason*, Collins, London, 1971.
Potter, Jeremy,	*A Trail of Blood*, Constable & Co., Ltd., London, 1970.
Tey, Josephine,	*The Daughter of Time*, Peter Davies, 1951; Penguin Books, Middlesex, 1966.

Note: Readers are referred to Dr. A.N. Kincaid's edited work, *The History of King Richard The Third*, by Sir George Buck, Alan Sutton, 1979, and his article *George Buck Senior and George Buck Junior*, in the March 1978 *Ricardian*. In the *Ricardian* article, Dr. Kincaid points out that the published Buck book we know is actually a reworking by George Buck, Esq., in 1646, of the book written by Sir George Buck in 1619. Dr. Kincaid concludes that the impostor, a great nephew, has turned his great uncle's well-documented and carefully researched work into a careless summary, with scanty documentation, giving as hearsay what was actually firsthand information.

British Library Harleian Manuscript 433, edited by Dr. Rosemary Horrox and P.W. Hammond, is being published by the Richard III Society of England. This Manuscript is the register of grants for the reigns of Edward V and Richard III. For an excellent explanation, see the article by Dr. Horrox in the Society's quarterly publication, *The Ricardian*, Vol. V, No. 66, September 1979, pp. 87-91.

About the Editor: William H. Snyder holds a Juris Doctor degree from the University of Denver. He was for many years on the staff of the United States Bureau of the Budget, in the Executive Office of the President. Later, he was a staff assistant to the Postmaster General and then was appointed Executive Secretary of the President's Advisory Board for the Post Office Department. His governmental duties involved reviewing and making recommendations concerning appropriations, legislations, organization, and management for natural resource, economic, Indian, and postal policies and programs. In 1971, he was elected Chairman of the Richard III Society, Inc., the American Branch of the Society. He serves also as an elected Vice-President of the parent society in England.

INDEX

Anne Neville, Richard III's Queen, 64-73, 82, 102, 134, 164, 204;
dies, 217-221

Barnet, battle of (1471), 50-51

Bosworth, battle of (1485), 232-239; appearance of, 243-244

Brackenbury, Sir Robert, Constable of the Tower, devotion to
Richard III, 98-99; the two Princes, 175-178; dies for Richard at
Bosworth, 228, 231, 236, 241

Buck, George, great-nephew of Sir George Buck — impostor, 289

Buck, Sir George, great-uncle of George Buck and author of *The
History of King Richard the Third*, 289

Buckingham, Henry Stafford, 2nd Duke of, 92; with Richard at
Stony Stratford, 118-121; entry into London, 123-124, 128, 136;
alerts Richard to plot, 139; bastardy of the two Princes, 143, 148;
takes charge of John Morton, 160; rewarded by Richard III, 164;
possible culpability for the two Princes, 173, 183, 185-186; rebels
— executed, 188-198

Butler, Lady Eleanor, daughter of the Earl of Shrewsbury, pre-
contract of marriage with Edward IV, 145-148, 156, 269-275

Chroniclers, 14-15, 144, 173-187, 257-267

Clarence, George, Duke of, 61, 63, 66-69, 74-75, 84, 146, 148, 206;
character, 39; marriage, 41-42; revolts against Edward IV, 43, 46;
Richard effects reconciliation, 48-49; death of, 89-94

Colyngbourne, William, 208-209

Dorset, Thomas Grey, Marquess of, 92, 109-110, 114, 116, 118-
119, 121, 123, 140, 184-186, 206, 225, 256

Elizabeth of York, eldest daughter of Edward IV, 110, 218-220,
222-223, 225

Edward III, 16-17, 109, 151, 161-162, 181, 188

Edward IV, confidence in Richard, 31, 39-40, 45-46, 103-107;
becomes Edward IV, 30; battles Lancastrians, 27-29; marriage,
40-41; defeats Warwick and Clarence, 43; escapes to Burgundy
with Richard, 44; returns with Richard, kills Warwick at Barnet
and recovers throne, 47-51; defeats Margaret of Anjou at
Tewkesbury, 51-52; death of Edward, son of Queen Margaret